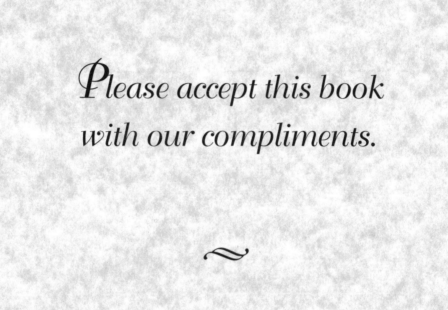

*P*lease accept this book
with our compliments.

~

THE
METROPOLITAN
AIRPORTS
COMMISSION

AMERICA'S NORTH COAST GATEWAY

"Twin Cities Enterprises" by H.R. (Bud) Meier
and Bill Farmer

Consulting Historian J. Robert Stassen
Photo Researcher Walter Hellman

Produced in cooperation with the
Metropolitan Airports Commission

Jostens Publishing Group, Inc.
Encino, California

AMERICA'S NORTH COAST GATEWAY

Minneapolis-St.Paul

International

Airport

by Karl D. Bremer

FRONTISPIECE: Photo by Richard Hamilton Smith

FACING: Courtesy, Metropolitan Airports
Commission/Alvis Upitis

PAGE 8, TOP: Photo by *Minneapolis Journal;*
courtesy, Minnesota Historical Society

PAGE 8, BOTTOM: Courtesy, Metropolitan
Airports Commission/Alvis Upitis

PAGE 11: Photo by Greg Ryan/Sally Beyer

PAGE 103: Photo by Greg Ryan/Sally Beyer

Jostens Publishing Group, Inc.—
Book Division
Editorial Director KAREN STORY
Production Director JAMES BURKE

Staff for *America's North Coast Gateway:
Minneapolis-St. Paul International
Airport*
Editor KAREN L. O'ROURKE
Photo Editor PATTY SALKELD
Editorial Assistant KATHY B. PEYSER

Project Coordinator MERLE GRATTON
Publisher's Representatives
RICHARD R. FRY, JOHN KOHLBACHER

Designer ELLEN IFRAH

JPG

Jostens Publishing Group, Inc.
Jack C. Cherbo, President

Library of Congress Catalog Card
Number: 93-78108

ISBN: 1-882933-00-1

CONTENTS

P A R T   O N E

Reaching for the Sky

Acknowledgments 7

Foreword 8

Introduction 9

Chapter One

Taking Flight 13

Wold-Chamberlain Field, the predecessor to the Minneapolis-St. Paul Airport, began operating in 1920, when an airmail route was established between the Twin Cities and Chicago. The airport grew rapidly, gaining a reputation for excellence early in its history.

Chapter Two

Soaring Ahead 27

During World War II the airport served military duty and soon after entered the age of international flight when Northwest began service to the Far East. Once renamed Minneapolis-St. Paul International, the airport expanded its facilities to keep pace with the Jet Age. Today MSP is among the nation's busiest and safest airports.

Chapter Three

Making Connections 49

Connecting markets from coast to coast, MSP serves as hub to Northwest Airlines, one of the nation's top five carriers. In addition, the area is served by six reliever airports, which comprise the third-busiest airport system in the United States.

Chapter Four

Welcoming the World 61

The Twin Cities and the Upper Midwest welcome visitors from around the world, making tourism one of the area's most important enterprises. Conventioneers, corporate executives, and vacationing families enjoy the region's offerings while enriching the local economy.

Chapter Five

Reaching Out 81

The MSP system continues to expand its global reach, and international carriers serve the nations of the Pacific Rim as well as those in Europe, thus assuring the Twin Cities a place in the global economy of the twenty-first century.

Chapter Six

Trading at Home and Abroad 93

Many *Fortune* 500 companies and other successful enterprises, old and new, make their homes in the Twin Cities. By promoting the import/export potential of the Upper Midwest and providing quality products and services to national and world markets, the local business sector assures the region continued economic growth.

Epilogue 102

PART TWO

Twin Cities Enterprises

Chapter Seven

The Airline Industry 105

Airlines, freight carriers, and companies specializing in aircraft sales and service play a vital role in the region's dynamic industrial scene.

Northwest Airlines, 106-107; KLM Royal Dutch Airlines, 108; Mesaba Aviation, Inc., 109

Chapter Eight

Networks 111

Courier services, ground transportation firms, communication companies, utilities, and businesses that provide aviation fuel link carriers to national and international markets.

InterNatural Designs, Inc., 112-116; National Interrent, 117; Northern States Power Company, 118-119; Hubbard Broadcasting, 120-121; AT&T, 122; Naegele Outdoor Advertising Company, 123

Chapter Nine

Airport and Airline Services 125

Travel agencies, ticketing services, retail shops, and food and beverage suppliers, as well as luggage, parking, security, weather, and maintenance services keep airports and airlines humming.

Host Marriott, 126-127; Calhoun Maintenance Company / St. Paul Flight Center, 128; American Amusement Arcades, 129; Smarte Carte, Inc., 130

Chapter Ten

The Professionals 133

Architects, engineers, and contractors; insurance firms; and educational, medical, and legal services provide essential support to airports, airlines, and related industries.

Kraus-Anderson Companies, 134-135; HealthSpan Health Systems Corporation, 136-137; Oppenheimer Wolff & Donnelly, 138-139; Mayo Foundation, 140-141; RFA / Minnesota Engineering, 142; Courage Center, 143; Robins, Kaplan, Miller & Ciresi, 144-145; HNTB Corporation, 146; Minnesota Community College System, 147; Central Engineering Company, 148; Wenck Associates, Inc., 149; Woodward-Clyde Consultants, 150; Bruce A. Liesch Associates, Inc., 151

Chapter Eleven

Finance and Development 153

The area's solid financial base provides a dynamic environment for economic opportunity and growth, while local developers, contractors, property management firms, and real estate professionals work to revitalize and create the urban landscapes of today and tomorrow.

Adolfson & Peterson, Inc., 154-155; The API Group, 156-157; National Trade Trust, 158-159; MacQueen Equipment, Inc., 160-161; Dain Bosworth, 162-163; SBM Company, 164; Hotel Capital Group, 165; Miller & Schroeder Financial, Inc., 166; Bell Mortgage Company, 167

Chapter Twelve

Conventions and Visitors 169

World-class convention centers, resorts, hotels and motels, restaurants, and cultural and sports attractions serve the important convention and tourism industries.

Residence Inn By Marriott, 170-171; Carlson Companies, 172; Holiday Inn Airport #2, 173; Minneapolis-St. Paul Airport Hilton Hotel, 174; Cedars Edina Apartment Community, 175

Chapter Thirteen

Manufacturers, High-Tech, and Import/Export 177

The Twin Cities' location and qualified work force draw manufacturers, high-tech industries, and import/export businesses to the region.

Diversified Dynamics Corporation, 178-179; Ceridian Corporation, 180-181; Control Data Systems, 182-183; Jostens, Inc., 184-185; Hypro Corporation, 186; Dri-Steem Humidifier Company, 187; Advantek Incorporated, 188-189; Horton Holding, Inc., 190; The Bergquist Company, 191; Dotronix, Inc., 192; Paramax, A Unisys Company, 193; Foley-Belsaw Company, 194-195; Minntech Corporation, 196; DataCard Corporation, 197; Metal-Matic, Inc., 198-199; Dresser-Rand Electric Machinery, 200; McLaughlin Gormley King Company, 201; Precision Associates, Inc., 202-203

Bibliography 205
Index 206

Air traffic controllers handled more than 430,000 aircraft operations in 1992 at Minneapolis-St. Paul International. The airport has one of the world's best safety records. Courtesy, Metropolitan Airports Commission/Alvis Upitis

ACKNOWLEDGMENTS

The following individuals contributed greatly to the construction of the history of Minneapolis-St. Paul International Airport for this project. Without their insight this book would have been far less interesting to write and read:

Vince Doyle   Robert Stassen
Milton Andersen   Walt Hellman
Dorothy Schaeffer   Harold Stassen

To my wife, Chris, and my parents,
Gene and Lodell Bremer

FOREWORD

The beginning of aviation in the Twin Cities dates back almost to the dawn of aviation itself and the flight of the Wright Brothers. Only five years after Orville and Wilbur Wright's historic achievement, two Minneapolis businessmen built an airplane and flew it successfully from a hill near Lake Minnetonka.

The remarkable photograph shown here demonstrates the courage and tenacity of Twin Cities aviation enthusiasts in the early part of the century. Despite its poor quality, the photo clearly shows the first airplane flight over the Minneapolis business district on January 12, 1913. The intrepid pilot is Alexander T. Heine and the structure on the left is the clock tower at Minneapolis City Hall. The temperature at the time of the flight was 19 degrees below zero.

The list of Twin Citians and individuals who helped make aviation history in Minneapolis-St. Paul is long. Charles Lindbergh, James Doolittle, Amelia Earhart, Eddie Rickenbacker, Glenn Curtiss, and Charles "Speed" Holman are just a few of the figures who played crucial roles in creating the industry that today is so important to Minnesota.

In 1943 the Minnesota Legislature passed an act creating the Metropolitan Airports Commission to develop a system of airports to meet the current and future air transportation needs of the community. The MAC, as it has become known in Minnesota, also was given the task of promoting aviation in the region.

This year the MAC celebrates its golden anniversary. The anniversary and the publication of *America's North Coast Gateway* give us the opportunity to thank present and past commissioners and employees who worked so hard and so effectively to build our airport system into one of the safest, most efficient, and best managed in the world. The anniversary also permits us to recognize and honor other individuals and companies, many whose stories appear in this book, who have supported our industry over the years.

The MAC was born during the depths of World War II and it participated in the shift from wartime to peacetime activity, the massive growth of air transportation in the postwar boom, the coming of the Jet Age and the attendant noise problems, deregulation, and the development of a major air transportation hub for Northwest Airlines.

It's been a rich 50 years for the MAC. However, the challenges of the next few years and of the twenty-first century will be no less demanding and require no less courage and determination in meeting them than was displayed by those aviation pioneers at the beginning of the century. Tomorrow will be as great an adventure as yesterday was and I, for one, wouldn't miss it for the world.

Jeffrey W. Hamiel
Executive Director
Metropolitan Airports Commission

INTRODUCTION

Minneapolis-St. Paul long has been at the crossroads of transportation.

The confluence of the Minnesota and Mississippi rivers had much to do with the development of the Twin Cities as a gateway to the north. Indians settled along the rivers to make use of these natural transportation corridors, which also provided sustenance from their waters and shores. Voyageurs followed, moving furs along the rivers that fed the Mississippi for shipment to East Coast and European markets. Still later came the keelboats and steamboats in the 1800s, hauling supplies for the growing settlements along the two rivers.

Roads were developed along the riverways as the territory was settled. The military soon recognized the strategic importance of the geography and Fort Snelling was established at the juncture of the Mississippi and Minnesota rivers in 1820.

Minnesota's population swelled from 6,000 in 1849 to 170,000 in 1861. To accommodate this growth, railroads spread from the Twin Cities throughout Min-

nesota in the mid-1800s. Linking the important transportation waterways of Lake Superior to the north and the Red River to the west with the Mississippi River at St. Paul was an early goal of railroad development in the state.

The first rails were laid in Minnesota in

1862 between St. Paul and St. Anthony. By 1872 there were 1,900 miles of railroad in Minnesota, eventually supplementing the rivers as a means of moving commodities such as grain, iron ore, timber, and manufactured goods to distant markets.

St. Paul became the nation's rail gate-

way to the developing Northwest. At one time there were 12 rail lines operating out of St. Paul, connecting the Twin Cities with both the Pacific and Atlantic coasts.

As commercial aviation sprouted its wings in the early 1900s Minnesota was at the forefront of its development. Northwest Airways was established in 1926 and from its base in the Twin Cities began to develop into one of the world's pioneers in air transportation.

Once again the Twin Cities' geographic location proved advantageous. Situated midway across the continent, Minneapolis-St. Paul served as the jumping-off point for air routes expanding west and to the Orient. Learning from the 1931 "north to the Orient" flight made by Charles and Anne Morrow Lindbergh, Northwest Airlines initiated the "Great Circle" route in 1947 over the Arctic to Korea, Japan, China, and

the Philippines, which brought cities along the northern boundaries of the United States 2,000 miles closer to the Orient than over the traditional transpacific route. In the 1970s hundreds of miles were shaved off travel to Europe as well by flying across the top of the world from the Twin Cities.

Minneapolis-St. Paul International Airport (MSP), ironically located near the confluence of the Minnesota and Mississippi rivers, continues to serve as a crossroads of commerce. Home to Northwest Airlines' major hub, the airport is served by nonstop or one stop-same plane flights to nearly 150 destinations, 15 of them international. In 1992 more than 21.4 million ticketed passengers from all over the world passed through its terminals.

MSP is America's North Coast Gateway and the world is at its doorstep. This is its story.

ABOVE: Due to airmail scandals in 1934, Army pilots were briefly assigned the task of flying the mail. Seen here in a photo taken that year, an Army pilot prepares for a flight out of Holman Field. Courtesy, Minnesota Historical Society

PRECEDING PAGE, TOP: An important early mode of transportation in the Twin Cities was the steamboat. Seen here around 1870 is the steamer *Montana* along the banks of the Mississippi River in St. Paul. Photo by Illingworth; courtesy, Minnesota Historical Society

PRECEDING PAGE, BOTTOM: For decades, beginning in the 1860s, railroads were vital to the transportation of commodities. Contrasted here are two Great Northern Railway trains—the original from 1862 and the modern all-steel version, photographed here in 1924. Photo by *St. Paul Daily News*; courtesy, Minnesota Historical Society

PART ONE

Reaching
for the Sky

CHAPTER ONE

TAKING FLIGHT

Many distinguished individuals were pioneers in the formation of Minneapolis-St. Paul International Airport. One such person was Charles "Speed" Holman, pictured here around 1930. This first operations manager for Northwest was also famous in his own right as an air racer, stunt flyer, and daredevil. St. Paul Downtown Airport (Holman Field) is named in his honor. Courtesy, Minnesota Historical Society

inneapolis-St. Paul International Airport, situated almost equidistant between the two Twin Cities, is one of the most conveniently located airports in the country. Ironically, the airport owes its splendid site more to the fortuitous failure of an automobile racetrack more than 75 years ago than it does to anything else.

Aviation already was firmly entrenched in Minneapolis-St. Paul when the need for a fully equipped airfield first was advanced.

The earliest known flight in the Twin Cities was made in January 1909, five years after the Wright brothers left the ground at Kitty Hawk. Ralph D. Wilcox and A.C. Bennett, partners in a northeast Minneapolis carburetor shop, built a 25-horsepower flying machine that Bennett flew off a hill overlooking Lake Minnetonka near Minneapolis. "They barely got off the ground," Wilcox's brother, who witnessed the flight, recalled 40 years later. "I've seen skiers go higher."

In 1910 boatmaker John O. Johnson flew a 600-pound biplane 200 feet over White Bear Lake before landing with engine trouble.

The first public airplane flight in the Twin Cities was staged in June 1910 by Glenn H. Curtiss in a 14-minute exhibition flight over the Minnesota State Fairgrounds.

The commercial value of transporting mail by air was recognized in 1910 with the introduction of federal legislation allowing the U.S. postmaster general to conduct experimental airmail flights throughout the country. The earliest such experimental flight in Minnesota took place on October 18, 1911, when aviator Hugh Robinson left Minneapolis' Lake Calhoun in a Curtiss "hydro-aeroplane" with 25 pounds of mail bound for New Orleans.

Destined to be the first to traverse the country north to south, Robinson planned to follow the Mississippi River making mail drops and pick-ups in sponsoring cities along the way.

"Over Lake Pepin the passengers in a Milwaukee train witnessed a thrilling race," the *Minneapolis Morning Tribune* reported. "The birdman was flying about 1,000 feet above the water. The crack train, burning the rails at 60 miles per hour, was soon outdistanced and the aviator disappeared in the distance ahead of the speeding train."

Before he reached Winona, 110 miles south of Minneapolis, Robinson fell into the river. Shortly after resuming his flight he ran out of gas and then was forced to land when he hit a wing-dam in the river and broke a pontoon.

Robinson made it as far as Rock Island, Illinois, setting a record for mail carried by air. But he abandoned his effort to continue to New Orleans over a dispute with sponsoring cities that he claimed reneged on their pledges to pay for his flight. Minneapolis, he said, was the only city to make good on its promise of $3,000.

Nonetheless, Robinson's effort further sparked the Twin Cities' interest in aviation. "Minneapolis, through the flight, will enter the ranks of the cities foremost in the placing [of] the art of aviation within the sphere of the practical," the *Morning Tribune* predicted.

Soon after the United States entered World War I in 1917 a group of 31 prominent businessmen organized the Aero Club of Minneapolis with the goal of assisting the federal government in recruiting and training young men from the region for the

In 1911, only seven years after the Wright brothers' flight on the North Carolina dunes, the first airmail flight in the Twin Cities took place. A few residents gathered on Lake Calhoun to witness the historic flight, piloted by Hugh Robinson. Courtesy, Minnesota Historical Society

war. Military flying escalated with the initiation of Army and Navy aeronautical ground training at Dunwoody Institute in Minneapolis.

Training flights were conducted at a 580-acre farm north of Minneapolis owned by Earle Brown, an Aero Club director who volunteered the use of it for free. By mid-1918 Dunwoody was turning out 50 fliers a month and ranked as one of the top three flight-training centers in the country.

Meanwhile, Minneapolis Postmaster E.A. Purdy, also an Aero Club director, in 1918 petitioned the postmaster general for the establishment of a trial airmail route between the Twin Cities and Chicago. The request was denied but efforts to bring Minneapolis into the airmail age persisted.

The Twin Cities' fascination with aviation didn't abate with the end of the war in November 1918. Instead, it shifted to the commercial and pleasure uses of flying. A number of aviation-related businesses were spawned following the war, operating from fields scattered throughout Minneapolis and St. Paul.

The uncontrolled and indiscriminate flying that resulted from these activities soon became a hazard, and in November 1919 the Civic and Commerce Association and licensed aviators in Minneapolis agreed to the first rules for flying over the city. They prohibited, among other things, stunt flying at an altitude of 3,000 feet or less and with passengers.

The following month the Aero Club

reorganized to broaden its membership to anyone interested in flying and kicked off a campaign to develop a flying field properly equipped and operated for all aviation interests. The club was joined in its drive by the Minnesota National Guard, which sought to establish an air squadron here.

The two groups agreed on the location for such a flying field—the now-defunct Twin City Motor Speedway—and their choice soon was endorsed by the Minneapolis Civic and Commerce Association and the St. Paul Association. The site, just south of the Minneapolis city limits bounded by S. 60th Street, S. 66th Street, S. 34th Avenue, and S. 44th Avenue, was relatively level and the track's infield would make a good landing site. Located halfway between the two cities of Minneapolis and St. Paul, the speedway offered plenty of room for expansion and suffered few aerial obstructions.

The Twin Cities Motor Speedway had been designed to make Minneapolis "the Indianapolis of the West" and featured bleacher seating for 100,000 and a two-mile concrete track. It held its first 500-mile race on September 4, 1915, and drew some of the country's top drivers, including Eddie Rickenbacker and Barney Oldfield. But by 1917 shoddy construction, poor management, and other problems beset the speedway and it went bankrupt.

The continuing efforts to secure an airmail route for Minneapolis finally succeed-

LEFT: The Snelling Speedway, an "Indy 500"-type track, was located just south of the Minneapolis city limits. After only a handful of major races and two short years of operation the speedway was abandoned. However, it quickly became an active airfield and the principal airport for the Twin Cities. Courtesy, Metropolitan Airports Commission

BELOW: A former World War I bomber inaugurated airmail service between Chicago and Minneapolis in 1920. Because of several crashes the service lasted only nine months. Courtesy, Minnesota Historical Society

ing strips, one 2,700 feet long and one 2,300 feet.

Speedway Field was ready for the inaugural flight of the Chicago-Twin Cities mail route on August 10, 1920, when a leftover World War I Martin bomber piloted by Walter Smith carried 30,000 let-

7,000 people and dozens of government and military dignitaries. The airport was named for local World War I aviator heroes Ernest Groves Wold and Cyrus Foss Chamberlain, the first two area pilots who gave their lives in combat during the war.

Wold, son of Theodore Wold, vice president of Northwestern National Bank in Minneapolis, was a first lieutenant with the U.S. Army's 1st Aero Squadron. He died while on a photography reconnaissance mission on the German front at Château-Thierry, France, on August 1, 1918.

Chamberlain, son of F.A. Chamberlain, chairman of the board of Minneapolis' First National Bank, was a sergeant pilot in the Lafayette Escadrille, a flying corps of American volunteers in France. He was killed in aerial combat at Château-Thierry, France, on June 13, 1918.

The dedication ceremonies, featuring "the greatest aerial parade in the Northwest's history," included air races, aerobatic competitions, and 40 airplanes. A single-file formation of the planes flew over the Milwaukee train station in downtown Minneapolis as ace World War I pilot Captain Eddie Rickenbacker arrived for the dedication. A giant Vought Experimental Marine Corps plane made the maiden flight from the newly designated Wold-Chamberlain Field. Rickenbacker followed, dropping flowers over the airfield.

"Why is it that the Twin Cities should be taking the lead in American communal aviation?" asked *Chicago Tribune* executive Ben Grey at the airport's dedication. "With all due respect to the citizens of the Twin Cities, I firmly believe the keen interest in aviation here is due to its geographic situation. Between the East and the West it is the liaison and hub. Any aviator flying from Chicago or New York west, or the reverse, knows that he will stop over in the Twin Cities. He knows of the superb landing field at the racetrack with all of its attendant mechanical facilities and hangars."

Historically, Minneapolis and St. Paul have competed vigorously for business. As aviation played an increasingly important role in commerce, joint operation of a single airport by the two cities became more difficult.

St. Paul withdrew its participation in Wold-Chamberlain early in 1926, citing

ed in 1920. The Aero Club reorganized again as the nonprofit Twin City Aero Corporation with Senator W.F. Brooks of Minneapolis as president and J.G. Ordway of St. Paul as vice president. The new corporation arranged to lease the speedway from the Snelling Field Corp., which now owned it, to accommodate the airmail flights. By May Minneapolis and St. Paul businessmen had raised $30,000 with which to level the field and erect an 80- by 90-foot wooden hangar to be leased to the U.S. Post Office free of charge.

The 160-acre speedway infield was accessed by a roadway that tunneled underneath the track. About 100 acres were used for a landing area, sufficient for two land-

ters. Crashes were common on early air mail flights, and after the Chicago-Twin Cities route lost four pilots and eight planes in the first nine months, it was discontinued on June 20, 1921.

The state appropriated $45,000 in July 1921 for the construction of three wooden hangars and other buildings on the north end of Speedway Field to house the newly formed 109th Observation Squadron of the National Guard; $2,500 annual ground rental was paid to the Twin City Aero Corporation for the National Guard buildings.

On July 10, 1923, Speedway Field was renamed Wold-Chamberlain Field in a lavish dedication ceremony attended by about

Dedicated as Wold-Chamberlain Field in July 1923, the airport commemorated two Minneapolis aviators, Cyrus A. Chamberlain (left) and Ernest Wold, who were killed in aerial combat over Château-Thierry, France, in World War I. Courtesy, Minnesota Historical Society

the need for an airport of its own closer to the downtown business district. A group of local civic leaders provided the funds to get a field started across the river from downtown St. Paul. And in June the city's voters approved a $295,000 bond issue for the purchase and development of about 150 acres at the site for an airport.

Congress had passed the Kelly Act in 1925 "to encourage commercial aviation and to authorize the postmaster general to contract for mail service." Under the act private airmail carriers were to receive 80 percent of the airmail revenues.

Business leaders hailed the advance of airmail service by the federal government once again, citing the interest savings in airborne transactions. "Millions are being saved by taxpayers over the country by the transferral of bank paper to financial points in short spaces of time," one newspaper reported, and efforts were renewed to revive airmail service to the Twin Cities.

The Chicago-Twin Cities airmail route was among the first 12 to be created by the postmaster general. Charles "Pop" Dickinson, a Chicago seed dealer with five airplanes, was awarded the route in March 1926.

Fifteen minutes after the inaugural flight left Minneapolis on June 7 en route to St. Paul and Chicago, Dickinson's pilot, Elmer Partridge of Chicago, plunged 1,000 feet to his death in a gale and dust storm near the Mendota bluffs. Dickinson's air-

mail flights were plagued with problems for the first month. His pilots began grousing publicly about the "out-of-date" aircraft they were forced to fly, to which Dickinson retorted: "These flyers have more temperament than opera stars. I am doing all I can to maintain the schedule."

Dickinson's misfortunes continued, however, and he eventually lost four of his five airplanes and all but one of his pilots quit. His good intentions notwithstanding, Dickinson gave the Post Office the required 90-day notice and on October 1 terminated his airmail contract.

Colonel L.H. Brittin, president of the St. Paul Association and an avid aviation supporter, became aware of the pending demise of Dickinson's airmail route and

immediately took the initiative to save it. After several unsuccessful negotiations with others, Brittin huddled with his friend William A. Kidder, manager of the Curtiss Northwest Airplane Company and operator of Kidder's Field near the fairgrounds in St. Paul. It was he and Kidder who were largely responsible for securing the support for the St. Paul airport, and Brittin solicited his friend's advice on how Dickinson's airmail contract could be continued.

Brittin and Kidder met with Henry Ford, also a proponent of the expansion of aviation nationwide, and a group of prominent businessmen in Detroit. By the end of that meeting, $300,000 had been pledged by stockholders in St. Paul and Detroit toward the organization of Northwest Airways Inc. in August 1926.

Within a month Northwest Airways was awarded the Chicago-Twin Cities mail route. Operating out of the old airmail hangar built by the Twin City Aero Corporation, the fledgling airline leased two open-cockpit planes—a Thomas-Morse Scout and an OX-5 Curtiss Oriole—and hauled the first sacks of airmail from the Twin Cities to Chicago on October 1. Three new Stinson Detroiter cabin planes went into service the next month, carrying only mail at first but adding passengers the following year.

While the Twin Cities' mail contract was undergoing some ownership changes, so was Wold-Chamberlain Field. As a result of St. Paul's withdrawal from Wold-Chamberlain, a movement developed to convert the airport to municipal ownership by the city of Minneapolis.

Because the Minneapolis Park Board was the only municipal agency empowered to buy land outside the city limits, it was deemed the most appropriate to operate the airport. In June 1926 Minneapolis aldermen John Ryan and O.H. Turner urged the Park Board to take the necessary steps to acquire the airport.

In September the Twin City Aero Corporation offered its purchase option on the field to the Park Board for $128,000. Aero Club president W.F. Brooks noted that the $2,500 annual ground rental now being paid by the Minnesota Air National Guard would be sufficient to service the debt on the airport.

With its sister city across the river already embarking on a major airport development program of its own, the chal-

ABOVE: Airmail service resumed in March 1926, when Chicago businessman Charles Dickinson was awarded the Post Office Department airmail contract between Chicago and Minneapolis. The crash of Dickinson's inaugural flight was the first of several misfortunes causing him to discontinue operations several months later. Courtesy, Minnesota Historical Society

RIGHT: Northwest Airways was established in 1926 to replace Dickinson's ill-fated Twin Cities-Chicago airmail service. Seen here around 1929 is the first nighttime airmail flight from St. Paul to Chicago. Courtesy, Minnesota Historical Society

ports. And at the Park Board's annual meeting in July a survey and report was presented that recommended the purchase of Wold-Chamberlain and laid out preliminary plans for its development.

The timing of the Park Board's decision couldn't have been better for generating public support for a municipal airport. Minnesota aviator Charles A. Lindbergh had just set the world abuzz with his nonstop transatlantic flight from New York to Paris May 20-21.

Lindbergh's historic trip fired the public's enthusiasm about air travel, and on July 5, 1927, Northwest Airways carried its first paying passenger from the Twin

lenge to Minneapolis was clear, W.A. Durst, chairman of the Minneapolis Civic and Commerce Association's airmail committee, told the Park Board. "St. Paul has tried to get the only airmail terminal of the Twin Cities and has not succeeded. Minneapolis has just as good a chance to develop as a transportation center . . . We do not like to see St. Paul get ahead of Minneapolis by developing an airport where we have none."

Observed the *Minneapolis Tribune*: "It is almost unthinkable that any intelligent, forward-thinking citizen will dispute the statement that Minneapolis as a municipality should own and operate a field of its own."

The Park Board in November asked the Board of Estimate and Taxation to include $150,000 in a five-year bond program for the purchase of Wold-Chamberlain. In March 1927 Governor Theodore Christianson signed enabling legislation allowing first-class cities to acquire and equip air-

Cities. Byron G. Webster, a St. Paul laundry executive, paid $50 for a one-way ticket from St. Paul to Chicago in a Stinson Detroiter flown by famed St. Paul aviator and Northwest operations manager Charles "Speed" Holman. Originating at Wold-Chamberlain, the flight was the first closed-cabin plane to be used by a commercial airline for passenger service.

When Lindbergh returned to Minnesota on August 24, 1927, for the first time in two years, he was greeted by throngs totaling 250,000 at Wold-Chamberlain Field, the St. Paul Airport, and at the parade in Minneapolis. Observed the *Minneapolis Morning Tribune*: "When the *Spirit of St. Louis* glided to rest on the landing field the Wold-Chamberlain port was black with humanity and 20,000 persons broke down police and military lines to sweep over the field and surround the plane."

Lindbergh's St. Paul Airport appearance was followed by a reception and banquet with 520 businessmen and other dignitaries. The men-only affair—women were expressly banned by Lindbergh's advance man—was described by the *St. Paul Pioneer Press* as "probably the most distinguished joint gathering in the history of the Twin Cities."

The Park Board moved to acquire Wold-Chamberlain about the same time as Lindbergh's visit. By then, Twin City Aero Corporation had defaulted on its payments and returned possession of the airport to the Snelling Field Corp. After negotiations over the initial appraisal of the property by the city, condemnation proceedings commenced against Snelling Field Corp. A settlement of $165,000 finally was agreed upon in April 1928, with $90,000 to be paid in cash and the remainder over 20 years at 5 percent interest.

Minneapolis issued $150,000 in bonds, which included the payment to Snelling Field Corp. plus an additional $24,000 for the owners of other properties included in the 325-acre purchase. The bonds also included $36,000 for improvements to the field and acquisition costs. On June 1, 1928, the Park Board took possession of Wold-Chamberlain Field. Although the name was changed to Minneapolis Municipal Airport, it would retain the name Wold-Chamberlain Field "for all time to come," insisted Park Board Superintendent Theodore Wirth. To ensure prudent and expeditious airport development, the Park

Board created a special aviation committee to work with commercial, military, and private aviation interests.

The airport's financial picture began to improve with the Park Board's take-over. The board increased the annual ground lease fee for the National Guard to $5,000. It approved a plan to lease 150- by 200-foot lots for hangar space at $100 a month. And Northwest Airways now was paying $200 a month for the old Aero Club hangar. The Park Board granted the first concessions contract to W.B. Michaud, who served sandwiches, soft drinks, popcorn, and peanuts from a tiny refectory building for 15 percent of gross sales.

Other events in 1928 furthered the expansion of aviation at Wold-Chamberlain as well.

The 9th Naval District earlier that year had announced its intentions to establish an air squadron unit at Wold-Chamberlain. The "Committee of 100," a group of businessmen, aviation enthusiasts, and pilots, was formed to beat the drum for aviation in Minneapolis. The committee built an 80- by 90-foot hangar on Wold-Chamberlain to house the Naval Reserve Aviation Squadron and agreed to turn it over to the Park Board on the condition that they charge the Navy only one dollar a

St. Paul Downtown Airport grew with the demand for more air service. Soon Northwest Airways' main base at the airport boasted a modern new hangar and terminal where its growing fleet of aircraft could be maintained. Seen here around 1932, crowds gathered to witness the start of the Winnipeg Goodwill Tour. Courtesy, Minnesota Historical Society

year for the ground lease.

Commercial air service began to pick up too. Northwest Airways introduced the 14-passenger Ford Tri-motor "Tin Goose" in 1928. In September it established the first coordinated air-rail link. Working with the Great Northern, Northern Pacific, Milwaukee, and Pennsylvania railroads, Northwest offered a service that included the transfer of passengers and freight between airplanes and trains, much as the railroad and steamboat lines had done 60 years earlier.

Northwest's airmail service was extended north of Milwaukee to the Fox River Valley cities of Fond du Lac, Oshkosh, Appleton, and Green Bay. The first regularly scheduled airplane express service linking Minneapolis with the Atlantic and Pacific coasts via its Chicago connection was established that year. Northwest Airways flew the routes for American Express,

which was pioneering this market. And on September 1, Northwest may have initiated the first fare war when it slashed its Chicago round-trip fare to $50 in order to compete directly with first-class rail travel.

Universal Air Lines Inc. ran scheduled operations to Rochester, Minnesota, and Chicago until April 1929, and Jefferson Airways operated scheduled service to Rochester from July 1928 through the following spring.

Universal built three new hangars on the field. With the Naval Reserve hangar, the three National Guard hangars, and the Northwest Airways airmail hangar, Wold-Chamberlain boasted a total of eight hangars housing 58 aircraft by the end of 1928.

That year the Municipal Airport posted a $7,948 profit on receipts of $11,011 and expenses of $3,063.

With all of the activity at the Municipal Airport and confident plans for the future of aviation there, significant upgrades to the field were imperative. Through the end of 1928 the Park Board had spent $33,433 on improvements to the airport. This included extensive grading and the removal of trees and some of the concrete racetrack.

Park Board Superintendent Wirth presented a million-dollar plan for improve-ments and the addition of 240 acres south of 66th Street to bring the total area of the airport to 565 acres. He also urged the city to pave the airport's access roads and extend streetcar service to the airport's entrance at 63rd Street. With other enhancements designed to eventually upgrade the airport to the Department of Commerce's highest rating, A1A, Wirth wrote in his annual report, "The port will be self-supporting and under proper man-agement should bring in revenue toward the payment of interest."

The Park Board's Aviation Committee drafted legislation to remove the limit on airport bonding authority granted to cities to allow for the airport's expansion. They were successful in the next legislative ses-sion in getting $450,000 in bonds autho-rized, of which $243,000 was sold to finance grading, a lighting system, and other improvements.

Wold-Chamberlain Field's first airport manager, Lawrence D. Hammond, a 35-year-old World War I pilot with airport operation experience, was appointed by the Park Board on January 3, 1929.

Three months later Northwest Airways hired its first station manager, M.E. (Mil-ton) Andersen. Working for "Speed" Hol-man for $80 a month, Andersen recalled his first job that would turn into a 40-year career with the airline.

On a tip from a friend who worked at Northwest, Andersen applied at the air-line's "office" on the airport. "They wanted somebody who was interested in working inside and not too interested in the air-planes," he said. In other words, would-be pilots need not apply.

The airline's first operations headquar-ters, he said, was in a rickety frame build-ing about the size of an average living room. A stove in the center of the room heated the building, and toilet facilities were provided by a two-holer outside. When it was moved to the other side of the field in 1930, Andersen remembered, "They hooked a Caterpillar tractor onto this office building and pulled it off to the other side of the field while I was in it."

Pilots had no radios, said Andersen, operating by "contact," or visual, flying only. Weather reports had to be telegraphed ahead to their originating air-port before they departed for the Twin Cities. "I'd look at the windsock and see the direction of the wind. The speed of the wind was judged by the condition of the sock. The 'visibility' was what you could see outside. Of course, that weather reflect-ed conditions at roughly two o'clock and by the time they got up here it was 6:00 or 6:30 and it could change by then, and often did."

The Park Board sought an appropria-tion of $40,000 in 1929 with which to erect a new airport administration build-ing. The proposed two-story facility would house airport administration offices; airline offices; passenger waiting areas; U.S. Cus-toms; Department of Commerce weather, radio, and administrative offices; a dormi-tory; and a pilots' lounge. The board pro-jected revenues from the snack bar alone would increase $4,000 to $5,000 a year.

By the end of 1929 about one-half of the old speedway track had been removed and about one-third of the field had been graded level. The airport showed a $1,335 profit for the year.

A lease was signed in February with Skelly Oil Co. for a gas station to service both planes and autos. The acquisition of 240 additional acres sought by Wirth for expansion of the airport finally cleared the appraisal and condemnation hurdles in early 1930 but was postponed due to more pressing needs of the airport.

The new administration building was begun in April and completed in record time by that fall at a total cost of $56,781. The two-story brick structure was dedicated in a ceremony featuring the French transatlantic flyers Dieudonne Coste and Maurice Bellonte on September 19.

Park Board Superintendent Wirth was convinced this would signal a new era in aviation in Minneapolis. "A high government official in the Aeronautics Service recently stated that this new building unquestionably had cinched aviation activities in the Northwest for this airport," he wrote in the board's annual report.

Minneapolis Municipal Airport showed its first operating deficit at the end of 1930, just under $5,000. Wirth intimated in his annual report that perhaps it was time to shift away from the philosophy that an airport "should bring in a substantial profit" and toward the concept that an airport "is an undertaking for the welfare of commerce and industry of the community and should be paid for by general taxation."

The state legislature obliged Wirth the following year, passing legislation enabling municipalities to levy up to .05 mills for the maintenance and operation of airports. The Park Board in October was granted authority to levy .03 mills beginning in 1932.

Northwest Airways bought one of Universal Air Lines' hangars in 1931 and relocated there when the old airmail hangar it previously occupied was moved to the north side of the field. The airline extended its service westward into North Dakota, and inaugurated service to Duluth using Sikorsky S-38 amphibians.

Northwest Airways' famed pilot and operations manager "Speed" Holman died May 17, 1931, in an air show crash in Omaha. More than 100,000 people attended his funeral, the largest ever in the Twin Cities. The St. Paul Airport later was renamed Holman Field.

Nearly three-fourths of the airport's grading was finished in 1931, a boundary lighting system was completed, a six-inch water main and a wire perimeter fence were installed, and a 1,300-foot concrete taxiway was built in front of the hangars and administration building. On the northeast corner of the airport 8.2 acres of land were added for an entrance. About $178,000 was spent on airport improvements that year.

Aviation activities at Wold-Chamberlain Field continued to grow. Transport passengers showed a 180 percent increase in 1931. Sight-seeing planes were up 125 percent that year, and visitors to the airport were up 54 percent. "Regardless of the markedly diminished business prosperity," the Park Board reported, "the use of air travel facilities is very much on the increase." However, the airport had a net loss again of nearly $5,400.

The Department of Commerce in 1931 began construction of an airway broadcasting and radio station a half-mile south of the airport. Radio station KCAQ commenced weather broadcasting operations in June 1932. A radio range station that projected a beam to aid air navigation was installed a year later.

The Minnesota National Guard moved its operations to St. Paul and its three hangars were taken over by the Naval Reserve Unit. A U.S. Marine Reserve Squadron was assigned to the airport and shared facilities with the Navy.

On January 15, 1932, Wold-Chamberlain Field received word that the Commerce Department had awarded it a Class A1A rating, the highest available. The upgrade in status was a big boost to the airport.

Service was initiated to Sioux City,

Iowa, by Hanford Tri-State Airlines. Sight-seeing passengers were up a phenomenal 186 percent in 1932. These sight-seeing flights lasted from seven to 15 minutes and cost from one to two dollars.

Transport passengers showed a more modest 9 percent growth that year. More than one million passengers visited Wold-Chamberlain Field between May and December.

American Airways (formerly Universal Air Lines) disposed of its holdings to the Northland Aviation Company, a locally owned concern that added a flying school and repair station to its operations.

Full weather bureau service came to Wold-Chamberlain when the Commerce Department was given space in the administration building. Weather maps were received on the agency's teletype machines.

With the first year of the tax levy, the airport showed a net income of $3,637 in 1932.

Hanford Airlines moved its operations from St. Paul to Wold-Chamberlain in 1933 and extended its service to Omaha, while Northwest Airways stretched its route farther west to Billings, Montana. The old airmail hangar was leased to Angelo "Shorty" DePonti and a partner, who ran Minnesota Aviation Sales and Service Co.

A firestorm of controversy erupted over federal airmail contracts in 1934. A congressional investigation into collusion and fraud involving the awarding of airmail routes by the postmaster general led to the sudden cancellation of all domestic routes nationwide by President Franklin D. Roosevelt on February 9, 1934.

The charges stemmed from the great latitude in handing out airmail routes that had been granted to the postmaster general by Congress. At one point Walter F. Brown, postmaster general under President Hoover, had invited a select few airlines to a private meeting in Washington to "carve up the airmail map," as one witness described it.

Although Northwest Airways was not involved in that infamous meeting, it nonetheless got dragged into the hearings. Colonel L.H. Brittin, vice president of the airline, took offense at being called as a witness and wound up serving 10 days in jail for contempt of the U.S. Senate following the disclosure of his attempt to destroy files related to the airmail route investiga-

tion. Brittin resigned from the airline several days before his contempt citation in order to spare Northwest futher embarrassment during the closed Senate hearings on the matter.

Airmail routes were stripped from commercial carriers and handed over to the U.S. Army, with disastrous consequences. The first day of service an Army mail plane crashed near Greenville, South Carolina, and before Roosevelt could return the mail to the airlines on March 10, a total of 10 Army pilots had died in crashes.

A conference of airlines was called and it was announced that no airline that had been involved in earlier airmail contracts would be allowed to bid on the new ones. The solution? Most of the airlines simply reorganized: Northwest Airways became Northwest Airlines, Inc., American Airways became American Airlines, Eastern Air Transport was now Eastern Airlines, and Transcontinental and Western Airlines added "Inc." to their names. By the end of

May Northwest was again hauling mail.

The temporary loss of airmail contracts put a dent in commercial transport activity at Wold-Chamberlain during the first half of the year but it returned to earlier levels within six months. Sight-seeing and tran-

sient passenger numbers were up 50 percent, while military flights had been curtailed by half.

Northwest increased its service to Chicago with three roundtrips daily and connected the Twin Cities with the West Coast when its airmail route was extended to Seattle. Its new 200-mph Lockheed 10-A Electra reduced the flight time to Seattle to 13 hours. Connections also were available to Winnipeg, Manitoba.

Hanford Airlines moved its headquarters to Wold-Chamberlain, sharing space with Northland Aviation, and extended its Sioux City-Omaha service to Kansas City.

Efforts begun a year earlier to secure federal funding for paving Wold-Chamberlain's runways continued throughout the year with no success.

Activity was up or maintained at an even keel in all areas of aviation at Wold-Chamberlain through 1935. Alterations were made to the administration building that year. Hanford Airlines moved its

New service was inaugurated between the Twin Cities and Sioux City by Hanford Tri-State Airlines. On hand for the occasion was famed aviator Eddie Rickenbacker (center). Courtesy, *Minneapolis Star Tribune*

headquarters to Sioux City after the Northland Aviation hangars it shared were bought by Hedberg-Freidheim of Minneapolis, which operated them as public hangars. And the Naval Reserve installed a 10,000-square-foot concrete apron at its hangar.

Wold-Chamberlain Field's reputation for having a crack snow-removal team originated with its earliest directors. "[Airport directors] Roy Johnson and Larry Hammond invented some of the most ingenious things to clear the runways," recalled Dorothy Schaeffer, who worked as assistant to airport directors at Wold-Chamberlain for 40 years.

One of those devices was developed in the winter of 1935-1936. Looking for a way to eliminate the hazard of snow windrows left on the airfield by plows, Hammond and a Park Board engineer adopted an idea they had heard about from Idaho mining camps: compact the snow rather than plow it.

Pulling three side-by-side 10-foot corrugated steel culverts filled with sand, a tractor could compact a 28-foot-wide swath at one time, leaving behind a surface hard enough to land on and take off from but no windrows or piles. The idea was so successful that the Department of Commerce asked Hammond for drawings of the equipment, and he was besieged by requests from airports around the country as well.

Construction on Wold-Chamberlain's long-awaited concrete runways was begun in August 1936. More than 150,000

LEFT: Angelo "Shorty" DePonti began operations at Wold-Chamberlain Field in the early 1930s serving transient aircraft as well as local customers. He continued to operate at the airport into the 1970s and was one of the most respected commercial operators in U.S. aviation circles. Courtesy, *Minneapolis Star Tribune*

BELOW: Runways began to be paved in the mid-1930s. This new construction employed hundreds of workers in the depths of the Great Depression at both Minneapolis and St. Paul airports. Courtesy, Minnesota Historical Society

square yards of concrete were poured in six-inch-thick slabs to create three 150-foot-wide runways in a triangular pattern, two of them 3,000 feet long and one 3,500 feet. The airport financed $50,000 of the project, providing the equipment and some materials; the federal Works Projects Administration (WPA) provided the labor and the remainder of the materials.

Despite a strike by some 500 WPA workers, the runways were completed in 50 days. On October 25 Howard Hunter, assistant national administrator for the WPA, presided over the runway dedication ceremonies before a crowd of 30,000.

Besides providing a hard, safe surface for airport operations, the paved runways also diminished the dust problem at the airport considerably. Retired Northwest station manager Milton Andersen, for one, didn't miss the dust: "In the summertime, with hot weather and a strong south wind, you'd go out there in the morning with a clean shirt on and inside of an hour it would be black from the stuff that would blow in. The windows would be closed but the stuff would still drift in. And no air conditioning!"

Hanford Airlines moved its northern terminus from St. Paul to Wold-Chamberlain in 1936, leasing the old airmail hangar. DePonti Aviation Co. (formerly Minnesota Aviation Sales and Service) bought the Northwest Airlines hangar and Northwest, now without a lease, began paying $100 a month for use of the landing field and ground facilities. Drainage at the airport was improved with grading, and all utilities were placed underground.

"We have been informed by a number of government officials, nationally known pilots, airline companies, and air-traveling businessmen that our Municipal Airport now unquestionably takes top ranking with the airports of the entire United States," the Park Board wrote in its annual report.

Transport aircraft and passenger counts rose by more than one-third in 1936. Aviation activities in most other areas also increased, and visitors to the airport topped one million again.

Growth at Wold-Chamberlain showed no signs of slowing. Northwest Airlines and Hanford Airlines expanded their operations at the airport, as did DePonti Aviation. The U.S. Department of Agriculture established a full weather station in the administration building that was manned

24 hours a day. And 45 wooden rental auto garages were constructed south of the administration building.

Northwest added seven new Lockheed Zephyrs on its Chicago and Seattle routes in 1937. Hanford Airlines changed its name to Mid-Continent Inc. in 1938 and expanded its service with Lockheed Electras. The only aviation activity that showed a decline was sight-seeing, which dropped 30 percent in 1937 and 1938 following a

50 percent jump in passenger charges.

Howard Hughes set a world speed record in 1938, when he flew a Zephyr around the world in 3 days 19 minutes. Hughes landed at Wold-Chamberlain Field July 14, his only American stop and the last stop on his historic flight before continuing on the final leg to New York City. Northwest ground crews serviced Hughes' plane in the shortest pit stop of his flight, Milton Andersen said. "I remember handing the receipt to him up in the cockpit."

Wold-Chamberlain Field was designated a "controlled" field by the secretary of commerce in March 1938. A temporary control room was set up on the roof of the administration building for visual traffic control, operated by assistant airport manager L.A. Johnson.

"At first they only had a light that they put on the airplanes for clearance to land,"

recalled retired Northwest pilot Vince Doyle. "We just looked at the tower for a green light for takeoff or landing. If you had to hold they gave you a red light. If they wanted you to return to the ramp it was a red light and white light flashing at you." These "light guns" later were augmented by radios.

Space was provided for the U.S. Post Office in a former garage on the field. Further improvements were made at the Naval

Northwest Airlines was not the only airline to grow and expand in the Twin Cities in the 1930s. Hanford Airlines had inaugurated service to Sioux City and Omaha and in 1938 changed its name to Mid-Continent Airlines. Courtesy, Bill Ellis Collection

Reserve base. Plans for adding a third floor to the administration building were initiated. And after several years of negotiations, the Park Board received permission from the War Department to construct a railroad spur across adjacent Fort Snelling land to connect with the airport.

Minneapolis raised the tax levy for the airport to the maximum .05 mills in 1938. Following the passage of the Civil Aeronautics Act of that year, the city joined the United States Conference of Mayors in urging the creation of a federal program for the development and expansion of publicly

One of the first methods of traffic control was the light gun, shown here in 1938 being operated from a temporary control room on top of the terminal building by Roy Johnson, assistant director at Wold-Chamberlain Field. Courtesy, Minnesota Historical Society

owned airports. Citing expenses related to federally mandated requirements imposed on airports, as well as free use of airport facilities afforded to federal agencies, the Park Board wrote, "Minneapolis can be expected to have reached the limit of financial support to the Municipal Airport."

The Park Board also for the first time entertained the notion of building a hangar and then leasing it back to an airline—Northwest—over an extended period. Northwest needed the new hangar to accommodate its new Douglas DC-3 airplanes, which it planned to put into service at Wold-Chamberlain in 1939.

The City Council in 1939 granted the Park Board's request for a $215,000 bond issue. Of that, $110,000 was to add a third story to the administration building featuring a glass-enclosed control tower on top. The remaining $90,000 was to build a new

147- by 130-foot municipal hangar to be occupied by Northwest Airlines. Northwest paid for construction costs beyond $90,000 and amortized the costs of the hangar, insurance, and ground rental over 20 years.

Both projects were started in the fall and completed the following year. All of the additional space in the administration building was spoken for before construction started, and the Park Board could already see the need for further expansion soon.

More than 1.5 million people visited the airport in 1939. Passenger traffic at Wold-Chamberlain Field increased 48 percent in 1938, and a 75 percent increase in local flights was noted that year. The price of small airplanes was becoming more affordable, causing a rise in student, private, and sight-seeing operations. Military operations at Wold-Chamberlain also rose significantly. The increasing number of flights prompted the addition of another control tower operator.

Northwest started service with its first 21-passenger airplane, the DC-3, in March 1939. The plane had a crew of two pilots

and stewardess service by registered nurses. The DC-3, says Doyle, had a major impact on the public's acceptance of air transportation. "That was the airplane that really convinced people it was a safe operation and not a daredevil type operation." Northwest carried more than 74,000 passengers the first year it put the DC-3 into service, up from 46,000 the year before.

As the 1930s drew to a close World War II was rapidly escalating. Wold-Chamberlain Field's strategic importance

to what almost certainly would be the United States' involvement in the war was becoming apparent.

Spurred in large part by the pending war needs, as well as the continuing increase in civilian flying, an ambitious plan for a major expansion of Wold-Chamberlain Field was developed in 1940. The plan called for nearly doubling the area of the airport, extension of runways to 5,000 feet, and the construction of additional taxiways, lighting, fencing, and other ancillary improvements.

National defense-related money soon was forthcoming: $430,000 was provided by the WPA as a Navy defense project for runway extensions, and a million-dollar expansion of the Naval Reserve base was approved that included a new hangar and repair and assembly shops.

It was a sign of things to come as the United States, and consequently Wold-Chamberlain Field, became drawn progressively deeper into World War II.

Northwest began service with its new DC-3 aircraft in March 1939. Over the next three decades the durable and comfortable DC-3 won millions of fans worldwide and cemented the public's acceptance of aviation as a safe and efficient mode of intercity transportation. Seen here with one of the new planes is Mary Jo Smith, whose profession as a registered nurse qualified her to be a stewardess for the airlines. Courtesy, Vince Doyle Collection

CHAPTER TWO

SOARING AHEAD

Wold-Chamberlain Field's role in national defense became increasingly more important with the onset of World War II. Several years after the war's conclusion spectators were still drawn to the glory of the fighting aircraft, as is evidenced by this 1949 open house which was visited by 75,000 Twin Citians. At the military base the B29 Super Fortress, seen here, proved to be a very popular attraction as part of the "War Birds" display. Courtesy, Bill Ellis Collection

 s the United States inched toward war, Wold-Chamberlain increasingly was seen as playing a vital role in the nation's defense. Besides its importance as a training center, Army chiefs reportedly favored the development of Wold-Chamberlain to guard against occupation of Canada by foreign troops.

The Minneapolis Park Board in 1940 worked out a plan with the federal Civil Aeronautics Administration (CAA) to develop Wold-Chamberlain Field into a Class 4 airport, the highest rating given by the CAA. The plan called for the acquisition of 90 acres to the north, 240 acres on the south, and an encroachment onto about 105 acres of Ft. Snelling. With the existing 340 acres, the acquisitions would more than double the size of the airport.

Aviation activity at Wold-Chamberlain steadily climbed. Passenger counts were up by 44 percent in 1940. Military operations at Wold-Chamberlain increased by 50 percent, and military training tripled under the Civilian Pilot Training program.

Wold-Chamberlain in October was included in a $40-million national defense airport development program. Six months later President Franklin Roosevelt ordered the start of a $2.1-million improvement program to make Wold-Chamberlain "one of the key airports in the national defense system and one of the largest and best equipped in the country."

A third floor was added to the airport's terminal and administration building with a modern, glassed-in air traffic control tower on top. Radio station KBPC operated from the tower, providing air traffic control to supplement visual control methods.

Northwest Airlines moved into a new hangar built by the Park Board and leased back to the airline over 20 years. Northwest promptly added a two-story shop and office building to the new hangar the following year. The Park Board built and leased a second hangar under a similar arrangement with Mid-Continent Airlines, which used it for the carrier's northern terminal and general services facilities.

Land for Wold-Chamberlain's expansion was acquired over the next two years, though not without appeals and lawsuits on a number of parcels. The Park Board

As the threat of war became more real, military activity at MSP doubled. Flight training became more intensive and expansion of facilities at the base was increased. Courtesy, Bill Ellis Collection

aggressively pursued the use of the adjacent Fort Snelling property but was rebuffed repeatedly by the War Department, despite the fact that military activities had become the dominant function of Wold-Chamberlain by that time.

The north-south runway was extended to 5,900 feet, concrete work was completed on all other airfield and ramp areas, a drainage system for the entire airport was installed, and sanitary sewer for all build-

ings was put in. A total of two million cubic yards of earth was moved and 200,000 square yards of concrete poured in Wold-Chamberlain's biggest spurt of growth to date.

On 32 acres deeded to it by the Park Board the Naval Reserve Aviation Base moved forward with the construction of barracks, hangars, and other buildings in a million-dollar expansion. By 1943 total investments in the base, which had attained Naval Air Station status, reached $9 million.

Contributing to the Navy's wartime research efforts was the Precipitation Static Research Program, established in one of its hangars at Wold-Chamberlain in 1942.

Using pilots and mechanics supplied by Northwest Airlines, the Navy conducted experiments designed to eliminate static that develops when planes fly through moisture, dust, and dry snow, blocking instruments and communications and navigational signals. Research on aircraft icing was conducted in another Navy research hangar.

Van Dusen Aircraft Co. opened for business in a small hangar in 1941, offering radio installation and metal fatigue testing services. DePonti Aviation converted three 100-foot hangars to one 300-foot unit and erected three new hangars. A piece of Wold-Chamberlain history, the original wooden airmail hangar built in 1920 that most recently had been occupied by Mid-Continent Airlines, was sold and moved to Northport field near White Bear Lake, where it still stands today.

In 1942 the Defense Plant Corp. provided Minneapolis Honeywell Regulator Co. $550,000 with which to build a research hangar. A 2,300-volt lighting system was installed and a six-foot chain-link security fence erected around the airfield. DePonti Aviation's hangars were leased to the Northwestern Aeronautical Corp. for an Army glider-building program. And demand for administrative space by the Army and airlines necessitated the conversion of the terminal building's last four hotel rooms to offices.

On May 16 Wold-Chamberlain's air traffic control tower and personnel were taken over by the Civil Aeronautics Administration and operated on a 24-hour basis. By October 1942 Wold-Chamberlain was restricted to military and airline flights only, and both Northwest and Mid-Continent had turned over many of their aircraft to the military for troop transport.

Even before the rapid expansion of

Wold-Chamberlain got under way in the early 1940s, efforts had begun among political and civic leaders to assess the long-term future aviation needs of the Twin Cities. Wold-Chamberlain and St. Paul's Holman Field had competed for air service since the start of airmail in the 1920s.

Some carriers served one airport or the other but many, including Northwest, attempted to serve both.

Such competition may have been healthy at the local level, but it did little to advance the Twin Cities' cause in the big picture of aviation, said some forward-thinking aviation enthusiasts.

Watching airplanes land at St. Paul and then 15 minutes later take off for Wold-Chamberlain, said former Minnesota Governor Harold Stassen, "I recognized how illogical that was from the standpoint of air travel. So when I was elected governor in 1938 I decided there ought to be one major municipal airport for the Twin Cities area and that it should be under a special municipal airport commission.

"Of course," he recalled, "when I urged it as governor there was a concern between St. Paul and Minneapolis as to whether this metropolitan area commission would tilt toward one city or the other."

Meanwhile, a group called the Air Freight Terminal Committee was created by the Minneapolis Park Board in 1941 to spur the development of an air freight ter-

LEFT: The summer of 1940 saw the addition of a modern air traffic control tower and the enlargement of the terminal building at Wold-Chamberlain Field. The following year an additional 327 acres of adjacent land was added to the airport. Courtesy, Bill Ellis Collection

BELOW: Barracks, new hangars, and other buildings were constructed at the Navy base as the airport was now on a total wartime footing. While the base functioned as a naval air station, major research projects on aircraft icing and static electricity were also conducted. Courtesy, Bill Ellis Collection

minal there. The group later changed its name to the Air Terminal Committee and broadened its scope to examine both passenger and freight facility needs.

"Minneapolis never has become the rail center it should have," said Minneapolis Alderman A.G. Bastis, who headed the Air Terminal Committee. "There is no reason why Minneapolis shouldn't be one of the three or four leading air centers in North America, if we start now with the prestige already won with Wold-Chamberlain Field and make plans to be ready for the upsurge of peacetime aviation when the war is over."

The committee produced a report in 1942 suggesting that while Wold-Chamberlain could be sufficiently expanded to meet at least postwar commercial aviation needs, the city should begin a search immediately for a site that could accommodate a second major air terminal if needed. That was the first of several planning efforts to locate a site for a new or replacement commercial airport in the Twin Cities over the past 50 years.

Although the committee was not assigned to address the issue of a joint Minneapolis-St. Paul airport, it indicated that should such an effort be pursued, "It is our observation that no better location for a joint commercial airport can be found than the present Wold-Chamberlain Field. It is nearly equidistant from the loop districts of Minneapolis and St. Paul and the

running time from each of the loop districts to and from the airport is substantially the same. In its enlarged aspect it can adequately serve both cities."

A site north of Minneapolis in Brooklyn Township was selected as most feasible for acquiring up to 1,500 acres for a possible second airport.

The Air Terminal Committee's report resulted in a legislative proposal to authorize "first-class" cities to issue up to $3 million in bonds to acquire or expand airports. That measure sparked discussions among

representatives from Minneapolis and St. Paul over the feasibility of a joint airport effort between the two cities.

Governor Stassen instructed Attorney General William Green to draft legislation for the creation of a metropolitan airports commission and began building a consensus for a commonly owned and operated Twin Cities air carrier airport. Many meetings were held among the players from both cities until agreement on most points was hammered out.

To ease the concerns about "tilting" toward one city or the other, Stassen pro-

ABOVE: Governor Harold Stassen, the youngest governor in Minnesota history, proposed a metropolitan airports commission consisting of balanced membership of Minneapolis and St. Paul interests. Founded in 1943, the commission centralized airport planning and effectively eliminated rivalry between the two cities regarding the main Twin Cities airport. Stassen is seen here (left) during a new hangar dedication in 1942. Courtesy, *Minneapolis Star Tribune*

LEFT: By the end of the 1930s Northwest Airlines began concentrating its operations at Wold-Chamberlain Field, decreasing its presence at Holman Field. Northwest suspended service at St. Paul from 1937 through April 1941, and permanently discontinued it in November 1941. Holman Field, however, still played a major role in Twin Cities air transportation, especially in the war effort. Courtesy, Frank Geng Collection

posed a balanced membership for the airports commission: a chair appointed by the governor who was a resident of a county not contiguous to either Hennepin or Ramsey counties, the mayors of both cities, a council member from each city, a commissioner from each city's board that has jurisdiction over airports, and a citizen member from each city.

"It had kind of a unique quality about it in the independent authority it had, separate from other governmental authorities," said Stassen. The concept was so novel that it would be years before it would be adopted elsewhere in the country.

Throughout the negotiations, wrote Minneapolis Park Board President Francis A. Gross, "There was much sparring, and at some of the early conferences little progress was actually made." There was some concern among the Minneapolis delegation that their city would be stuck paying for improvements and maintenance of Holman Field, which many considered to be a "sink-hole," in exchange for giving up a share of Wold-Chamberlain.

But progress eventually was made, often at the urging of Governor Stassen, who saw the creation of a metropolitan airports

commission as more than simply a way to resolve competition between two cities. Stassen saw this as a first step toward establishing the Twin Cities as a major international gateway.

"In advocating it I said if we developed a major airport, I could foresee that this could be the place in the future for planes to take off and go over Alaska, to go to Japan and the rest of the Orient," said Stassen. "I gave that as a kind of picture of what the Twin Cities could become—a major center through which, because of its location, planes of the future could curve over the pole. That was one of the things I was criticized for. They said that I was dreaming."

Stassen's thinking ultimately was proved to be right on target.

Minneapolis' support was won over when an appropriation of one million dollars was added to the bill for improving metropolitan area airports. The appropriation was to be repaid with a tax over 10 years.

Legislation creating the Metropolitan Airports Commission (MAC) was passed in 1943. It was one of Stassen's last acts as governor before he resigned to join the

Navy as a lieutenant commander.

The MAC was charged with promoting air transportation and developing the metropolitan area as an aviation center, while at the same time minimizing the environmental impact of the airport on the residents of the metropolitan area.

Its first chairman was Lewis Castle of Duluth.

One of the MAC's first actions was to commission a study that would guide the new agency in the development of the region's air transportation facilities. Completed by the end of the year, this plan recommended developing Wold-Chamberlain Field as the Twin Cities' major air terminal. Holman Field should be developed for "major special services," the plan advised. And a whole system of secondary airports

Seen here in 1943 is the first meeting of the Metropolitan Airports Commission, with members (from left) Ell Torrance; Francis A. Gross, Minneapolis; John J. McDonough; Milton W. Griggs, St. Paul; chairman Lewis G. Castle, Duluth; Marvin L. Kline, Minneapolis; William A. Parranto; Fred M. Truax, St. Paul; and Harry P. Burgum, Minneapolis. Courtesy, Metropolitan Airports Commission

throughout the metropolitan area, including one to the north of the Twin Cities to be held as a reserve major air terminal site, also should be developed, it stated.

The plan was adopted by the MAC, but the takeover of Wold-Chamberlain was not painless. Days before the Minneapolis Park Board was to hand over the keys to the airport, two separate lawsuits were filed challenging the constitutionality of portions of the law that established the airports commission.

The MAC eventually was upheld in both lawsuits before the Minnesota Supreme Court. On August 14, 1944, the MAC assumed control of Holman Field, which was being operated by the military, as well as all other aviation activities within a 25-mile radius of Minneapolis and St. Paul. The following day the MAC took over Wold-Chamberlain, changing its

name to Minneapolis-St. Paul Metropolitan Airport/Wold-Chamberlain Field.

A challenge to the MAC's authority to set its own standards for aviation activities within a 25-mile radius of the Twin Cities came in 1945, when the airports commission refused to grant licenses for the operation of two privately owned airports in Minneapolis, Cedar and Nicollet. Operation of the airports would compromise the safety of Wold-Chamberlain, the MAC ruled, and the owners filed suit in Ramsey County. But after an unfavorable ruling in the lower court, the MAC prevailed on appeal to the state Supreme Court.

With its authority upheld once again by the high court, the MAC pressed on with its airport system development plan, which initially included Wold-Chamberlain, Holman, new airports in Bloomington and Robbinsdale, University Airport north of

Minneapolis, Fleming Field in South St. Paul, and an undetermined site east of St. Paul.

At the time of its takeover by MAC in 1944, Wold-Chamberlain Field consisted of 722 acres with four paved runways, the longest of which was 5,900 feet. However, with new-generation aircraft coming into service that would require longer runways, another expansion was imminent. Northwest already had given notice that by April 1947 it would begin operations of its new Boeing 377 Stratocruisers, a plane requiring more runway than Wold-Chamberlain could provide.

With the termination of World War II in 1945 Wold-Chamberlain began the transition back to civilian operations. The Army research hangar occupied by the Minneapolis Honeywell Regulator Co. was turned over to the MAC under the federal

ed air cargo operations.

Military flights still comprised nearly half the aircraft operations at Wold-Chamberlain even two years after the war was over. General aviation flights—many of them ex-G.I.s getting their ratings after the war—accounted for almost as many, while airlines represented only about 10 percent of the total operations in 1947. By 1950 aircraft movements at Wold-Chamberlain were cut in half due to declining military activity and the removal of flight training to other secondary fields.

Public hearings again were held on the future of the airport in 1947, the development of secondary airports in the MAC system, and whether a site to the north in Anoka County should be acquired for a future second air carrier airport to either replace or supplement Wold-Chamberlain. The hearings drew heated testimony from residents around Wold-Chamberlain opposed to its further expansion due to noise, something the MAC would hear often in the years to come.

ABOVE: Not only did passenger service boom following the end of the war but an entire new aspect of the industry—air cargo—took off. The first shipment of fruit by Air Express included gifts to city and state officials, including Mayor Hubert Humphrey of Minneapolis (left) and Mayor John McDonough of St. Paul. Courtesy, Minnesota Historical Society

LEFT: During the war Holman Field served as a major modification center for B-24 Liberator Bombers. The center, operated by Northwest Airlines, employed 6,000 people during the war and produced 3,286 aircraft by war's end. This modification crew assembled for a group photo in front of a B-24 around 1944. Courtesy, Minnesota Historical Society

The determination after this round of hearings was to continue developing Wold-Chamberlain as the Twin Cities' major commercial airport. In February 1948 the MAC authorized the purchase of an additional 1,800 acres of land west of the airport in Richfield for the construction of

Surplus Property Act and then leased to Northwest Airlines. A U.S. Army Transport Command hangar built in 1943 also was deeded back to the commission.

The final glider was flown from Northwestern Aeronautical Corp. in July and DePonti Aviation's hangars were leased to Hinck Flying Service, Parker Aviation, and Lakeland Skyways.

Air cargo activity began to develop after the war. The first large commercial cargo flight arrived at Wold-Chamberlain in November 1945 carrying a load of fresh produce for Super Valu grocery stores on a Flying Tigers Line C-46. By the next year Sky Freight Line was flying in fresh fish from Boston, Slick Airways was transporting produce from California and Texas to Minnesota markets, and Trans-Continent Air Express, American Airlines Cargo, and Twentieth Century Airlines also had start-

and a possible cross runway of 10,000 feet. Development of the Anoka site, which never would come close to the scale of the MAC proposal, did not begin until 1951 and it eventually joined the MAC's reliever system of secondary fields.

The MAC immediately recognized the importance of attracting new air service to Minneapolis-St. Paul if the development of Wold-Chamberlain as a major North American air transportation center was to take place as planned. When the commission was organized in 1943, Wold-Chamberlain was served by only two airlines: Northwest, with service across the northern tier from Chicago to Seattle, and Mid-Continent, serving points south to Kansas City.

In its first year the MAC authorized its participation in airline route cases before the Civil Aeronautics Board and budgeted $20,000 for studies to improve air service.

and only the fourth transcontinental airline in the country.

Northwest, capitalizing on its wartime experience flying troops and cargo to Alaska and the Aleutian Islands, was awarded routes to the Orient via the "inside route" through Edmonton, Canada, and Anchorage in 1946.

Charles and Anne Morrow Lindbergh had pioneered the over-the-pole route with their famous "north to the Orient" flight 15 years earlier in 1931 flying a Lockheed Cirrus floatplane. This so-called "Great Circle" route brought New York 2,000 miles closer to Japan than the conventional mid-Pacific route.

Service to Tokyo, Seoul, Shanghai, and Manila was inaugurated from Minneapolis-St. Paul on July 15, 1947, on Northwest's 50-passenger, four-engine Douglas DC-4.

ABOVE: Hal Carr, executive vice president of Wisconsin Central and later president of North Central Airlines, led the most successful of the new regional carriers that emerged after the war. Courtesy, Sherm Booen Collection

LEFT: Peacetime brought to Northwest and the other carriers a need to reequip their aircraft fleets. By 1950 Northwest had ordered DC-4s, which it would use to inaugurate its new service to the Orient; Martin 202s, an aircraft with a star-crossed history at Northwest; and the immensely popular Boeing Stratocruiser, shown here parked at the MSP terminal during an open house. Courtesy, Vince Doyle Collection

one new runway and the extension of two existing runways.

The Federal Aid to Airports Act was passed in 1946, providing federal funds to airports on a 50-50 matching basis. The MAC's first money under the program was not forthcoming until 1949, however. That year it received two grants of more than $600,000 for the extension of the north-south runway, construction of a new 6,500-foot runway, and an 1,800-foot extension of the northeast-southwest runway. By 1950 the MAC had received nearly $1.8 million in federal aid under the act.

The MAC moved in 1950 to acquire 1,200 acres in Anoka County for the development of a second major airport, which it felt would be needed within 10 to 15 years. As proposed, the Anoka County site would feature two parallel 10,000-foot runways

The commission set two goals: to secure single-carrier service to the nation's top population centers—New York City, Chicago, Los Angeles, Philadelphia, Boston, Detroit, Pittsburgh, San Francisco, St. Louis, Cleveland, Baltimore, Washington, and Buffalo; and to secure direct service to every region in the country.

Northwest Airlines set out on a major expansion after the war and began converting some of its DC-3 Army transports to commercial use even before the war was over. In June 1945 Northwest inaugurated service between the Twin Cities and New York City via Milwaukee and Detroit, becoming the first airline to provide service to both coasts from Minneapolis-St. Paul

Northwest president Croil Hunter recognized that the Orient would be an important market when the war ended. He pushed the U.S. government to award Northwest route authority to serve Japan, China, Korea, and the Philippines, service the airline inaugurated in July 1947. The inaugural ceremony featured Minneapolis Mayor Hubert Humphrey as one of the principal speakers. Courtesy, Metropolitan Airports Commission

The following year the airport's name was changed again to reflect its new status. It was now Minneapolis-St. Paul *International* Airport/Wold Chamberlain Field.

Inland Aviation in 1946 was awarded a route extension from Huron, South Dakota, to the Twin Cities. With the merger between Inland and Western Airlines, which started service at Wold-Chamberlain in April 1947, single-carrier service to Los Angeles became available, albeit with plane changes at Rapid City and Denver.

Capital Airlines inaugurated service at Wold-Chamberlain in December 1947 with service to Detroit and Washington, D.C.

Wisconsin Central Airlines, a small intrastate airline based in Clintonville, Wisconsin, that would later move its main base to MSP International as North Central Airlines, started service to Minneapolis-St. Paul, St. Cloud, Hibbing/Chisholm, and Duluth on February 24, 1948. All inaugural flights except the Twin Cities-

feeder carrier in Ohio and Indiana. The application wasn't approved for four years. At the end of the year North Central moved its main base to Minneapolis-St. Paul.

Limited space at Wold-Chamberlain forced the airline to take up offices several miles from the airport. Rising operating costs began to outstrip revenues, however, and despite a 42 percent increase in passengers in 1953 over the previous year, the airline lost money for the second consecutive year.

Hal N. Carr, who at age 25 had been an executive vice president at Wisconsin Central in 1947 and then left, was brought back as president of the airline in 1954. The industry's youngest airline president,

ABOVE: Work on the $47-million expansion program at MSP began in 1957. By September 1959 the new terminal building, with its "sawtooth" roof, was taking shape. Courtesy, Metropolitan Airports Commission

LEFT: Dorothy Schaeffer, assistant airport director at Minneapolis-St. Paul International Airport for several years, became the highest-ranking and most influential female airport official in the United States by the time she retired in 1984. She was one of the Metropolitan Airports Commission's first employees in 1943 and is shown here on the right with Vice President Hubert Humphrey (left), MAC Commissioner and St. Paul City Councilman Len Levine, and Carole Levine. Courtesy, Metropolitan Airports Commission

Hibbing segment were cancelled that day due to cold weather.

Within a year operating revenues at the fledgling airline passed one million dollars, passenger counts tripled, and Wisconsin Central employed 40 pilots—10 of them based in Minneapolis-St. Paul.

Wisconsin Central Airlines' presence at Minneapolis-St. Paul continued to expand. In 1952 it changed its name to North Central Airlines and applied to the CAB for a merger with Lake Central Airlines, a small

Carr returned North Central to profitability within months. By June 1955 North Central had passed the one-million-passenger mark and boasted 900 employees and 20 airplanes that flew to 43 cities in six states.

Carr aggressively kept pushing new route applications before the CAB through the 1950s. In 1958 North Central was awarded routes to 18 more cities and began competing with the main trunk carriers at some airports. The airline started replacing

its DC-3s with Convair 340s in 1959 and a $350,000 maintenance hangar for the new Convairs was built at MSP International.

North Central wasn't the only airline to outgrow its facilities at MSP as a result of the robust growth of aviation in the decade following World War II.

Northwest broke ground in 1949 on a $1.15-million maintenance base comprising three hangars. In 1956 the airline entered into an agreement with the MAC to provide a $15-million overhaul of the operations and general headquarters facility at MSP. The complex was built on a 76-acre parcel adjacent to the site of a proposed new multimillion-dollar terminal and leased back to the airline over 30 years. With more than one million square feet of floor space under one roof, the five-hangar structure was the largest in the Upper Mid-

west and featured the longest clear spans of any building in the world.

Northwest moved its Holman Field overhaul facilities into the hangar complex in 1959, and the airline's new general offices were occupied in 1961. Total cost for Northwest's new main base was $18 million.

All the while, Northwest was developing an extensive route system from MSP that ultimately would secure the carrier's position as the dominant airline serving the Twin Cities. In addition, Northwest was selected as a prime contractor with the military for the Korean Airlift from 1950 to 1952, flying more than 1,000 roundtrips between Seattle and Tokyo via the "Great Circle" route it had pioneered through the Aleutian Islands.

MSP during the postwar era began to outgrow its terminal and administration building. Besides increased demand for space to accommodate airline ticket counters, baggage operations, and administrative offices, the airport needed more room for other ancillary services.

With four scheduled airlines operating at MSP after the war, the terminal building was about to burst at the seams. Two abandoned Navy hangars were moved to the west side of the terminal in 1947 and joined together to form a quick and economical addition.

A 24-hour nursery was opened in the terminal building in 1947. A coin changer, amusement machines, and soda pop machines were installed. Parking meters made their first appearance at MSP the following year, accompanied by MAC Ordinance No. 1, which allowed the tagging of illegally parked cars. A refreshment stand in the terminal was opened in 1949.

An open house in 1949 drew 75,000 people to the airport, where 22 planes were on display. Northwest and Mid-Continent flew 318 passengers on 15 sight-seeing flights for $2.50 a person. Later that year a telescope was placed in the spectators' enclosure for the throngs of non-flying visitors the airport was starting to attract.

"I used to have to pop popcorn for the

The Blue Concourse, seen here in 1961 during its construction, was one of the two original passenger concourses at MSP and was designed to load passengers from the ramp. Jet loaders and a second level to the concourses would come later in the decade. Courtesy, Metropolitan Airports Commission

popcorn machines," recalled Dorothy Schaeffer, who served as assistant to the airport director from 1942 until 1984. "We had one in the observation deck and we had to keep that full on weekends. It was just jammed on Saturdays and Sundays. People were crazy about aviation then—they always have been."

In 1950, the first year the airport's observation deck was opened, it drew 264,000 visitors. "Kids would come out there on their bikes and they'd stay out there all day," said Schaeffer. "They were into everything. Whenever I'd catch them I'd toss them out of the building."

By 1955 MSP was serving more than one million passengers a year with 50,000 air carrier operations annually. New carriers continued to be attracted to Minneapolis-St. Paul and existing carriers were expanding routes as fast as the CAB would allow them.

After more than a decade of pursuing land at Fort Snelling for MSP's expansion and running into opposition from the War Department, Veterans Administration, and veterans' groups, 427 acres of the military reservation finally was deeded to the MAC in 1955. The original stone fort and other historical buildings were not included and are still standing today.

Design studies were undertaken for a new passenger terminal at MSP and on October 27, 1958, ground was broken. Scheduled for completion in 1961, the terminal was the chief component of a $47-million expansion program the MAC proposed that also included a new control

tower, new access roads, and upgrading of runways and taxiways.

The 600,000-square-foot terminal was designed to handle a peak passenger load of 14,000 per day based on forecasts of four million passengers annually by 1975.

One of its most innovative features was the separation of passenger services on the top level from baggage, cargo, and ground transportation services on the bottom level. The upper passenger level was served by an elevated roadway with a built-in snow-melting system, while the lower level was served by a separate road.

The futuristic glass-and-concrete structure featured a striking "sawtooth" roofline with 17 folds, doorless "doors of air" (which since have been replaced), and two concourse piers with a total of 24 aircraft loading positions, or gates. Its open-ended design was aimed at easy expansion of airline ticket counters, office space, waiting concourse, and concessions. If needed, the main building could be doubled in size. A mezzanine space above the ticket counters

and concessions would allow for the utilization of an additional 40,000 square feet of space for offices without enlarging the terminal.

Fifty feet of clear space was left in front of the 330 feet of ticket counters. The passenger waiting area adjacent to the ticketing facility seated 1,200, with some space reserved for additional retail concessions. On the inside of this area was space for a newsstand, drugstore, gift shop, and other retail stores; a barber shop; nursery; telephones; and parcel lockers. On the field side of the area was a dining room, snack bar, and coffee shop served by a common kitchen.

On the ground level of the terminal building was a 200-foot-long self-claim baggage counter, along with car rental

ABOVE: The new terminal was formally dedicated in January 1962. The following week the airlines made the move from the old west side terminal. The interior of the new terminal is seen here in this 1976 photo. Courtesy, Minnesota Historical Society

RIGHT: By 1970 passenger-loading bridges had been added to both concourses at Lindbergh Terminal, and a new tower adjacent to the fire station (background) had begun operation. Courtesy, Metropolitan Airports Commission

agencies, telegram counter, post office, pressroom, first aid, and direct access to the ground transportation platform.

Each concourse pier, named "Blue" and "Red" because it would be easier for travelers to remember, was 450 feet long and featured ground-floor gate lobbies, each designed to serve four aircraft loading positions. An open observation deck was provided on the roof of each pier. Like the main building, the two concourse piers were designed for ease in expansion and adaptation to enclosed aircraft boarding bridges that were anticipated for future use.

Airport, airline, and other tenant offices were located throughout the main building and concourse piers.

"The latest in engineering knowledge and techniques along with very thorough

architectural planning will keep Wold-Chamberlain's new terminal building as up to date as the jet planes of the future," proclaimed Gerald F. Paulson, chief structural engineer with Thorshov & Cerny Inc., architects of the new facility.

The $8.5-million terminal was dedicated on January 13, 1962, and an open house the next day drew 100,000 people. The first flight arrived at the new terminal one week later.

The Wold-Chamberlain terminal "is one of the finest examples of forward planning in the United States today," noted Governor Elmer L. Andersen as he cut the ceremonial ribbon with a pair of gold scissors. Minneapolis Mayor Arthur Naftalin described the new terminal as "a symbol of the soaring upward and outward of the

human spirit."

Other major improvements at Wold-Chamberlain besides a new terminal building included a 2,500-space parking lot, a new $1.3-million Western Airlines hangar, a $1.35-million Northern States Power substation, a $1.25-million underground fueling system, and a $500,000 air traffic control tower.

Development of facilities and air service at MSP thrived during the 1960s. By the time the new terminal opened, Ozark Airlines and Eastern Air Lines had entered the Minneapolis-St. Paul market in 1957 and 1960, respectively, joining Northwest, Western, United, North Central (formerly Wisconsin Central), and Braniff (formerly Mid-Continent). American Airlines inaugurated service at Wold-Chamberlain in 1965.

On January 5, 1961, the first scheduled jet aircraft flight passed through Wold-Chamberlain, a Northwest Airlines DC-8 en route from Chicago. Braniff Airlines began scheduled jet service from Minneapolis-St. Paul almost four months later with Boeing 720B jets to Mexico City, followed by Western, United, and Northwest over the next three months. To accommodate the Jet Age, Runway 11R/29L was extended to 10,000 feet in length by the end of the year.

Airlines built up their jet fleets throughout the 1960s and by the early 1970s the new generation of widebody aircraft began to arrive at Minneapolis-St. Paul. Northwest inaugurated Boeing 747 "jumbo jet" service at MSP on June 22, 1970, and started DC-10 service two years later.

The new air traffic control tower was completed in 1964. North Central Airlines in 1967 broke ground on its new $17-million main base and headquarters on 102 acres at the south end of the airfield, which opened in October 1969. United moved into a new $2-million hangar/cargo facility in 1968. And Northwest started construction in 1969 on an $18-million hangar expansion in which it would service its widebody 747s and DC-10s.

The terminal's Green Concourse was opened in 1968 as a transient aircraft facility. DePonti Aviation moved to Gate 35 on the Green Concourse to service transient aircraft, as did U.S. Customs and Immigration and public health inspectors and all "third-level" airline ticketing facilities.

Toward the end of the 1960s, airlines

were starting to yearn for routes between the Twin Cities and Europe. Rights to serve Europe were difficult to acquire, requiring complex international negotiations and even ratification by the White House.

In 1967, 38,000 passengers flew from Minneapolis-St. Paul to Europe through other airports and it was estimated that another 12,000 would use a Twin Cities gateway if it were established. The CAB in 1969 classified the Twin Cities as "the largest generating point (origin of business) in the United States without single-plane or single-carrier service to Europe."

Recognizing that an "over-the-pole" route to Scandinavia was only 300 miles farther from Minneapolis-St. Paul than from congested East Coast airports, Northwest, Pan Am, and Western all had applied to the CAB for routes between the Twin Cities and Europe by 1969. In June of that year Northwest and Pan Am began operating single-plane "interchange" service (planes and crews of both airlines alternately used) between the Twin Cities and Lon-

don, with one stop in Detroit.

MAC's executive director at the time, Henry Quitu, envisioned a bright future for the Twin Cities' international service due to its geographical location and coined the term "America's North Coast Gate-

way" in reference to MSP. The MAC was instrumental in helping Northwest win the nonstop route to London's Gatwick Airport before deregulation, a route Northwest still flies today.

Northwest's single-carrier transatlantic passenger service started in 1979 with service from the Twin Cities to Copenhagen, Stockholm, and Glasgow. Nonstop service to Oslo and Frankfurt came later.

After the multimillion-dollar modernization of MSP in the early 1960s, aircraft and passenger traffic soon outstripped earlier forecasts. The four-million-passenger level predicted by 1975 was surpassed in 1967. FAA forecasts in 1969 predicted 10 million passengers by 1975 and 17 million by 1980; aircraft operations at MSP International were expected to more than double between 1967 and 1975 and nearly triple by 1980, according to the FAA. At

ABOVE: The first of the widebody jets, the 368-passenger 747 of Northwest Airlines, began scheduled operations on June 22, 1970, with service to Detroit and New York. Nicknamed "The Aluminum Overcast," the 747 soon became a favorite for passengers and for NWA president Donald Nyrop, seen here in 1972, who recognized the popularity and the tremendous revenue-generating capability of the new aircraft. Courtesy, *Minneapolis Star Tribune*

RIGHT: The new MSP control tower, erected near the site of the original terminal building and tower, was nearing completion when this photo was taken in late 1963. Courtesy, Metropolitan Airports Commission

Based in the Twin Cities, North Central Airlines also needed new facilities to maintain its new fleet of DC-9 aircraft. Construction on the airline's $17-million main base and general office was begun in 1967. Courtesy, Metropolitan Airports Commission

that rate, some predicted, MSP would reach capacity by 1977.

Based on these revised forecasts, MAC entered another long, painful, and ultimately fruitless process of picking a second major Twin Cities airport site at the end of the decade.

The fight that was waged in the late 1940s over the fate of Wold-Chamberlain and a possible second airport paled by comparison. After another series of inflammatory hearings and public comment, the MAC's controversial decision to acquire a site at Ham Lake in Anoka County for a second major airport, while keeping MSP in operation, was rejected by the Metropolitan Council in 1969. The Met Council felt MSP should be downgraded and eventually abandoned in favor of a new site.

Despite opposition from the U.S. Department of the Interior and Met Council over environmental problems with the Ham Lake site, as well as threats of a lawsuit from the city of St. Paul over potential contamination of its water supply from the site, the MAC voted again to acquire the site. Its vote again was overruled by the Met Council.

In 1972 the MAC and Met Council came to an agreement on the Ham Lake location. But by that time, the MAC began to get cold feet about the aviation forecasts upon which it was relying and for the second time abandoned its effort to develop a second major Twin Cities airport.

As a result of this latest round of controversy over a new airport, there was an attempt in the Minnesota legislature in 1973 to make the MAC a branch of the Met Council. The effort failed, but the commission's makeup was expanded to include representatives from suburban metropolitan area communities in addition to Minneapolis and St. Paul.

In the late 1960s and 1970s, continued growth of passengers' business required expansion of the Lindbergh Terminal with the addition of the Green and Gold concourses. By 1967 four million passengers passed through the facility—a level not forecast until 1975. Courtesy, Metropolitan Airports Commission/Alvis Upitis

The move made sense because by that time, MAC owned reliever airports in rural Hennepin, Anoka, Washington, and Dakota counties and noise problems were affecting many other communities beyond Minneapolis and St. Paul.

MSP generated publicity of a more favorable nature in 1969, when Universal Studios selected the airport for the filming of the blockbuster movie *Airport*.

Shooting on the film, which featured an all-star cast of Burt Lancaster, Maureen Stapleton, Dean Martin, George Kennedy, and Helen Hayes, began in February. The first scene—a mythical "Trans-Global Airlines" B-707 borrowed from Flying Tigers mired in the snow off the southwest corner of the north-south runway—required excavation of the airfield.

Ironically, Minnesota's severe winter weather, the chief reason MSP was chosen for shooting the film, didn't cooperate for much of the filming and crews had to resort to blowing bushels of fake plastic snowflakes around to simulate a blizzard.

Shooting continued through the springtime inside the terminal and on the airfield. At one point the terminal was crowded with nearly 700 "extras," but most filming took place between 7 p.m.

and 3:30 a.m. to minimize disruptions of regular operations. The movie premiered on March 18, 1970, in MSP's Les Voyageurs restaurant.

Expansion at MSP continued unabated through the 1970s. In June 1970 Runway 11L/29R opened for its full 8,200-foot length. The first baggage carousels were put into service in the terminal building that year. When completed, the five carousels would be able to serve 1,000 passengers at one time. The Servicemen's Center opened in November, staffed by volunteers 24 hours a day. In its first year the center served more than 18,000 military personnel.

Northwest's Gold Concourse opened in 1971, along with its new cargo facility, crew headquarters, and flight simulator

facility. Construction on the parking ramp in front of the terminal building continued and the second deck opened, adding 850 spaces.

Expansion of the Green Concourse followed in 1972, as well as another addition to the parking ramp. An in-pavement lighting system was installed on the runways in 1974. And the bane of the coinless traveler, pay toilets, began to be removed from the terminal in 1975 in accordance with a new state law requiring at least half of them to be free.

Another state law that proved to be popular—and years ahead of its time—was the Minnesota Clean Indoor Air Act. The law, which drew nationwide attention, placed restrictions on smoking in public buildings such as airport terminals for the first time. In 1993 the terminal buildings at both MSP and St. Paul Downtown Airport became totally smoke-free.

Many smaller carriers started service at MSP in the 1960s and 1970s, including Mohawk Airlines (which later became Allegheny) serving upstate New York and parts of New England; MATS Airlines serving Iowa, Illinois, and Indiana; Mesaba Airlines with flights to northern Minnesota; Midstate Air Commuter with service to Wisconsin; Central Iowa Air-

RIGHT: MSP received much publicity with the release of the Universal Studios film, *Airport*, based on the Arthur Hailey novel. The film was shot at Wold-Chamberlain Field and many airline and airport employees were used as extras. One of Hollywood's most successful disaster films, the film featured Dean Martin and Jacqueline Bisset. Courtesy, Universal Studios

lines, and Air Wisconsin.

In 1975 the MAC bought United's six-year-old hangar with its unusual "hyperbolic paraboloid" roof and converted it to the Hubert H. Humphrey International Charter Terminal to serve the growing number of charters operating at MSP. The terminal opened in 1976 with expectations of serving 100,000 passengers a year.

Air cargo activity at MSP mushroomed during the 1970s. North Central started

BELOW: Controversy erupted in 1969 with the decision by the Metropolitan Airports Commission to build a new airport at Ham Lake in Anoka County. During a stormy commission meeting St. Paul mayor and MAC commissioner Tom Byrne hands MAC chairman Lawrence Hall a telegram from Northwest Airlines threatening to cancel expansion plans for its main base and move major maintenance on its 747 fleet to another city. The decision to move the airport was later set aside. Courtesy, *Minneapolis Star Tribune*

ABOVE: With construction of the Green and Gold concourses completed, MSP was ready for the expansion that would come with deregulation and the development of hubs by both Republic and Northwest Airlines. The Red and Blue concourses are shown in the foreground with the Gold Concourse on the right and the Green to the left. Parking ramps constructed in the late 1980s are shown between the two new concourses. Courtesy, Erdahl Aerial Photos

RIGHT: Named for Minnesota's favorite son, Hubert Humphrey, a converted United Airlines hangar became MSP's new charter and international arrivals facility. More than one million passengers were accommodated at the Humphrey Terminal in 1992. Courtesy, Metropolitan Airports Commission/Alvis Upitis

construction on a new cargo facility and began moving into it by the end of the year. Western opened a new air cargo terminal building in 1975. And Northwest introduced its new all-cargo B-747 freighter.

Deregulation of the airline industry in 1978 spurred another building boom at MSP in the 1980s. Before deregulation nine carriers served Minneapolis-St. Paul; after deregulation 24 airlines were flying in and out of the Twin Cities.

Among airlines entering the Twin Cities in the wake of deregulation were PeoplExpress and TWA (1978); Southern Airways (1978), which merged with North Central in 1979 to become Republic Airlines; Continental and Midway (1981); Texas International (1982); Sun Country (1983), which was a charter operation founded by former Braniff pilots; and Delta and Frontier (1984).

A new $20-million, seven-level parking ramp opened in 1984, adding another 2,000 spaces. A $28-million expansion of the Gold Concourse completed in 1986 featured the airport's first "people-mover," a half-mile moving sidewalk running the length of the concourse. The Green Concourse was expanded again, and a bridge was built connecting the Red and Gold concourses within the secured area. Numerous improvements also were made in concessions throughout the entire terminal, including the opening of a McDonald's restaurant on the Gold Concourse in 1985.

In 1985 the Wold-Chamberlain terminal building was dedicated as the Charles A. Lindbergh Terminal in honor of Minnesota's most famous aviator son.

By the mid-1980s the effects of deregulation on weaker airlines were starting to be felt. The merger of MSP's two biggest airline tenants, Northwest and Republic, took place in 1986, making it the nation's fourth-largest carrier. Frontier filed for bankruptcy after 39 years of operation. New York Air and PeoplExpress merged

into Continental, Delta bought Western in 1987, and Ozark merged with TWA.

Passenger counts at MSP increased by 64 percent from 1983 to 1987, while aircraft operations grew by only 21 percent during the same period. The apparent disparity in figures reflects the increasing use of larger aircraft and higher occupancy rates. Air cargo and mail tonnage nearly doubled during that time.

Marriott began a $7-million renovation of its terminal concessions in 1986, adding 11 shops and food service outlets. A $4.5-million expansion and renovation of the Humphrey International Terminal was completed in 1987. The MAC's capital improvements budget for 1988 included $30 million for a new eight-level, 2,200-space parking ramp to be completed in 1989; $45 million for Northwest and Mesaba airline hangars, which would be repaid through long-term leases; and $19.9 million for ground transportation facilities, reconstruction of access roads, and enclosed skyways connecting parking ramps with the main terminal.

Although noise has been an ongoing problem at the airport since the 1940s, the MAC is known worldwide for its persistence and innovation in trying to find amicable noise-abatement solutions while continuing to meet the area's air service needs.

In 1986 the MAC adopted a compre-

Federal Express became one of the world's most successful airline enterprises by developing a cargo business and providing service to its customers at levels unsurpassed in the industry. Courtesy, Metropolitan Airports Commission/Alvis Upitis

hensive noise-reduction plan that promised to reduce the average daily noise at MSP. A ban on training flights enacted that year eliminated about 1,200 flights a month, and the merging of Northwest's and Republic's operations in 1987 resulted in the reduction of about another 100 flights a day.

The next year the MAC held hearings on a controversial "noise budget" ordinance that would allow each airline to generate only a certain amount of noise. The proposal was shelved, however, after Northwest and the FAA threatened to sue on the basis of federal prohibition of interference with interstate commerce.

The MAC then negotiated agreements with carriers for voluntary reductions to bring noise down to 1984 levels, but the city of Minneapolis threatened to sue if mandatory noise reduction measures weren't enacted.

The airlines eventually agreed to reduce noise levels to at least 24 percent below the August 1986 high, or to approximately 1984 levels. The MAC's aggressive noise-reduction efforts have continued with a

$100-million soundproofing/property acquisition program for noise-affected schools and homes. It also has installed 24 permanent noise-monitoring microphones in neighborhoods around the airport that accurately record noise, identify aircraft, and record flight track data.

The agreements with the airlines, although voluntary, succeeded in progressively reducing noise levels for five years.

Forecasts by the MAC and Metropolitan Council in 1988 predict an increase in passenger traffic at MSP from 19.3 million in 1991 to 39 million in 2020. The airport could accommodate such growth at its current site through 2020 and even beyond if several recommended improvements are implemented. These include a new 8,000-foot north-south runway, a terminal twice the size of the existing one, and 30 additional aircraft gates.

The proposed new runway on the west side of the field (independent from all existing runways) would require the acquisition and elimination of residential areas in Richfield and commercial properties in Bloomington. A new terminal also would be built on the west side of the airport. Existing terminal and parking facilities would be removed from between the Gold and Green concourses and replaced by aircraft parking gates. All concourses and the new terminal would be connected by an underground people-mover system. Total cost of the expansion is estimated at $1.5 billion.

An alternative is to build a second air carrier airport in the metropolitan area at a cost of at least $4 billion. Under a "dual-track" process established by the state legislature, the MAC and Met Council have pursued a strategy of continuing to improve the existing MSP facilities, while at the same time searching for a potential new airport site in case one is needed.

The Metropolitan Council identified a 115-square-mile area in Dakota County south of the Twin Cities where a new airport might be built. The MAC then nar-

senger facility charge," collected from all originating and connecting passengers at the airport.

From its humble beginnings in the middle of a defunct auto racetrack in 1920 to being the nation's 15th-busiest airport, Minneapolis-St. Paul International has come a long way.

Today Minneapolis-St. Paul International Airport/Wold-Chamberlain Field covers 3,100 acres. It is served by 10 major airlines, 8 regional airlines, 19 charter carriers, and 15 cargo carriers, with single-plane passenger service to 125 domestic and 15 international destinations. In 1992 MSP saw more than 21 million passengers pass through its gates and hosted over 415,000 aircraft operations.

rowed that down to a specific site within the area and by 1996, the legislature will decide to expand MSP, build a new airport, "bank" land for future construction of a new airport at such time as it may be needed, or do nothing.

Meanwhile, MSP hasn't stopped building. Through 1996, $70 million in roadway and terminal improvements are planned, funded primarily by a $3 head tax, or "pas-

As it looks ahead to the twenty-first century, the Metropolitan Airports Commission once again must assist the legislature in determining the fate and future of Minneapolis-St. Paul International Airport.

ABOVE: Braniff International was the first major casualty of deregulation when it suspended operations in May 1982 and filed for bankruptcy. The handwritten note posted at the MSP ticket counter told Braniff passengers how they could make alternate arrangements. Courtesy, *Minneapolis Star Tribune*

LEFT: Formed by the merger of the Twin Cities-based North Central Airlines and Southern Airways, Republic Airlines emerged as a major deregulation-era airline. Republic became an intense competitor with Northwest at two main hubs shared by both companies—Minneapolis/St. Paul and Detroit. Republic was led by former Continental Airlines president Stephen Wolf, who helped to bring about the merger with Northwest in 1986. Courtesy, *Minneapolis Star Tribune*

CHAPTER THREE

MAKING CONNECTIONS

A mother and son prepare for some night flying in the countryside surrounding Lake Elmo Airport east of St. Paul. Photo by Greg Ryan/ Sally Beyer

One of the most well-developed airport systems in the country operates in the shadow of Minneapolis-St. Paul International. While MSP handles all commercial air traffic in the Twin Cities metropolitan area, the vast majority of "general aviation" activity, which comprises everything else, occurs at the MAC's six reliever airports.

More than 876,000 operations took place at the Twin Cities' six relievers in 1992, twice the operations at MSP. About 2,000 aircraft are based at these airports, which also support a wide range of aviation services.

The MAC operates MSP and the six relievers, while the Metropolitan Council, an intergovernmental planning agency, is responsible for coordinating the aviation system and other regional systems with individual city and county comprehensive plans.

The MAC's first proposed airport system in 1946 included Wold-Chamberlain, Holman Field, airports at Bloomington and Robbinsdale, University Airport north of New Brighton, one airport east of St. Paul, and Fleming Field in South St. Paul.

This plan was modified to include Flying Cloud Airport in Eden Prairie instead of Bloomington, a site in Crystal instead of Robbinsdale, Anoka County, and Oakdale, which later was replaced by Lake Elmo.

The commission had no shortage of advice from the local aviation community in formulating its airport system plan. The Greater Twin Cities chapter of the National Aeronautics Association, for example, ambitiously forecast a need for 20 to 40 additional fields in the Twin Cities.

The commission acquired its first reliever airport, Flying Cloud in what is now Eden Prairie, on September 1, 1948. On December 6, 1948, the modified system plan was adopted by the commission and it has remained essentially the same ever since. That same day the MAC voted to acquire the Crystal Airport site.

While it isn't likely that a new general aviation facility will be needed soon in the Minneapolis-St. Paul region, one area in northwestern Hennepin County has been identified as a potential site for a new reliever airport in the Twin Cities if demand requires it. However, development of any new airports in the Twin Cities, or

significant expansion of any of the existing relievers, ultimately will depend on whether MSP remains at its present site or a new international airport is built elsewhere.

Let's take a tour of the Minneapolis-St. Paul reliever airports system and check the pulse of general aviation in the Twin Cities.

ST. PAUL DOWNTOWN AIRPORT

St. Paul Downtown Airport is the crown jewel of the Metropolitan Airports Commission reliever airport system. Located just across the Mississippi River from the downtown business district of the capital city, and only 15 minutes from downtown Minneapolis, St. Paul Downtown Airport is closer than MSP to both cities' core business districts, a fact prominently promoted in the airport's marketing.

A group of civic leaders helped persuade the city of St. Paul to buy the initial 150 acres of land for Holman Field, known then as St. Paul Airport, in 1926. A 3,400-foot sod landing strip was developed, followed by a second 2,500-foot turf strip and a municipal hangar.

On July 5, 1927, Northwest Airways carried its first passenger from St. Paul Airport. Airline passenger service continued to expand at St. Paul Airport and Northwest established its main base there in 1930. That same year the Minnesota National Guard's 109th Air Squadron moved from Wold-Chamberlain Field.

The airport was renamed Holman Field in 1932 in honor of Charles "Speed" Hol-

man, a famous local race and stunt pilot who later became Northwest's first pilot and operating officer. Holman was killed performing stunts in an Omaha air show in 1931.

Holman Field was expanded by 90 acres in 1929 and fill from dredging operations on the river was used to build up some of the floodplain land on which the airport sat. Throughout the 1930s additional improvements and land acquisitions were made at Holman Field through the federal Work Projects Administration, as well as more dredging and filling. These included paving runways, taxiways, and aprons, installation of lighting and other utilities, and construction of a new administration/terminal building.

All this construction took a heavy toll on Northwest's ability to conduct scheduled operations at Holman Field, however, and the airline pulled all scheduled service out of St. Paul in 1941.

Holman Field took on an important role during World War II, when the War Department took over the field and established a major B-24 bomber modification facility there in 1942. Northwest Airlines operated the modification facility, which employed more than 5,000 workers and turned out 3,000 specially equipped aircraft, much of it done in secret.

When the MAC took over Holman Field in 1944 it still was under lease to the War Department. The control tower was operated by the Civil Aeronautics Administration. The modification center was turned over to Northwest for a main base

and the MAC petitioned the federal government in 1947 for the return of the airport to the local authority.

Holman Field was transferred to the MAC in 1948 and an additional 349 acres on the south and west sides of the airport were acquired for further construction by 1950 of a new control tower, lighting, and aprons.

St. Paul Downtown Airport today is the primary reliever for MSP and is heavily used by business aircraft. Fleets of several major Twin Cities corporations are based here, as well as aircraft used by state agencies. About 250 aircraft are based at St. Paul Downtown. In addition, the U.S. Army Reserve and Army National Guard maintain a number of helicopters here for training missions.

Corporate pilots favor St. Paul Downtown Airport because of its close proximity

LEFT: Regent Aviation expanded to spacious new facilities on the west side of St. Paul Downtown Airport in 1989 and has continued to grow. The full-service FBO completed a new 32,000-square-foot maintenance hangar in 1993. Courtesy, Regent Aviation

FAR LEFT: St. Paul Downtown Airport is closer than MSP International to both downtown Minneapolis and St. Paul, making it an attractive alternative for corporate pilots flying into the Twin Cities. About 250 aircraft are based there, including many corporate jets. Photo by Greg Ryan/Sally Beyer

25 acres of developable land on the southwest side of the field that may be used with some wetlands mitigation.

St. Paul Downtown Airport has embarked on an aggressive marketing program in the past two years. An ad campaign targeted at corporate pilots touted St. Paul Downtown as "the Twin Cities' best-kept secret," but that secret is starting to get out.

Airport manager Greg Fries and fixed-base operators on the field report a significant increase in out-of-state itinerant corporate aircraft visiting St. Paul Downtown as a result of the major national and international events held in the Twin Cities recently. Many of them, they say, are repeat customers.

Aviation business at St. Paul Downtown Airport is prospering as evidenced by recent expansions and additions:

■ Regent Aviation: 24-hour, full-service FBO that relocated to new facilities on the west side of the field in 1989. A new 32,000-square-foot maintenance hangar was completed in 1993 that also will house a new avionics shop.

The company also operates a pilot shop in the airport terminal building and a seaplane base on the adjacent Mississippi River during the summer months. Other services available at Regent include Phillips 66 100LL and jet-A fuel, full maintenance services that soon will include a turbine shop, meeting facilities, car rental, courtesy shuttle to MSP and other locations, and in-flight catering.

■ St. Paul Flight Center: full-service FBO with 42,000 square feet of rental hangar space and a new turboprop maintenance department added in 1992. St. Paul Flight

to both cities, long runway and Instrument Landing System (ILS), and no delays for takeoffs and landings. The airport gained a national reputation as a world-class facility by hosting several major influxes of corporate aircraft in recent years: the 1991 World Series; the Special Olympics in 1991, which drew more than 200 Cessna Citation jets flying 1,500 handicapped athletes in from 30 cities; the 1992 Super Bowl and NCAA Final Four; and the 1992 American Bonanza Society Convention, which was attended by over 250 Beechcraft Bonanzas from across the country.

St. Paul Downtown Airport had 152,378 operations in 1992, typically handling about 420 operations a day. Its air traffic control tower operates from 7 a.m. to 10 p.m.

St. Paul Downtown's triangle-shaped airfield comprises a 6,700-foot primary runway, 14/32, which can accommodate any corporate jet flying, and secondary runways 8/26 (3,646 feet) and 12/30 (4,115 feet). Runway 32 is served by an ILS and there is a nondirectional beacon approach for Runway 30. All runways are lighted and served by parallel taxiways. Navigational aids include visual approach slope indicators (VASIs) on Runways 12/30 and 26 and runway end identifier lights (REILs) on Runways 14/32 and 30.

According to MAC Reliever Airports manager Gary Schmidt, an ILS has been proposed for Runway 14. "It would really assure the corporate pilots that they'll have access to the field under all weather conditions." Schmidt hopes the system can be installed by 1996.

There are few opportunities for expansion of St. Paul Downtown Airport beyond its existing 540 acres, but there are about

systems, and searchlights.

A new helicopter charter company is expected to begin operations at St. Paul Downtown Airport by 1994.

St. Paul Downtown Airport and Fleming Field are home to the Confederate Air Force, a volunteer group that is committed to keeping World War II aircraft flying. The group puts on an annual air power display in August the week following the Oshkosh, Wisconsin, International Fly-In, drawing some 20,000 spectators.

ANOKA COUNTY/BLAINE AIRPORT
Anoka County/Blaine Airport is the MAC's busiest reliever airport, with 195,650 operations in 1992. About 400 aircraft, mostly single-engine but some turboprop, jet, and rotorcraft, are based here. The 1,900-acre field is located in the city

ABOVE: St. Paul Flight Center opened a new turboprop maintenance department in 1992, evidence of the thriving corporate aviation community at St. Paul Downtown Airport. The operation is one of two full-service fixed-base operators on the field. Photo by Greg Ryan/Sally Beyer

RIGHT: Lives depend on the aircraft flown by LifeLink III, a critical care service at St. Paul Downtown Airport. LifeLink III, a tenant at St. Paul Flight Center, operates two helicopters and two fixed-wing aircraft fully equipped to handle all types of medical emergencies. Photo by Greg Ryan/Sally Beyer

Center also has car rentals and Amoco 100LL and jet-A fuel.

■ Wings Inc.: Part 141 flight school affiliated with Inver Hills Community College and Northwest Airlines training facilities. Wings Inc. also offers seaplane training at a base near Brainerd in north-central Minnesota.

■ Aviation Maintenance Inc.: single-engine, light twin, and turbine maintenance services; airframe maintenance.

■ Minnesota Jet: turbojet aircraft management, operation, and charter services, including time-critical organ transplants.

■ R.C. Avionics: maintenance and installation of all major lines of avionics, specializing in strobes, instrument panel fabrication, fuel metering systems, infrared

of Blaine in southern Anoka County, 30 minutes north of downtown Minneapolis and St. Paul.

Anoka County Blaine Airport originally was intended to serve as a secondary commercial airport with parallel 10,000-foot north-south runways. The MAC acquired 1,200 acres for Anoka County/Blaine Airport in 1950, but the airport never saw a day of commercial service.

After considerable protests from neighboring residents, the MAC in 1954 ordered the expansion of the airport by about 400 acres to accommodate various noncommercial uses: the National Guard's 109th Air Squadron, then stationed at Holman Field in St. Paul; the 440th Fighter Bomber Wing Reserve, located at MSP; the University of Minnesota's aviation activities, which had been conducted at University Airport airport south of the Anoka site until the MAC bought it through condemnation; and private aircraft owners.

The MAC's decision to expand the airport was appealed and hearings on the matter were reopened a year later but it ultimately was upheld.

Anoka County Blaine Airport today has two intersecting runways—a 4,855-foot

primary (17/35) and a 4,000-foot crosswind (8/26)—served by connecting parallel taxiways. All runways are lighted. Runway 35 is equipped with REILs and VASIs are on Runway 17/35.

A new parallel runway and taxiway (17R/35R) and extension of 8/26 have been recommended for Anoka County/Blaine. And MAC Reliever Airports manager Schmidt says he expects funding for an air traffic control tower can be secured by 1994.

Anoka County/Blaine Airport offers a wide range of aviation services for recreational and corporate pilots:

■ Cirrus Flight Operations: full maintenance and overhaul services; Phillips 66 100LL and jet-A fuel, including self-service fueling; weather services hangar and tie-down rentals.

■ American Air Center: full maintenance services; Phillips 66 100LL fuel; weather services; pilot supplies; flight instruction; Cessna and Piper single- and multi-engine aircraft rental.

■ Northern Aviation: piston-engine maintenance; Part 141 flight school; Cessna and

Anoka County/Blaine Airport, the busiest airport in the Twin Cities' reliever system, sees nearly 200,000 operations a year. About 400 aircraft are based here and the field is served by a wide range of aviation services. An additional runway and taxiway have been proposed for Anoka County/Blaine Airport to accommodate its expected growth. Courtesy, Metropolitan Airports Commission/Alvis Upitis

Piper single- and multi-engine aircraft rental.

■ Bolduc Aviation Specialized Services: certified FAA repair station; engine overhauls; engine accessory rebuilding.

■ Anoka Flight Training: Cessna Pilot Training Program flight school with simulator; Cessna, Beechcraft, and Piper single- and multi-engine aircraft rental; Phillips 66 100LL and auto fuel; full maintenance and overhaul services; hangar and tie-downs for rental.

■ Aircraft Electronics: service and sales for all major lines of avionics, including autopilots.

■ Thunderbolt Aviation: single-engine and

light twin aircraft maintenance and annual inspections; sheet metal and fabric repairs.

In between aircraft maintenance work, Thunderbolt Aviation owner John Ysker has been building a hybrid "airplane-car" in his shop. The 21-foot-long craft is powered by a 350-horsepower engine and will travel 300 miles per hour in the air and 60-65 miles per hour on the ground, Ysker claims. He expects to finish it by 1997 or 1998. "I think it's a marketable unit," he says.

The University of Minnesota flight department maintains a Beechcraft King Air and Baron at Anoka County/Blaine Airport for use by its faculty and staff.

FLYING CLOUD AIRPORT

Flying Cloud Airport is a bustling center of general aviation activity in the western Minneapolis suburb of Eden Prairie serving business and recreational fliers and even an air museum. The airport saw 198,306 operations in 1992, with about

500 aircraft based here.

On September 1, 1948, Flying Cloud became the first reliever airport to be acquired by the MAC. At the time it was a privately owned and operated 135-acre, grass-strip airport with a small terminal building. By 1952 a north-south runway was paved after pilots petitioned the MAC for a hard-surface runway.

Today the 560-acre field has two parallel runways—9R/27L (3,909 feet) and 9L/27R (3,599 feet)—and a 2,694-foot crosswind runway 18-36. Runway 9R is equipped with a VASI and approach light system. Runway 27L has a VASI and REILs, and a VASI also is on 18. The air traffic control tower operates from 7 a.m. to 9 p.m.

The MAC has proposed to extend and widen Runway 9R/27 to 5,000 feet by 100 feet to allow Flying Cloud to better serve as a corporate reliever to MSP. Observes MAC's Schmidt: "If Minneapolis-St. Paul International stays where it is, each of the reliever airports will have to take a bigger share of the corporate traffic. And it does provide a greater margin of safety."

The extension would require acquisition of land on the west end of the runway. Total cost of the project has been estimated at $4 million.

Flying Cloud Airport has an active aviation business community with six fixed-base operators and a variety of other services and attractions.

Perhaps Flying Cloud's most unusual aviation attraction is the Planes of Fame Air Museum, a private collection of 25 World War II fighters, bombers, and trainers owned by Bob Pond and housed in 50,000 square feet of hangar space. All the planes are "functional and ready to go,"

says museum manager Jim Duffy. "It's one of the premier collections in the world."

Planes of Fame has supplied vintage warplanes for a number of motion pictures and commercials. And for $75 you can take a ride in an open-cockpit Stearman biplane to experience flying "the way it was meant to be," says Duffy. About 200 volunteers assist with maintaining and restoring the planes. The museum is open six days a week year-round.

Other businesses on Flying Cloud include:

■ Elliott Flying Service: Beechcraft distributor and service center; full maintenance services; avionics shop; nondestructive test-

ing; prop balancing; pressurization testing; air charter; in-flight catering; car rental; limousine service; pilot supplies; hangar rental; 100LL and jet-A fuel.

■ Thunderbird Aviation: flight school with 26 aircraft; full maintenance and overhaul services; hangar and tie-down rentals; charter service; Phillips 66 100LL fuel.

■ ASI/Modern Aero: Piper aircraft dealer and parts distributor; service center for Piper, Mooney, and Aerospatiele; flight instruction; aircraft rental; Avnet/Pride 100LL and jet-A fuel; hangar and tie-down rental; car rental.

■ Modern Avionics: avionics repair shop for all major lines.

■ Flying Cloud Executive Aviation/Aviation Charter: air charter operation specializing in air ambulance services; full maintenance services; hangar and tie-down rentals, Phillips 66 100LL and jet-A fuel.

ABOVE: Student pilots use a simulator for more realistic single- and multi-engine flight training at Flying Scotchman on Crystal Airport. The Part 141 flight school employs a fleet of 12 Cessnas and a Beech Duchess. Photo by Greg Ryan/Sally Beyer

RIGHT: Specialized aircraft repair businesses like Maxwell Aircraft Services round out the Crystal Airport aviation community. The company performs all types of propeller repair at its 30,000-square-foot shop on the airport. Photo by Greg Ryan/Sally Beyer

FACING PAGE: Helicopter Flight's fleet of five Robinson choppers at Crystal Airport provides helicopter instruction, charter services, and aerial photography. Photo by Greg Ryan/Sally Beyer

■ American Aviation Company: flight instruction; piston and turbine maintenance and overhauls; aircraft rental; avionics and instrument repair and installation; pilots' gift shop.

■ General Aviation Services: flight training; aircraft sales, rental and charter; aircraft maintenance; hangar rental; 100LL and jet-A fuel.

■ Aircraft Sales Inc.: aircraft sales and brokerage firm for singles through jets.

■ The Upholstery Shop: full interior refurbishment and modification facility for airline, corporate, and general aviation aircraft; fireblocking; sound deadening; orthopedic seat work; cabinetry and entertainment system installation.

CRYSTAL AIRPORT
Crystal Airport adjoins the northeastern Minneapolis suburbs of Crystal, Brooklyn

Center, and Brooklyn Park. The 430-acre airport is easily accessible via U.S. 169 for the recreational and business flyers who use it.

Residential neighborhoods completely encompass Crystal Airport so the likelihood of expansion there is virtually nil.

Crystal Airport was the second airport acquired by the MAC in 1948. Construction didn't begin until the summer of 1950, and an additional 34 acres of land was purchased the following year for run-

way extensions and noise relief for adjacent neighbors.

Recent activity at the airport includes a major renovation at one of the field's fixed-base operators, Crystal Shamrock.

Crystal Airport's air traffic control tower operates from 7 a.m. to 9 p.m. It has three 75-foot-wide paved runways—parallel runways 13L/31R (3,264 feet) and 13R/31L (3,267 feet) and crosswind runway 5L/23R (2,499 feet)—and 2,123-foot turf Runway 5R/23L. Runways 13L/31R and 5L/23R are equipped with VASIs and runway edge lights. A VOR-A approach is available on 31R and REILs are on 13L/31R.

Operations at Crystal Airport in 1992 numbered 179,546. About 325 aircraft are based at Crystal, nearly all piston-engine with an occasional business jet. There are about 250 hangar buildings, mostly single-plane. Wiley Enterprise owns about 100 and the remainder are privately owned or at FBOs.

Following are aviation businesses and

services available at Crystal Airport:

■ Crystal Shamrock: full-service FBO, FAA-certified repair and overhaul facility and Part 141 flight school; Cessna dealer; Texaco 100LL, jet-A and auto fuel; complete maintenance and line services; upholstery work; avionics repair; Cessna and Piper rental aircraft; 10 hangar spaces and 45 tie-down spaces.

■ Flying Scotchman: Cessna service center and Part 141 Cessna Pilot Center flight school with single- and multi-engine simulators; 12 Cessnas and Beech Duchess rental aircraft; Phillips 66 100LL fuel; full maintenance services.

■ Helicopter Flight: helicopter charter and flight instruction using four Robinson R-22s and one R-44; aerial photography; rotor and fixed-wing maintenance services; hangar storage space.

■ Maxwell Aircraft Service: specialized propeller repair for all types of aircraft.

■ Northland Aircraft Services: full-service FBO; flight training; aircraft rental; 100LL and jet-A fuel sales; full maintenance services; hangar and tie-down rental; pilot supplies; car rental.

■ Crystal Skyways: flight training; aircraft rental; 100LL and auto fuel sales; maintenance; tie-downs.

AIRLAKE AIRPORT
AirLake Airport is the southernmost field in the MAC's reliever airport system. A large industrial park is located just north of the airport and agricultural and scattered residential uses make up the remainder of the airport's surrounding areas.

Located near the Dakota County communities of Lakeville and Farmington 22 miles south of Minneapolis and St. Paul, AirLake Airport is home to about 100 based airplanes, mostly single-engine and light twins. Aircraft operations at 565-acre AirLake Airport grew from an estimated 52,000 in 1987 to 81,087 in 1992.

AirLake's single Runway 11-29 is 4,100 feet long. Runway and landing lights are radio controlled. According to MAC's Schmidt, AirLake's 20-year plan calls for extending the existing runway to its original 5,000-foot length and the addition of a

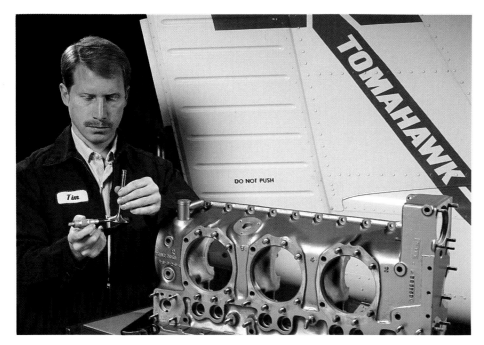

Full piston-engine maintenance services are performed at Flyteline Services, one of two fixed-base operators on AirLake Airport. Flyteline is a Phillips 66 Performance Center and Cessna Pilot and Service Center. Photo by Greg Ryan/Sally Beyer

new crosswind runway if traffic demands it. However, AirLake generally has operated well below its capacity.

Additional hangar space could be built on the southeast corner of the 565-acre field if needed.

Although AirLake is located in a comfortable rural setting, it's easily accessible to the Minneapolis and St. Paul downtown business districts via Interstate 35 four miles west of the airport and Cedar Avenue on the airport's eastern boundary.

Flight training students, private recreational fliers, and a few business pilots comprise AirLake's aviation community.

Aviation services available at AirLake include:

■ Flyteline: Phillips 66 Performance Center; Cessna Pilot and Service Center; Part 141 flight school, including computerized FAA testing facilities; aircraft rentals.

■ Multiflight: Part 141 flight school; Cessna and Piper aircraft rental; 100LL fuel; pilot supplies; full maintenance services; hangare and tie-down rental.

LAKE ELMO AIRPORT
Lake Elmo Airport is surrounded by

rolling farmland in Washington County on the eastern edge of the Twin Cities metropolitan area. The countryside around the airport is dotted with small clusters of homes on large lots separated by expansive pastures and patches of hardwoods. The St. Croix River, a National Scenic Riverway on the Minnesota Wisconsin border, lies about five miles to the east.

Primarily serving recreational fliers, the airport is easily accessible via Interstate 94 three miles south and Minnesota highways 5 and 36 to the north.

Lake Elmo Airport was acquired by the MAC in December 1949, the result of a compromise between proponents of a site farther south and the city of Stillwater northeast of Lake Elmo, which also wanted an airport of its own. After extensive public hearings the 320-acre site was purchased for $38,300.

Lake Elmo's two runways, 13-31 and 3-21, bisect in a "T" with connecting taxiways around two sides of the triangular-shaped airfield. Traffic at Lake Elmo grew from an estimated 63,000 operations in 1987 to 69,950 in 1992. Operations are projected to grow to more than 88,000 by 1998.

About 150 single- and twin-engine piston aircraft are based at Lake Elmo Airport. The field's FBO population dropped from three to one in 1992, when Mayer Aviation acquired Elmo Aero and a fire claimed the airport's third FBO.

According to Schmidt, improvements

planned for Lake Elmo Airport include upgraded navaids, such as a VOR or NDB, lengthening of the field's primary runway, and an extension to the crosswind runway. Improvements at Lake Elmo are expected to make the airport more attractive to overflow traffic from nearby St. Paul Downtown Airport as that need increases.

Services available at Lake Elmo Airport include:

■ Mayer Aviation: full-service FBO; flight school with simulator; Phillips 66 80 octane, auto, and 100LL fuel; full maintenance services and overhauls; 35 hangar spaces and 12 tie-downs; single-engine Piper and Cessna aircraft rental; pilot supplies.

In addition to the six MAC-operated designated reliever airports, the area's aviation community is served by another 14 fields within 50 miles of the metropolitan area:

■ South St. Paul Airport (Fleming Field), a city-owned facility in South St. Paul and the only non-MAC-operated airport in the

LEFT: Aircraft operations at AirLake Airport in rural Dakota County 22 miles south of the Twin Cities grew from 52,000 in 1987 to 81,087 in 1992. Near the communities of Farmington and Lakeville, the airport also is easily accessible to downtown Minneapolis and St. Paul. Courtesy, Metropolitan Airports Commission/Alvis Upitis

BELOW: Mayer Aviation rents single-engine Piper and Cessna planes and provides a full range of other services for recreational flyers, including 100LL, 80 octane, and auto fuel sales. Photo by Greg Ryan/Sally Beyer

■ New Richmond Municipal Airport, a publicly owned field near New Richmond in western Wisconsin with a 3,000-foot paved runway and 2,240-foot turf runway.

■ Osceola Airport, a city-owned airport in Osceola, Wisconsin, south of New Richmond, with a 3,000-foot paved runway and a 2,240-foot turf runway.

■ Carlton Municipal Airport, a privately owned, public-use field with two turf runways in Goodhue County 30 miles south of the Twin Cities.

■ Winsted Municipal Airport, a city-owned facility near Winsted in McLeod County with a 3,245-foot turf runway.

■ Northport Airport, a privately owned airport in suburban White Bear Lake.

reliever system. It has a 4,000-foot paved runway.

■ Benson Airport in northeastern Ramsey County, a privately owned airport that serves area glider enthusiasts.

■ Buffalo Municipal Airport, a publicly owned field in Wright County 20 miles northwest of Minneapolis.

■ Cambridge Municipal Airport, a publicly owned field near Cambridge in Isanti County 30 miles north of the Twin Cities.

■ Faribault Municipal Airport, a publicly owned facility with a 4,700-foot runway near Faribault 50 miles south of the Twin Cities.

■ Forest Lake Airport, a privately owned, public-use airport with a 2,575-foot turf runway near Forest Lake in Washington County 30 miles northeast of St. Paul.

■ Glencoe Municipal Airport, a publicly owned facility with a 3,420-foot turf runway near Glencoe in McLeod County 30

miles west of Minneapolis.

■ LeSueur Municipal Airport, a city-owned airport with a 3,000-foot paved runway near LeSueur in LeSueur County 40 miles south of the Twin Cities.

CHAPTER FOUR

WELCOMING THE WORLD

Built in 1904, the Minnesota State Capitol in St. Paul is an Italian Renaissance-style masterpiece. The capitol is one of the cornerstones of St. Paul's "Cultural Corridor."
Photo by Richard Hamilton Smith

Minnesota for many years undersold itself as a tourist destination. The state long had to combat its image as frozen tundra whose main export was record-breaking cold temperatures. Even its most well-known nickname—the Land of 10,000 Lakes—was pegged conservatively. The number of lakes actually is closer to 15,000.

All that has changed. Today tourism is a $7-billion-a-year industry in Minnesota, placing it among the top five industries in the state. The Minnesota Office of Tourism, coupled with a whole host of major national sporting and other events held here in recent years, has raised the visibility of Minnesota to an all-time high.

In 1991 Minnesota played host to nearly seven million domestic business and pleasure travelers, another half-million Canadian neighbors to the north, and 195,000 other international visitors.

All those visitors aren't just passing through, either. Minnesota is the final destination for more than 80 percent of them, spending an average of nearly four nights in the state. The Twin Cities seven-county metropolitan area alone is the destination of half of all out-of-state visitors during the fall and winter months and attracts about one-third of those traveling in the spring and summer.

Meetings and conventions are an important part of the Twin Cities' tourism industry, and both cities are continually upgrading their facilities to accommodate them. There are more than 15,000 hotel rooms available in the Minneapolis-St. Paul metropolitan area.

The new Minneapolis Convention Center opened in 1990 with 280,000 square feet of exhibition space under three unique domed halls and a 28,000-square-foot ballroom. The facility drew more than a quarter-million conventioneers to downtown Minneapolis in 1992 and already has bookings for major events years in advance.

The St. Paul Civic Center features a 16,500-seat arena with 73,000 square feet of exhibition space. The Civic Center is scheduled for a $90-million renovation in the mid-1990s.

Minnesota's first-rate transportation systems make it easy for visitors to get here.

Minneapolis-St. Paul International Airport is the main hub for locally based

The Michelangelo-influenced St. Paul Cathedral, one of the city's grander architectural landmarks, resides at the east end of prestigious Summit Avenue. Photo by Greg Ryan/Sally Beyer

Northwest Airlines. The airport is served by a dozen other major passenger and freight carriers and numerous charter and commuter airlines, with more than 1,000 arrivals and departures daily between the Twin Cities and destinations around the globe.

Minneapolis-St. Paul lies at the crossroads of east-west Interstate Highway 94 and north-south Interstate Highway 35, and Interstate 90 traverses the southern half of the state. And the Twin Cities and north-central Minnesota are served by Amtrak's east-west "Empire Builder" passenger trains daily.

Minnesotans always have known why people are attracted to the Twin Cities. The rest of the country in recent years has started to catch on as well.

Travel expert Arthur Frommer in 1986 named the Twin Cities one of the top 10 vacation destinations in the world. *Money* magazine ranked the Twin Cities seventh in its 1990 "best places to live" survey. *Newsweek* magazine in 1989 cited St. Paul as one of the country's 10 "hottest" cities to watch in the 1990s. "Minneapolis-St. Paul is among America's cleanest, safest metropolitan areas," *Fortune* magazine said when it ranked the Twin Cities second best in the country for business in 1990.

So what's the attraction here? After all, this is America's North Coast, not the vaunted East or West Coast. Let's take a look around and find out.

"If each of the Twin Cities hums to a different tune, they harmonize on the main themes: There is still hope for the American city; an urban landscape can still nurture the human species."
—*National Geographic* magazine, November 1980.

The tale of these two cities begins in their architecture. While St. Paul's distinctly European flavor contrasts sharply with Minneapolis' shimmering cosmopolitan

ABOVE: The St. Paul City Hall and Courthouse building is a splendid example of Art Deco inside and out. The interior features the 36-foot onyx *Indian God of Peace,* which stands illuminated in a recently renovated black atrium. Photo by Greg Ryan/Sally Beyer

TOP: The Minnesota House of Representatives meets annually in these ornate chambers of the state capitol. Photo by Greg Ryan/Sally Beyer

newness, both cities have some magnificant architectural treasures of historical significance worth noting.

Summit Avenue, the longest preserved stretch of Victorian-era mansions in the country, is St. Paul's most exclusive address. The 4.5-mile parkway is an architectural delight, running from railroad magnate James J. Hill's fabulous 1891 red sandstone mansion and the Michelangelo-influenced St. Paul Cathedral on one end, past F. Scott Fitzgerald's residence, the governor's mansion and dozens of even grander stone palaces, to the bluffs high above the Mississippi River on the other.

St. Paul's Landmark Center, a former federal courts building where mobsters were tried in the Roaring Twenties, is a majestic pink marble castle in the midst of downtown. With its multiple towers, turrets, and gables, the neo-Romanesque building now houses numerous arts groups and galleries.

Minneapolis' answer to the Landmark Center is its City Hall. Built in 1906 at a cost of $3.5 million, this five-story granite fortress is topped with a four-faced clock tower that rises nearly 345 feet in the air.

The Minnesota State Capitol in St. Paul, completed in 1904, is an Italian Renaissance-style masterpiece designed by Cass Gilbert, who later went on to design the U.S. Supreme Court building. The capitol boasts the world's largest unsupported marble dome, and its floors are laid with more than 20 types of imported marble.

The St. Paul City Hall and Ramsey County Courthouse is one of the finest examples of Art Deco architecture anywhere. The highlight is the building's Memorial Hall, a black colonnaded atrium in which a massive 36-foot onyx sculpture, the symbolic *Indian God of Peace,* stands guard.

Other Twin Cities architectural highlights include the Alexander Ramsey House in St. Paul's Irvine Park, home of Min-

Rice Park in downtown St. Paul shimmers with light in the wintertime. The park is flanked by the coppery-warm Ordway Theatre, the St. Paul Public Library, the fortress-like Landmark Center, and the elegant St. Paul Hotel. Photo by Greg Ryan/Sally Beyer

One of the oversized characters of Minneapolis' Heart of the Beast Puppet and Mask Theatre—surefire crowd-pleasers wherever they turn up—towers over a waterborne float in the annual May Day Celebration at Powderhorn Park. Photo by Richard Hamilton Smith

nesota's first governor; St. Paul's Minnesota Museum of Art and Minneapolis' Foshay Tower, both monuments to Art Deco; the Grain Belt Brewery, a Gothic 1891 brewhouse on the banks of the Mississippi River in north Minneapolis; and the newer Cesar Pelli-designed Norwest Center, a dominant figure on the Minneapolis skyline.

Minneapolis and St. Paul share a rich tradition of appreciation for the arts that goes back to before the turn of the century. Mildred Lucile Hartsough wrote in 1925: "It was in the period beginning about 1880 that newspapers in Minneapolis and St. Paul began to reflect the general feeling that the metropolitan character of a city depended on something more than economic progress, and to take interest in a less material side of life. Social and dramatic events and the growth of educational

facilities, especially the University of Minnesota, received increasing attention. Musical development was especially noted during that period, and the evidence indicates that the progress made in that field was rapid."

That tradition is evident in today's Twin Cities more than ever.

There are 90-plus live theaters—more than any area outside of New York—in Minneapolis and St. Paul, presenting traditional plays, comedies, musicals, experimental theater, and touring Broadway productions.

Theater not your passion? Then try the 130 art galleries, 20 classical music groups, 15 museums, 10 dance companies, and dozens of live music clubs featuring a menu of rock, jazz, rhythm and blues, country, and folk music unsurpassed anywhere. And just for laughs, check out the thriving Twin Cities comedy club scene, a bigger market than either New York or Los Angeles.

The crown jewel of the Twin Cities' theater community is the Tony Award-winning Tyrone Guthrie Theater. One of America's leading repertory theaters and

the largest regional theater in the country, the Guthrie is home to an outstanding resident acting company.

When English director Sir Tyrone Guthrie in the early 1960s chose Minneapolis as the site for a new repertory theater company outside of the New York mainstream, he startled many in the industry. In retrospect, though, it appears to have been a logical reward for this area's long-standing heritage of cultural awareness.

In addition to the Guthrie, there is a wealth of lesser-known gems that will challenge the ability of even the most avid theater-goer to keep current.

The highest concentration is in the West Bank Theatre District between downtown Minneapolis and the University of Minnesota. Mixed Blood Theater features funny, provocative, and unpredictable plays that blend social commentary with theatrical excellence in a century-old renovated firehouse. Dudley Riggs' Theatre at "Seven Corners" on the West Bank is nationally known for its witty satirical revues and original music comedies.

Downtown Minneapolis at the Hen-

nepin Center for the Arts you can take your pick from the Illusion Theater, Theatre de la Jeune Lune, and Theatre Exchange, all known for bold and innovative productions. The center, housed in a historic 1890 Romanesque structure, also is home to several dance companies, choral groups, arts organizations, and restaurants.

The Great American History Theatre in St. Paul fills a unique niche with original works on the history, folklore, and social issues of the region. Among its recent sub-

jects: St. Paul natives F. Scott and Zelda Fitzgerald, a 1930s Depression Christmas musical, and a Scandinavian vaudeville production.

For eye-popping visual excitement check out In the Heart of the Beast Puppet and Mask Theatre in Minneapolis. These imaginative souls use the ancient tradition of puppet and mask theater to explore contemporary social issues, events, and values.

The giant-size Heart of the Beast caricatures are a hit with children and adults alike.

St. Paul's acclaimed Penumbra Theatre Company is Minnesota's only professional black theater, counting among its regular offerings works by Pulitzer Prize-winning St. Paul playwright August Wilson.

The Old Log Theater in suburban Minneapolis is the oldest continuously running theater in the country. Originally established in a converted log stable in 1940, the Old Log now presents the best of Broadway comedy and British farce in a

ABOVE: Zenon Dance Company is one of several nationally recognized dance companies in the Twin Cities. The area also has a large independent dance community. Courtesy, Zenon Dance Company/Ann Marsden

ABOVE RIGHT: The St. Paul Chamber Orchestra makes its home and worldwide reputation at the Ordway Theatre. Photo by Richard Hamilton Smith

RIGHT: Minneapolis' Tyrone Guthrie Theater has won awards both for its striking building design and its fine repertory theater. *Iphigeneia at Aulis* was one of the theater's 1992 productions. Courtesy, Guthrie Theater/ Michal Daniel

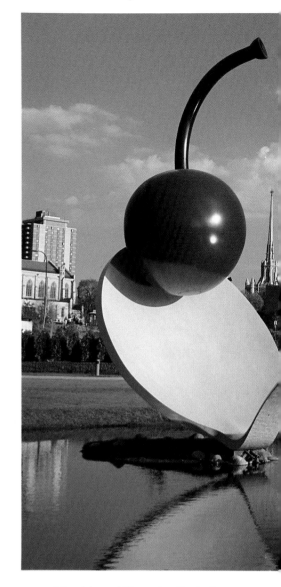

655-seat dinner theater located on 10 wooded acres.

Even children have their own theater community in the Twin Cities. The Children's Theatre Company is the nation's leading theater for young people, featuring plays from children's literature, folk tales, fantasies, and original works. The Youth Performance Company works with actors

The Romanesque-style mansion housing the American Swedish Institute in south Minneapolis holds a collection of artifacts depicting 150 years of Swedish heritage in America. Photo by Greg Ryan/Sally Beyer

ages nine to 21. And St. Paul's Children's Museum regularly presents performing arts events for children.

The Twin Cities' vibrant dance community produces more than 100 dance events a year. A number of nationally recognized professional dance companies are based here—the Nancy Hauser Dance Company, Zenon Dance Company, and New Dance Ensemble—augmented by a large independent dance community.

Minneapolis and St. Paul's deep appreciation for the performing arts extends to their historic vaudeville and performing arts theaters. In recent years the Twin Cities have preserved three of their finest in St. Paul's World Theater and Minneapolis' Orpheum and State theaters.

The World Theater is one of only a few remaining "two-balcony dramatic house" theaters in the country. It was restored to its 1910 elegance in 1986 as the former home of public radio's popular live weekly broadcast, "A Prairie Home Companion." None of its 916 seats are more than 87 feet from the stage, giving audiences a warm sense of intimacy with performers. The World's superb acoustics are complemented with state-of-the-art audio recording and broadcast facilities, making it a favorite of professional production companies.

Across the river, both the historic Orpheum Theater and the State Theatre on Minneapolis' Hennepin Avenue have been serving audiences almost continuously since 1921. Today they're owned by the Minneapolis Community Development Agency and have been given a new lease on life as part of the agency's efforts to revitalize Hennepin Avenue as a major entertainment destination.

The historic 2,800-seat Orpheum, the country's second-largest vaudeville house when it opened, is a splendid setting for touring Broadway productions and a wide range of musical events. The Beaux Arts-style theater with its recessed domed ceiling has been preserved from further deterioration and is continually being upgraded. Minnesota native Bob Dylan performed an acclaimed series of five concerts at the Orpheum in 1992.

The spectacularly ornate State Theatre reopened to rave reviews in 1991 after a multimillion-dollar restoration. The 2,200-seat State, with elements of Italian Renaissance, Moorish, and Byzantine Revival design modes, features a heavily ornamented glazed terracotta facade outside. Inside, a 100-foot-high proscenium arches over the stage flanked by monumental festooned pilasters and molded plaster figures. Elaborate murals adorn the walls and recessed curved ceiling, and six huge crystal chandeliers remain intact. The State reopened with the Minnesota Opera's production of Rodgers and Hammerstein's *Carousel* and continues to offer local productions, first-run Broadway shows, popular music, and other events.

The performing arts have two modern-day treasures in St. Paul's Ordway Music Theatre and Minneapolis' Orchestra Hall.

Elegance and class prevail at the Ordway Theatre, where liveried footmen greet visitors at the curb. Designed by renowned St. Paul-born architect Benjamin Thompson, the Ordway is the prestigious address of the St. Paul Chamber Orchestra, currently conducted by Hugh Wolff, the Minnesota Opera, and the Schubert Club, one of America's oldest musical societies. The stunning $45-million European-style theater/concert hall/opera house exudes warmth with its mahogony, copper, and brick textures, and both its 1,815-seat

LEFT: Claus Oldenburg's 29-foot *Spoonbridge and Cherry* spanning a pond is one of the Minneapolis Sculpture Garden's most popular attractions. The 10-acre garden is located across from the Walker Art Center and Guthrie Theater. Photo by Greg Ryan/Sally Beyer

BELOW: The Minneapolis Institute of Arts houses a permanent collection of 80,000 objects representing more than 4,000 years of history. Photo by Richard Hamilton Smith

neapolis coffeehouses in the early Sixties for fame in New York, to the trademark "Minneapolis sound" of superstar native Prince and local Grammy Award-winning producers Jimmy Jam Harris and Terry Lewis, to the inventive rock and roll of the Replacements and Husker Du.

"An open-minded population willing to listen to new things," the *Star Tribune*'s Bream says, has helped propel the Twin Cities' phenomenal popular music scene. In addition, he cites a lifelong appreciation for music that is nurtured here through the educational system, church choirs, and strong institutional support for musical arts. The fortunate result is a local musical cauldron that boils over with diversity.

You don't need to go to Chicago for rhythm and blues—you'll find it around every corner on the Twin Cities club circuit. Cool spots for hot blues include Minneapolis' West Bank, where local favorites Willie Murphy, Big Walter Smith, and the Butanes Soul Revue pack the houses regu-

main hall and 315-seat auxiliary hall offer impeccable acoustics.

Orchestra Hall is home to the internationally acclaimed Minnesota Orchestra, under the direction of Edo de Waart since 1986. The hall is noted for the large, specially engineered plaster cubes protruding from its ceiling that serve as sound diffusers and account for its fine ascoustic properties. Orchestra Hall's outdoor plaza features a variety of musical events in the summertime, including the orchestra's free Symphonies for the Cities series and the wildly successful Viennese Sommerfest that runs for several weeks.

The Twin Cities rank second only to New York in the number of symphony concerts performed annually.

Concert halls and theaters aren't the only place you'll find culture in the Twin Cities. Pick up one of the free local newsweeklies and you'll be astounded at the amount of live music you can hear in Minneapolis and St. Paul nightclubs on any given night. Says Jon Bream, music critic for the Minneapolis-based daily *Star Tribune*. "Per capita we probably have a more vibrant and versatile music scene in the cities than any other major metropolitan area. There are more places in which to

play live music here than anywhere, including New York City."

Minneapolis-St. Paul in 1988 ranked eighth among the nation's top 20 markets for touring artist bookings, second only to Chicago in the Midwest.

The Twin Cities are known around the world for their contributions to popular music, from Dylan, who left the Min-

larly along Cedar and River-side avenues; downtown Minneapolis' Glam Slam, the Fine Line Music Cafe, the Times Bar, and First Avenue; and St. Paul's "Frogtown" neighborhood, where the Blues Saloon regularly hosts the best in national acts in a cozy, second-story juke joint setting.

Folk music long has had an audience in the Twin Cities; Minnesota Public Radio took that nationwide with its weekly live broadcasts of Garrison Keillor's "Prairie Home Companion" in the 1980s, a show that essentially was staffed by local folk musicians. Guitar virtuoso Leo Kottke, Prudence Johnson, and the seminal Sixties folk-blues trio of Koerner, Ray and Glover all have their roots in the Twin Cities and continue to play in the area.

Gospel music flourishes in the Twin Cities, ringing forth from churches and bars alike. You can even get your Sunday morning religion at the Fine Line Music Cafe's gospel brunch.

Twin Cities jazz aficionados are well-served in both the concert halls and clubs. St. Paul's Dakota Bar and Grill has won praise from such greats as Harry Connick, Jr., and Max Roach, and provides local players a first-class room in which to play. Dixieland, big band, bebop, experimental, and fusion are all represented in the local jazz community.

If it's galleries and museums you're after, put on your walking shoes. The Twin Cities are loaded with them.

Minneapolis' Walker Art Center adjoining the Guthrie Theater holds a permanent collection of more than 5,000 pieces from the major movements of twentieth-century American and European art, including T.B. Walker, Edward Hopper, Franz Marc, Georgia O'Keefe, and Alexander Calder. With 53,000 square feet of exhibition space, the Walker has distinguished itself as an organizer of such landmark exhibits in the 1980s as "Picasso: from the Musee Picasso, Paris," the Dutch Mod-

ABOVE: The Minnesota Timberwolves are the state's newest professional sports franchise. The National Basketball Association team plays at Target Center arena in downtown Minneapolis. Photo by Focus on Sports

FACING: Kirby Puckett is arguably Minnesota's most popular sports superstar ever. The Minnesota Twins' center fielder began his pro career with the Twins and would like to finish it here as well. Photo by Focus on Sports

ernists show "De Stijl: 1917-1931," and "The 20th-Century Poster: Design of the Avant Garde."

The Walker also is an important catalyst in the performing arts, annually offering more than 150 events in dance, theater, new music, and poetry and fiction readings. Its film exhibition program continues to grow, with some 300 films and video-tapes shown each year, often showcasing new work by emerging American and European filmmakers.

Take a bag lunch and stroll across the

street from the Walker Art Center to the 10-acre Minneapolis Sculpture Garden. Here you can amble along tree-lined walkways, stopping to view the assortment of 40 or so twentieth-century sculptures scattered throughout the grounds. One of the highlights of the garden is *Spoonbridge and Cherry*, a 29-foot fountain that features a gigantic gray spoon with a red cherry in its bowl spanning a pond against a backdrop of the Minneapolis skyline.

The Minneapolis Institute of Arts in Minneapolis houses an expansive permanent collection of 80,000 objects representing every age and cultural tradition over 4,000 years of history. Among the institute's significant holdings are paintings by Rembrandt, Goya, Degas, and van Gogh; 10,000 photographic images by such masters as Alfred Stieglitz, Edward Steichen, Walker Evans, Ansel Adams, and Richard Avedon; a collection of ancient Chinese bronzes and jades; and rare works from African, Pacific, pre-Columbian, and North American Indian cultures.

St. Paul's Minnesota Museum of Art features special traveling exhibits and contemporary Upper Midwest artists at its Landmark Center Galleries; its Deco-flavored Jemne Building Galleries displays exhibits drawn from its permanent collection of American and non-Western art.

The American Swedish Institute in south Minneapolis is a treasure trove of artifacts from 150 years of the Swedish experience in America, housed in a stately Romanesque mansion adorned by Swedish craftwork and furnishings. Traveling Scandinavian art exhibits also are featured.

Step into the dinosaur age at St. Paul's Science Museum of Minnesota, where four prehistoric skeletons form the centerpiece of the new Paleontology Hall. The museum is internationally known for the production of its 3D-like, surround-screen "Omnimax" films on volcanoes, barrier reefs, rain forests, and other nature-related themes.

The Twin Cities Marathon attracts thousands of participants from around the world with its scenic course criss-crossing blufftops above the Mississippi River and scenic parkways drenched in fall colors. Photos by John Kelly III

The Mississippi River provides a variety of recreational opportunities, from floating stage productions aboard the Centennial Showboat Theatre to crewing with the U of M rowing team. Photo by Greg Ryan/Sally Beyer

For an interesting twist, take the family to the Children's Museum at Bandana Square in St. Paul. Hands-on exhibits, live performances, and story telling are used in innovative ways to expose young people to new ideas, scientific concepts, and forms of expression.

And for museum fare that's a bit more off-beat, consider Minneapolis' Questionable Medical Devices Museum in St. Anthony Main, the Baseball Museum across from the Metrodome downtown, the Firefighters Memorial Museum, where more than 40 classic fire engines are on display, or the Schubert Club's Musical Instrument Museum at Landmark Center in St. Paul.

Minneapolis-St. Paul is in the big leagues when it comes to another type of culture—sports. No other comparable market in the country supports three professional sports teams as the Twin Cities do with Minnesota Twins Major League baseball, Minnesota Vikings NFL football, and

Minnesota Timberwolves NBA basketball.

Twin Cities sports fans are no strangers to championship teams either. The Vikings have played in four Super Bowls over the years and the Twins have brought home two World Series championships since 1987.

The local sports community is competition-crazy even when its own teams aren't involved. In 1991 alone attendance records were set here for the U.S. National Figure Skating Championships, U.S. Open Golf Championship, and the International Special Olympics Games. In 1992 the Super Bowl came to the Twin Cities, the northernmost site for the game ever.

The Twin Cities have a sports arena for every occasion. The Twins and Vikings, as well as the University of Minnesota Gophers, play in the climate-controlled comfort of the Hubert H. Humphrey Metrodome in downtown Minneapolis, a 60,000-seat indoor stadium covered by an air-supported Teflon roof. The Timberwolves' home court is at Target Center in Minneapolis, the area's newest sports facility. The newly renovated St. Paul Civic Center is a regular host for national championship collegiate hockey tournaments and other sporting events.

Amateur sports competition has taken

off in the Twin Cities in recent years. Minneapolis-St. Paul hosted the U.S. Olympic Festival in 1990, the International Special Olympics in 1991, and the National Collegiate Athletic Association Final Four basketball tournament in 1992.

The Minnesota Amateur Sports Commission was created in 1987 and $29 million in state funds were appropriated for the construction of amateur athletic facilities. The showpiece is the National Sports Center in suburban Blaine, which opened in 1990 with a multipurpose indoor sports arena for weightlifting, wrestling, soccer, and track; a lighted, 12,000-seat outdoor stadium for soccer and track-and-field competition; and a 5,000-seat cycling velodrome with the only all-weather wood track in the United States. Sixty miles north of the Twin Cities in St. Cloud is the new National Ice Hockey Center, featuring two Olympic-size ice rinks.

Come October, many sports enthusiasts turn participant and join an international cast of thousands in the Twin Cities Marathon, the country's most scenic urban race. The course takes runners on a winding tour through Minneapolis and St. Paul neighborhoods and parks during the peak of fall colors.

Open space is important to Twin

Citians. With 67,000 acres in 153 parks, the Minneapolis-St. Paul metro area has one of the most extensive urban park systems in the country. There are 45 miles of connecting hiking/biking paths in the Twin Cities, some of them linked to trails leading to the quiet countryside far beyond the cities' limits.

Some of your best bets: Como Park in St. Paul, with sprawling picnic grounds, an excellent free zoo, and floral conservatory that's ablaze with color even in the deep-freeze of midwinter; Lake Harriet in Minneapolis, where almost nightly musical performances are featured in the summer at the park's pavilion; Rice Park in downtown St. Paul, a block-square center of a variety of performing arts activities surrounded by the towering Landmark Center, St. Paul Public Library, Ordway Music Theatre, and St. Paul Hotel; Minnehaha Falls in south Minneapolis for hiking and soaking up the cool spray of the waterfalls; and St. Paul's Phalen Park, another picnicking favorite with good fishing in Lake Phalen.

Speaking of lakes, Twin Citians are never far from water. More than 95 percent of all Minnesotans live within five miles of recreational shoreline. In fact, there's more shoreline in Minnesota than in California, Hawaii, and Florida combined.

Needless to say, with three rivers and 200 recreational lakes in the metropolitan area, fishing is a popular pasttime. Twin Cities anglers year-round catch walleye, northern pike, bass, trout, catfish, muskie, sturgeon, and the ever-present panfish in waters that are easily accessible to the public.

Sprawling Lake Minnetonka southwest of Minneapolis, Lake Phalen on St. Paul's East Side, Minneapolis' Nokomis Lake, White Bear Lake, and Bald Eagle Lake north of St. Paul offer challenging fishing for amateur and expert anglers alike, from slab-size, lip-smacking crappies to rod-bending northern and muskie.

The upper St. Croix River 20 miles east of St. Paul on the Wisconsin border has some of the area's best smallmouth bass fishing. Below Stillwater, the St. Croix regularly yields monster catfish in the 40-pound-plus range, sturgeon, and limits of walleye.

The St. Croix River is one of America's most pristine rivers and the first to be protected under the National Scenic River-ways System in the 1970s. Besides fishing,

the St. Croix offers serene backwater canoeing and camping in its upper reaches and boating and picnicking along its lower sections.

The Mississippi River has experienced a phenomenal resurrection as a Twin Cities recreational resource over the past decade and today offers many opportunities along its miles of urban shoreline and beyond.

Trout-fishing enthusiasts can head southeast of the Twin Cities a couple of hours for their pick of several blue-ribbon trout streams.

A little over two hours to the north is Mille Lacs Lake, Minnesota's most productive walleye hole. Entire cities of ice houses sprout up on this huge lake in the winter-time, luring thousands of hardy ice-fishing

You'll run into just about any type of character at the Minnesota State Fair, including arm-wrestling behemoths. The 12-day fair is a cornucopia of sights, sounds, tastes, and thrills. Photo by Greg Ryan/Sally Beyer

fans armed with ice augers and snowmobile suits.

The Twin Cities metropolitan area has plenty of hunting opportunities as well. Whitetail deer are hunted in outlying portions of the metro area, along with ruffed grouse, pheasant, and wild turkey.

The Minnesota Valley Wildlife Refuge in Bloomington, an 8,000-acre oasis of woodlands in the Minnesota River Valley, is one of only four urban National Wildlife Refuges in the country.

More than a million visitors a year trek to the Minnesota Zoo in suburban Apple Valley, a 485-acre preserve with 2,000 inhabitants, nearly 60 of them endangered. Some of its more unusual residents are its

Victorian koala bears, Japanese snow monkeys, and Southeast Asian sun bears. Also popular are its coral reef exhibit with 100-plus species of tropical fish and six species of sharks, the educational World of Birds show, and the zoo's 12 kilometers of cross-country ski trails.

Displaying animals is only part of the zoo's mission, though. Equally important are the wide range of conservation, educational, and species survival activities in which the zoo is engaged.

The Minnesota Landscape Arboretum is 905 acres of rolling hills, native woods and prairies, and gardens operated by the University of Minnesota in Chanhassen west of the Twin Cities. A truly living learning experience, the arboretum is open year

round and is accessible by foot or by tram tours through the woods.

Minnesotans celebrate life with every changing season. In the Twin Cities, it's personified in St. Paul's Winter Carnival held in late January and early February, and Minneapolis' midsummer Aquatennial. Both of these popular civic affairs bring out hundreds of thousands of participants for such events as milk-carton sailboat races and ice sculpting. In 1992 the largest ice

Minnehaha Falls takes on a whole new appearance under the gentle shroud of a fresh dusting of snow. Minnesotans learn to take advantage of the winter months and use city parks year-round.

INSET, TOP: Ice sculptures in downtown's Rice Park, one of the many attractions of the St. Paul Winter Carnival, glisten in the winter twilight with Landmark Center in the background.

INSET, BOTTOM: Minnesotans learn to appreciate winter at an early age. One of the younger participants in the St. Paul Winter Carnival checks out the ice sledding conditions at Como Lake.

Photos by Greg Ryan/Sally Beyer

ABOVE: Ethnic holidays such as Norway's Set-tende Mai on May 17 are celebrated throughout the year in the Twin Cities. Photo by Richard Hamilton Smith

FACING: The Mall of America, North America's largest indoor shopping and entertainment complex, features at its center Camp Snoopy, an entire amusement park under one roof. Photo by Greg Ryan/Sally Beyer

structure ever constructed, a dazzling 165-foot ice palace, was built in St. Paul for the 1992 Winter Carnival, drawing 2.5 million spectators.

The Minnesota State Fair is America's largest, running 12 days and attracting 1.5 million visitors to a 300-acre site midway between Minneapolis and St. Paul in late August and early September. Scores of other regional and ethnic celebrations take place in the Twin Cities area throughout the year—the Lao Family New Year celebrated by the Twin Cities' Southeast Asian community in November, St. Paul's Festival of Nations in the spring, and the Minnesota Renaissance Festival in Shakopee, a six-week cornucopia of arts, music, and food in a 400-year-old English country fair setting held mid-August through September. Drive in any direction from the Twin Cities and you'll find small towns that celebrate everything from peppers and pump-

kins to the lowly carp.

Is shopping your bag? The Twin Cities are rated as one of the nation's premier shopping meccas. *Sales and Marketing Management* magazine in 1990 ranked Minneapolis-St. Paul third in the nation in retail sales per capita. Retailing giant Dayton-Hudson is headquartered in Minneapolis, and most other leading national department stores have outlets here.

Southdale in suburban Minneapolis was the country's first indoor shopping mall. Today shopping at malls has become a way of life in the Twin Cities, where the Mall of America, the largest indoor shopping and entertainment complex in North America, opened in 1992. Even downtown Minneapolis and St. Paul have gone indoors. Most buildings in both business districts are linked by several miles of enclosed walkways that criss-cross the cities one floor above street level, allowing shoppers and downtown workers to traverse the city uninhibited by the weather outdoors.

Downtown retail centers in Minneapolis include the upscale Gaviidae Common on Nicollet Mall, with prime tenants Saks Fifth Avenue and Neiman Marcus, the Conservatory and City Center. Browse the warehouse district for artwork and antiques, and the West Bank or Uptown areas for something a little more funky.

St. Paul Center in the heart of downtown features 110 shops and restaurants.

In St. Paul's Lowertown District, Galtier Plaza features an array of owner-operated shops, theaters, and services. Bandana Square near the Midway District houses a variety of specialty and apparel shops and restaurants in a collection of renovated 1880s railroad buildings. Drive down Grand Avenue for more eclectic shopping and poke around St. Paul's neighborhood antique stores for some real bargains.

Stillwater, 15 miles east of St. Paul, is a cluster of interesting shops and antique stores in an old brick river town along the scenic St. Croix.

You can travel around the world in Twin Cities restaurants. Ranging from the exotic (Afghani, Ethiopian, Thai, Vietnamese) to Mediterranean (Greek, Italian, Lebanese) to European, Minneapolis and St. Paul can satisfy your foreign tastes. Continental and regional specialties abound—being the Midwest there are several excellent steak houses here—as well as a broad selection of vegetarian dining.

Quirky eateries worth sampling in the Twin Cities include Mickey's Diner, a classic 1930s railroad dining car and historic site in downtown St. Paul; The Original Coney Island, a sleepy little joint that's been serving steamy, mouth-watering coneys across the street from Mickey's since 1923; the New Riverside Cafe at the corner of Cedar and Riverside in the West Bank district of Minneapolis for home-cooked, organic vegetarian fare served by friendly hippies; and Mayslack's Polka Lounge in northeast Minneapolis, where mountainous garlic-drenched roast beef sandwiches are the order—and just about the only order—of the house.

If gambling is your ticket, there are plenty of opportunities to wager a dollar right here in the Twin Cities area. Minnesota's Indian tribes have seized a goldmine of an opportunity in on-reservation gambling enterprises. There are 14 Indian-operated casinos statewide, several within easy driving distance of the Twin Cities. Mystic Lake Casino in Shakopee and Treasure Island Casino at Red Wing offer free metro area busing to their Las Vegas-style casinos that feature 24-hour blackjack, video slots, and high-stakes bingo action. Grand Casino at Hinckley farther north also is easily accessible from the Twin Cities. St. Croix Meadows in Hudson, Wisconsin, 20 miles east features greyhound racing nearly all year.

CHAPTER FIVE

REACHING OUT

The integration in 1993 of operations between Minneapolis-St. Paul-based Northwest Airlines and Amsterdam-based KLM Royal Dutch Airlines placed MSP at the crossroads of world aviation. Photo by Greg Ryan/Sally Beyer

he unprecedented announcement of integrated operations between Minneapolis-St. Paul's Northwest Airlines and Amsterdam-based KLM Royal Dutch Airlines in 1993 signaled the advent of a new era in air transportation: the globalization of the world's airline industry.

The move planted Minneapolis-St. Paul International Airport square at the crossroads of world aviation.

Minneapolis-St. Paul International Airport and Amsterdam Schiphol Airport serve as the dual hubs for the world's first global airline system. Daily flights operated jointly by Northwest and KLM between the two airports will provide seamless connections worldwide for both passengers and cargo, further ensuring Minneapolis-St. Paul International's position as America's North Coast Gateway.

Said Northwest president and chief executive officer John Dasburg: "Travelers and shippers now can take advantage of the strength of two large international route systems. Northwest and KLM benefit by sharing revenues and expenses to operate more efficiently."

The Northwest-KLM system comprises the world's third-largest airline system and serves more than 300 destinations in 100 countries on six continents.

The partnership between the two airlines was forged close on the heels of a 1992 "Open Skies" agreement signed by the United States and the Netherlands that allows airlines from both countries to fly anywhere in the two countries. KLM already had a 20 percent ownership stake in Northwest and had been operating nonstop B-747-400 service between Minneapolis-St. Paul and Amsterdam since 1991. Consequently, the two carriers were well-positioned to take swift advantage of this new agreement.

Northwest Airlines grew up with Minneapolis-St. Paul International Airport. From its beginnings in 1926 as a fledgling carrier hauling mail between the Twin Cities and Chicago in two open-cockpit airplanes, Northwest has evolved into the world's fourth-largest airline operating more than 360 airplanes.

The airline's primary maintenance base is at Minneapolis-St. Paul International. Its corporate headquarters and state-of-the-art

The partnership between KLM, based at Amsterdam's Schiphol Airport (inset), and Northwest has forged an important link between the canals of the Dutch city and the lakes and rivers of the Twin Cities. Photo by John Elk III; inset photo courtesy, Schiphol Airport.

training facilities, the Northwest Aerospace Training Corporation, are located in the nearby community of Eagan.

Northwest's current fleet comprises a broad mix of Boeing 747 passenger planes and freighters, McDonnell-Douglas DC-10, B-757, B-727, Airbus A320, MD-80, and DC-9 aircraft.

With its "Airlink" regional airline partners, Northwest serves more than 240 destinations in 22 countries throughout North America, Asia, Europe, and Australia. Its domestic route system spans 43 states.

Minneapolis-St. Paul is Northwest's main domestic hub; its other passenger hubs are in Memphis, Detroit, and Tokyo, with international gateways in Boston and Seattle.

The historic partnership with KLM is not the first time Northwest has broken new ground in international air service. Northwest pioneered the "Great Circle" northern route to Asia flying troops over the Yukon to Alaska and the Aleutian Islands during World War II, and in 1946 was authorized by the Civil Aeronautics Board to fly routes to the Orient via Edmonton, Canada, and Anchorage. The following year Northwest initiated service to Tokyo, Shanghai, Seoul, and Manila.

Today Northwest has probably the best transpacific air service between the United

ABOVE AND RIGHT: Daily nonstop service between MSP and London's Gatwick Airport will get you there in time for the changing of the guard. Other European destinations with non-stop or direct service from the Twin Cities include Frankfurt and Paris. Courtesy, London Gatwick Airport (above); photo by Cliff Hollenbeck (right)

LEFT: Northwest's direct service to Germany's Frankfurt-Main International is one of several important links between Minnesota and European markets provided by the airport. Courtesy, Frankfurt Airport

ABOVE AND RIGHT: Sydney's Kingsford Smith Airport is among Northwest Airlines' extensive network of Pacific Rim destinations. The port on Australia's southeast coast of the Tasman Sea is one of the commonwealth's cultural and financial centers. Courtesy, Sydney Airport (above); photo by Dave G. Houser (right)

In addition to being one of Europe's leading aviation hubs, Amsterdam also is a cultural hub of Europe. KLM's presence has been key to the development of tourism in the Netherlands. Photo by Dave G. Houser

States and Asia of any carrier, as well as a strong intra-Asia route system.

Northwest operates direct B-747 service daily between Minneapolis-St. Paul and Tokyo's new Narita Airport. Connecting service on Northwest to other points in Asia is available from Minneapolis-St. Paul via Boston and Detroit. Other destinations within Asia include Osaka, Nagoya, and Fukuoka, Japan; Seoul, Korea; Okinawa; Manila, Philippines; Beijing, Taipei, and Shanghai, China; Hong Kong; Singapore; Guam; Saipan, Palau; and Bangkok, Thailand.

Air service to the Pacific Rim, destination for nearly 30 percent of Minnesota's manufactured exports, is critical to Minnesota's international trade needs. Japan is the second-largest market for Minnesota-made manufactured goods. Total manufactured Minnesota exports to Japan grew from $484 million in 1987 to $839 million in 1990. That represented 2.2 percent of all U.S. manufactured exports to Japan.

Northwest's service between Minneapolis-St. Paul and Europe includes direct flights to Frankfurt, Germany, London's Gatwick Airport, and Paris' Charles de Gaulle Airport. Northwest also has service between the Twin Cities and Edmonton, Toronto, and Winnipeg, Canada.

With the addition of the KLM/Northwest daily DC-10 service to Amsterdam Schiphol Airport, Minneapolis-St. Paul passengers now can make connections to more than 80 additional international destinations on KLM and its affiliated carriers in Europe, Africa, and Asia.

Schiphol is one of the world's most highly rated airports by passengers of all nationalities. From its single terminal with 40-plus duty-free shops to its multilingual staff to its front-door rail service into Amsterdam, Schiphol was designed with passengers in mind. It's no wonder Schiphol is one of Europe's fastest-growing gateways.

The success of KLM's entry into the Minneapolis-St. Paul market has been phenomenal, says Robert Swan, KLM's northern region general manager in Minneapolis. KLM began service at MSP in April 1991 with nonstop service to Amsterdam three times a week. Two years later that was expanded to daily service.

"This is really a hub feeding a hub," explains Swan. "We have a very strong

business market to Amsterdam because from there you can connect to almost anywhere in the world in a very short time."

Mark Abels, Northwest Airlines' vice president for corporate communications, notes that Northwest's and KLM's route structures complement one another. "If you'd paint the route map of Northwest and the route map of KLM on a globe, they'd fit together perfectly."

By the year 2000, 83 percent of the world's airline traffic will be generated in six markets: transatlantic, transpacific, Europe-Asia, intra-Europe, intra-Asia, and intra-United States. Northwest-KLM is the only airline system with a strong presence in all six markets, says Abels, a fact that bodes well for the partnership's future.

The KLM-Northwest partnership means more Europe-bound passengers nationwide will fly through Minneapolis-St. Paul to get there. "Business and pleasure travelers alike are learning that you don't have to go through other crowded U.S. ports to get to Europe," says Swan. "MSP is a pretty gentle place to leave from."

Metropolitan Airports Commission executive director Jeff Hamiel says it makes good business sense for international airlines to operate at Minneapolis-St. Paul. "The shortest route between the United

ABOVE AND RIGHT: Minnesota has had strong ties to Scandinavia since the state was settled. NWA/KLM daily service between MSP and Amsterdam allows for connections to more than 80 new international destinations, including Sweden's Stockholm Arlanda Airport. Photo by Dave G. Houser (above); courtesy, Luftfartsverket/ Thomas Wingstedt (right)

States and both Europe and Asia is the 'Great Circle,' and we're right on it," says Hamiel.

Delays at MSP are going to be fewer than at other more crowded international gateways, and airline fees are in the lowest 20 percent of all airports. "Our cost of operations to airlines here is about $3 per passenger. That is one of the lowest per-passenger costs in the country." Despite its low fees, the airport has remained profitable without a local property tax levy since 1969.

Airlines need not be concerned about operating conditions at MSP, despite Minnesota's sometimes severe winters. "If you compare us with any city across the northern tier in the United States, Minneapolis-St. Paul International clearly has the finest reputation for being open under all types

ABOVE: United Express is a code-sharing partner of United Airlines, providing important feeder service into hubs such as MSP. Courtesy, Metropolitan Airports Commission/Alvis Upitis

RIGHT: Mesaba Aviation, a code-sharing partner with Northwest, is based at MSP and provides commuter service to many Upper Midwest destinations. Courtesy, Mesaba Aviation, Inc./Brady T. Willette

Aviation, a Northwest Airlink regional carrier, and Sun Country Airlines, a charter vacation destination operator.

Mesaba Aviation began commuter operations in 1973 flying a single Cessna 421 between MSP and Grand Rapids, Minnesota. Today Mesaba operates a fleet of 15 Fokker F-27s and 21 Fairchild Metro SA-227s with service throughout the Upper Midwest.

The regional carrier has been consistently profitable, steadily adding to its route structure over the years. Mesaba provides an important link between secondary air markets and the international hub at Minneapolis-St. Paul.

Sun Country Airlines began operating charter flights at MSP in 1983 and has

of adverse weather conditions," says Hamiel.

The proof is hanging on the wall at the airport. Minneapolis-St. Paul's crack snow crews have won the International Aviation Snow Symposium's prestigious Bernt Balchen Award for excellence in airport snow and ice control four times, most recently in 1991. And pilots have consistently rated MSP as one of the world's safest airports.

Direct passenger service is available from Minneapolis-St. Paul International to 131 domestic and 15 international destinations. In addition to Northwest and KLM, which account for nearly 80 percent of all traffic at MSP, the airport is served by seven other major passenger carriers: American, America West, Continental, Delta, TWA, United, and USAir. Twenty charter carriers and seven regional carriers also operate at MSP.

Air cargo has grown dramatically at Minneapolis-St. Paul in recent years. Between 1985 and 1991 air cargo/airmail carriers at MSP weighed in with an impressive 85 percent increase in metric tonnage. In 1992 air cargo tonnage rose another 12 percent to

304.1 metric tons, including mail.

International air cargo got a boost at MSP in 1993 with the expansion of its on-airport foreign trade zone, which allows shippers to conduct certain activities within a specified area at the airport without paying import duties.

Northwest owns the world's largest 747 freighter fleet, providing MSP with twice-weekly transpacific service.

Fifteen cargo airlines operate at Minneapolis-St. Paul International, including Federal Express, UPS, Emery Worldwide, Airborne Express, DHL Airways, Zantop, and Burlington Express.

Minneapolis-St. Paul International Airport is home to two other important links in the region's air service network: Mesaba

been profitable ever since. In 1991 Sun Country was the fourth-largest charter carrier in the country, selling Eagan blocks of seats to wholesale tour operators. Sun Country's corporate headquarters is in Eagan. Its maintenance base and a fleet of eight B-727s and two DC-10s are at MSP.

From Minneapolis-St. Paul Sun Country flies to Las Vegas and Orlando year-round. Other sun-drenched vacation destinations include St. Thomas and St. Croix in the U.S. Virgin Islands, Montego Bay, Jamaica, Barbados, and several destinations in Mexico. Charters to Anchorage and Oslo normally operate in the summer.

The quality of air service at Minneapolis-St. Paul International gets high marks from business travelers in the Twin Cities.

Says Northwest's Abels: "You cannot over-estimate the value of not only a major air-line hub here but an international gateway. That is an advantage that few other cities in this size market can match."

Arlene Englert, manager of travel management services for the 3M Company in Maplewood, agrees. The level of service traditionally enjoyed at Minneapolis-St. Paul International has facilitated 3M's expansion worldwide over the years to become one of the most recognized names in U.S. business.

3M spends $80 million a year on commercial air travel, one-fourth of that international travel. More than 25,000 trips a year are made in and out of Minneapolis-St. Paul, where its corporate headquarters and substantial manufacturing facilities are based.

Jon K. Andersen of International Resource Group Inc., a Minnetonka-based international business development firm, says air service is a key consideration of companies seeking to start up or do business here. "Global access like we enjoy in the Twin Cities means that freight gets to its destination faster. It means travel times are much reduced. It makes it a lot easier to attract new investments into the Twin Cities."

Dresser-Rand manufactures custom electric motors for major oil companies, utilities, and engineering firms that often are shipped by air. The company has been in business in Minneapolis for more than 100 years.

Says Don Anderson, sales director: "We serve markets and have installations around the world. It's important for us to travel for service, and for us to be accessible to our customers so they can come in here and be involved in the production cycle. Without the level of air service we enjoy here, both domestic and international, that would not be possible."

Maplewood-based 3M Company, whose products are known around the world, depends on the excellent air service at MSP International to conduct its business globally. 3M personnel take more than 25,000 commercial airline trips a year in and out of the Twin Cities. Courtesy, 3M

At a time when many airports are scrambling just to keep the carriers and flights they have, Minneapolis-St. Paul International is experiencing solid growth in both its domestic and international passenger and cargo service. It's no coincidence that, commensurate with that growth, Minnesota's star has risen in the global marketplace.

As Minneapolis-St. Paul International Airport continues to make connections between Minnesota and the rest of the world, there is every reason to believe that star will continue to rise.

CHAPTER SIX

TRADING AT HOME AND ABROAD

Minneapolis has become a major financial and retailing center in the Midwest while maintaining a high quality of life in an urban environment. Photo by Greg Ryan/Sally Beyer

he Twin Cities of Minneapolis and St. Paul are the economic and cultural watershed of the Upper Midwest. A fertile region for innovation and creativity, the Twin Cities are living proof that an urban society can prosper and grow without sacrificing the qualities of life that made it attractive in the first place.

While in many respects the difference between St. Paul and Minneapolis may appear to be "the difference between pumpernickel and Wonder Bread," as radio personality Garrison Keillor once observed, the long tradition of making things work here more often is the result of the shared attributes of the two cities. Capitalizing on a symbiotic relationship that is at once competitive and complementary, Minneapolis and St. Paul have emerged today as America's North Coast Gateway.

Consider these facts and it's not hard to see how Minneapolis-St. Paul has developed into one of America's most sought-after places to live and do business:

A broad industrial base that comprises the headquarters of 33 *Fortune* 500 companies and 11 of the nation's 400 largest privately held firms; a quality-driven work ethic that pervades the region's labor force, among the best educated in the country; an efficient and well-maintained transportation infrastructure; an arts community that boasts more live performances than anywhere in the country; a long tradition of good government that cares about its people; a healthy respect for the environment; an abundance of natural resources providing a smorgasbord of recreational opportunities in and around Minneapolis and St. Paul.

"Search America from sea to sea and you will not find a state that has offered as close a model to the ideal of the successful society as Minnesota."
—Neil R. Peirce and Jerry Hagstrom, *The Book of America*, 1983.

Minneapolis-St. Paul today is a metropolitan area of 2.4 million people representing a little over half of Minnesota's total population. The Twin Cities experienced above-average population growth in the 1980s while maintaining below-average levels in the problems that most often accompany urban growth—unemploy-

ABOVE: St. Paul, the government center for most state and federal agencies in Minnesota, also has a great resource in the Mississippi River. The city is expected to embark on a major commercial and recreational development of the city's Mississippi riverfront in the near future. Photo by Greg Ryan/Sally Beyer

FACING PAGE, TOP: The Twin Cities' vibrant arts community can be seen everywhere, from some of the finest theaters in the country to street parades like this one celebrating May Day in Minneapolis' Powderhorn Park. Photo by Richard Hamilton Smith

ment, crime, and pollution.

The Twin Cities don't have to spend much time trumpeting their excellence— plenty of others are doing that for them. Minneapolis and St. Paul over the past few years have landed near the top of virtually everyone's "best" lists.

Forbes magazine placed a dozen Twin Cities firms on its "200 Best Small Companies" list in 1990, more than any other state. Seven Twin Cities firms made *Business Week*'s "100 Best Small Companies" list in 1990. *World Trade* magazine selected Minneapolis-St. Paul as two of the 10 best North American cities for international business. And *Electronic Business* magazine in 1990 named the Twin Cities one of the country's top four "hot growth spots."

The Twin Cities' greatest assets are their people. Wrote *Fortune* in its 1990 assessment of Minneapolis-St. Paul: "In certain areas of the U.S. you can still find plenty of the smart, enthusiastic, loyal workers you need ... Minneapolis-St. Paul offers the twin benefits of well-educated workers and a terrific work ethic."

Few would disagree that the high value Minnesotans place on education has a lot to do with why the Twin Cities seem to work so well. The state's nearly 91 percent

high school graduation rate is the highest in the country, and 20 percentage points above the national average. Forty-five percent of the state's budget is dedicated to local school districts and post-secondary education.

Minnesota ranks among the top three states in the nation in ACT college entrance exam scores and among the top four in the number of higher-education students per capita.

The University of Minnesota often seems to dominate the Twin Cities' higher education scene. But in addition to the U of M Minneapolis and St. Paul campuses, the metropolitan area is home to 11 private four-year colleges, one state university, six two-year community colleges, and six state technical colleges.

The University of Minnesota-Twin Cities, a "land-grant" public university with an enrollment of about 42,000, is among the country's largest. A recent national

report ranked 17 of the U of M's graduate programs in the top 10 of their field. Chemical engineering and geography programs were rated number one in the United States.

The University of Minnesota is the backbone of research conducted in the Twin Cities. Research expenditures at the U of M in 1989 were nearly $200 million, sixth in the nation among public universities. Technology transfers between the university and industry have helped fuel many of the region's most successful products.

The University of Minnesota's medical school is world renowned for its pioneering in heart surgery—the world's first open-heart surgery was performed here in 1954—and as the world's busiest transplant center. It's no coincidence that medical technology is one of the Twin Cities' leading industries, with such products as transplant devices, pacemakers, and biomedical equipment being developed and made locally.

Fifty-five percent of the U of M's Institute of Technology graduates stay in the state to work, enriching the work force for Minnesota's cutting-edge computer and

electronics industries.

The school's agriculture college provides important research for the Twin Cities' extensive food-processing and agribusiness industry, which includes such giants as Cargill, General Mills, International Multi-foods, Pillsbury, and Land O' Lakes.

And the U of M's highly regarded forestry programs have played a key role in the development of Minnesota's $2-billion timber and wood products industry.

The liberal arts tradition runs deep in

The annual Father's Day father-child run at Minneapolis' Lake Nokomis Park is a multigenerational favorite. Healthy living combined with a strong work ethic make for an excellent work force in Minnesota. Photo by Greg Ryan/Sally Beyer

the Twin Cities' private college community. St. Paul has the highest concentration of private colleges per capita to be found anywhere, among them Macalester College, a first-rate liberal arts college styled

ABOVE: The Twin Cities' extensive food-process-ing and agribusiness industries benefit greatly from the U of M's extensive food science pro-grams at its St. Paul campus. Courtesy, Univer-sity of Minnesota/Dave Hansen

LEFT: Agricultural research conducted at the University of Minnesota's St. Paul campus is an important link in the state's number one indus-try. These sunflowers are part of research plots planted at the U of M's ag school. Cour-tesy, University of Minnesota/Don Breneman

after the great Ivy League schools; the College of St. Catherine's, the largest Catholic women's college in the country; and William Mitchell College of Law, whose alumni include former U.S. Supreme Court Chief Justice Warren Burger and Supreme Court Justice Harry Blackmon. Other highly regarded private schools in or near the Twin Cities include Augsberg College in Minneapolis, Hamline University and St. Thomas University in St. Paul, and St. Olaf College and Carlson College in Northfield.

The six community colleges in the metropolitan area provide broad opportunities for students seeking specialized two-year degrees. Eighteen community colleges statewide offer associates degree programs

in more than 100 areas of study.

The Twin Cities' six technical colleges are part of a statewide network of 34 publicly operated technical schools, second largest in the country. The technical college system offers 300 program majors and supplies a major portion of the region's highly skilled workers.

It's been upon the stable underpinnings of quality education and a conscientious work ethic that Minneapolis and St. Paul have built a diverse and healthy economic base comprising world-class leaders in a wide range of fields.

With a local economy not reliant on any single sector—the region's top 95 employers account for only 22 percent of the entire work force—the Twin Cities' unemployment rate historically has stayed well below national levels. The Twin Cities have a higher percentage of professional, paraprofessional, and technical jobs than the nation as a whole. And the region's per capita income consistently has topped the national average by at least 15 percent over the past decade.

Manufacturing is the Twin Cities' biggest income-producing sector, accounting for 25 percent of total gross earnings in 1988. Electronic equipment, scientific controls, medical equipment, food processing, publishing, and fabricated metal products represent the bulk of the Twin Cities' manufactured products.

High-tech industries have a prominent profile among the Twin Cities' manufacturing sector. Manufacturers of computer-related equipment, medical devices, software, and electronics dominate that group. Among the Twin Cities' leading high-tech firms are Honeywell, Ceridian Corporation (formerly Control Data Corporation), Paramax (a Unisys Company), Minntech Corporation, Cray Research, Medtronic, and St. Jude Medical.

The service industry, while second-largest in income production, is the Twin

Cities' fastest-growing sector in terms of jobs. Banking, insurance, advertising, transportation, food distribution, and retailing are the chief service industries based here, including Northwest Airlines, Minnesota Mutual Life, Super Valu, Norwest, Cargill, and Dayton Hudson.

Twin Cities industries rank well above the national average in research and development expenditures per capita. And in 1988 the state was fifth in the number of patents issued per capita.

Minnesota increasingly is being seen as a major player in international markets. The state's exports grew by 54 percent from 1987 to 1990. Minnesota companies exported $6 billion worth of manufactured

General Mills food products long have been a staple of pantries everywhere. Minneapolis has been home to a number of food-processing com-panies such as General Mills since its heyday as a grain milling center in the 1800s. Photo by Jim Sims

goods in 1991 to more than 160 countries. Two-thirds of those exports were technology-based products.

Leading the list of manufactured goods exports from Minnesota is industrial machinery, followed by scientific instruments, electronic equipment, and transportation equipment.

Agricultural commodities and processed foods accounted for almost $2 billion in exports from Minnesota in 1991, nearly 5 percent of America's total agricultural exports. Minnesota ranks among the top five states in exports of soybeans, dairy products, sunflower seeds/oil, and feed grains.

International investments in Minnesota are also on the rise. Foreign affiliates in Minnesota increased by 70 percent between 1985 and 1989. Canada is the largest foreign investor in the state at $3.4 billion, followed by the United Kingdom at $1 billion and Japan at $800 million.

Japanese investments in Minnesota have taken the sharpest turn upward in recent years with an average annual growth rate of 51 percent during the 1980s, well above the national average.

Creative arts are a growing industry in the Twin Cities. Minneapolis-St. Paul is the fourth-largest film/video production market in the country. The area long has been a hot spot for commercial filming and jingle production, and more than 1,000 screen and stage actors work in the Twin Cities. Combine that with an abundance of skilled production workers and state-of-

ABOVE: Minnesota's $2-billion-a-year wood products industry provides both manufacturing jobs in the Twin Cities, such as this Andersen Corporation window plant, and timber-harvesting jobs in northern Minnesota. Andersen windows are recognized around the world for their high quality and energy efficiency. The company employs about 4,000 workers at its plant in Bayport, east of St. Paul. Courtesy, Andersen Windows, Inc.

the-art audio, video, and film production facilities, such as rock superstar Prince's Paisley Park Studios, and it adds up to an enticing location for filmmakers.

Efforts to draw more film crews to the area have paid off; in 1990-1991 ten feature films were shot in Minnesota, most of them in the Twin Cities, and the region is fast becoming known as an economical alternative to traditional film locations such as New York and Los Angeles.

Audio production also is big business here. In 1990 alone, six Number One singles on *Billboard*'s "Hot 100" were recorded in Minnesota and produced by a Minnesota-based producer.

And with some 200 advertising agencies, Minneapolis-St. Paul is sixth in the nation in ad billings.

Both Minneapolis and St. Paul downtown business districts have seen extensive growth in office space growth in recent years; 12 million square feet were added in Minneapolis alone between 1980 and 1992. Additionally, the new Minneapolis Convention Center, with nearly 300,000 square feet of exhibit space, was completed in 1990.

The Twin Cities is a good place to start a business as well. Minnesota is 5th in the nation in small business loans and 13th highest in terms of venture capital funds per capita. A wide range of financial and technical resources also is available through the state Department of Trade and Economic Development.

The region truly is an international multimodal transportation hub. Economic growth and world trade in the Twin Cities have been facilitated by the development and maintenance of a solid transportation infrastructure linking Minnesota with the rest of the world.

In addition to the extensive domestic and international passenger and freight services available at Minneapolis-St. Paul International Airport and its six reliever fields, the area is served by virtually every other mode of transportation as well.

Fourteen barge lines ply the Mississippi

River in the Twin Cities, carrying such commodities as agricultural products, bulk fuels, and aggregates to ports all over the world on the nation's largest navigable river system. Some 150 trucking firms operate in Minneapolis and St. Paul. The Soo Line Railroad, based in Minneapolis, and 10 other railroads have offices locally. And the Twin Cities are in close proximity to the Lake Superior port of Duluth 150 miles north, the largest freshwater port in the world.

You can step back in time on a Mississippi River steamboat cruise. The paddlewheel steamboats *Jonathan Padelford*, *Josiah Snelling*, and *Anson Northrup* operate local cruises out of St. Paul and Minneapolis daily during the summer and on weekends in the spring and fall. The New Orleans-based paddlewheelers *Delta Queen* and *Mississippi Queen* steam north to St. Paul about six times a year to pick up passengers for St. Louis and points in between.

The Twin Cities' urban street and highway system is the fifth largest in the country. But even so, more than 70 million

Minneapolis-based Honeywell is a world leader in aviation electronics and guidance systems. This control panel equipped with Honeywell systems is made for space aviation applications. Courtesy, Honeywell

companies are located in the Minneapolis-St. Paul area. A key factor in the location decision of these firms is access to a major airport with direct, frequent service to numerous U.S. cities. It is clear that without adequate air service levels, this economic development would not have occurred," the report states.

Business, civic, and political leaders alike cite the importance of a major hub airport like Minneapolis-St. Paul International in attracting businesses and industries to the area—and keeping them here.

Curt Carlson is founder and chairman of Minnetonka-based Carlson Companies. In addition to its Radisson Hotels and restaurants, the company owns Carlson Travel Network, North America's largest travel agency.

"Many of us remember it was not too many years ago when almost every place we needed to travel to involved a transfer in Chicago to some other airline," says Carlson. Today, thanks to the well-developed air service in Minneapolis-St. Paul, "We enjoy global access to world markets, often direct flights."

Frequent and dependable air service is essential to the Twin Cities' substantial medical products industry as well.

passengers a year ride the Metropolitan Transit Commission bus system. Studies currently are under way for a light-rail transit system in the metro area, with a route to the airport among the first proposed.

Minneapolis-St. Paul International Airport is a powerful economic engine. A 1991 economic impact study identified more than 24,000 jobs in Minnesota directly dependent on the airport. Another 9,000 jobs are created due to expenditures by visitors to the Twin Cities who arrive via the airport. And, the study found, more than 35,000 additional jobs in the Twin Cities' 65 leading industrial and service firms heavily depend on the airport.

"The Twin Cities area is home to over 1,500 technology-intensive firms," the air-

port economic impact study reported. "Furthermore, 26 of the top 1,000 publicly held corporations are headquartered in Minneapolis, and 15 *Fortune* 500 industrial companies and 16 *Fortune* 500 service

St. Jude Medical manufactures prosthetic heart valves and other biomedical devices in suburban Little Canada for shipment worldwide. Medical technology is one of the Twin Cities' leading exports. Courtesy, St. Jude Medical

ABOVE: Paisley Park Studios, owned by international rock superstar and Minneapolis native Prince, have been a magnet for dozens of major record, film, TV, commercial, and concert tour productions. Paisley Park's state-of-the-art facilities are located in suburban Chanhassen west of Minneapolis. Courtesy, Paisley Park Enterprises

BELOW: Dayton Hudson, one of the country's largest retailers, is based in Minneapolis and includes among its many outlets Target discount stores coast to coast. Courtesy, Dayton Hudson Corporation/Steve Niedorf

Medtronic, Inc., a Minneapolis-based manufacturer of cardiac pacemakers and other medical implant devices, relies on overnight air freight for delivery of its time-sensitive products.

"It is important that these products not sit on the shelf for long periods of time," says Medtronic spokesperson Dick Reid. "We fill orders on a day-to-day basis with Federal Express. Air freight—even air courier service—is critical to a medical device company like Medtronic."

Additionally, says Reid, "Our business depends very heavily on close relationships with physicians. And medical professionals are always coming here for training courses." A major hub airport in the metropolitan area has been key to establishing and maintaining those relationships, he says.

Robert M. Rosner, vice president of Minntech Corporation in suburban Plymouth, says his company's delicate computerized medical equipment often must travel by air because other modes of transportation are too rough for the instruments' sensitive electronics.

Located only 30 minutes from an international hub with air service as good as MSP, says Rosner, "We're centrally located by air to our major international markets in Western Europe and the Far East."

The internationally renowned Mayo Clinic in Rochester, 70 miles south of Minneapolis-St. Paul, also is heavily dependent on MSP's international air service.

Providing patients' needs ranging from annual check-ups for heads of state to time-critical organ transplants, the Mayo Clinic has earned a worldwide reputation for excellence in medical care, and its proximity to MSP has been a key link in developing that reputation in the global community.

The Twin Cities' thriving tourism and convention industries benefit mightily from the presence of Minneapolis-St. Paul International.

"Our industry is called destination marketing," says Tom Getzke, St. Paul Conven-

tion and Visitors Bureau vice president. "In order to be a destination you have to be able to get here. Accessibility—both nationally and internationally—is the key and Minneapolis-St. Paul International has both."

And, he says, the close proximity of MSP to both downtown business districts is a major plus in the eyes of convention and meeting planners.

Regular nonstop service to European and Pacific Rim destinations has enabled the Twin Cities to land increasing numbers of international events that otherwise would have gone elsewhere, says Getzke.

For example, in 1992 St. Paul hosted the World Congress on Bovine Medicine that attracted more than 3,000 veterinarians from 48 countries.

Greg D. Ortale, president and chief executive officer of the Greater Minneapolis Convention and Visitors Association, agrees. "Without the level of air service that we have in the Twin Cities, our ability to attract major national and international conventions and trade shows would be significantly reduced."

Concludes Kenneth B. Peterson, St. Paul's director of planning and economic

Minnesota exports of food and agricultural products topped $2 billion in 1991, nearly 5 percent of America's total agricultural exports. Photo by Greg Ryan/Sally Beyer

development: "Minneapolis-St. Paul International Airport and its accompanying reliever airports system play a vital role in attracting new economic development to the Twin Cities area. Equally important, a well-rounded air transportation system is essential to retaining the diverse industrial and service base already located here."

EPILOGUE

More than 70 years after its resurrection from a racetrack to an airport, Minneapolis-St. Paul International Airport is only just beginning to realize its potential as America's North Coast Gateway.

The synergy between the airport and the economic and cultural vitality of the Twin Cities and Upper Midwest is powerful. MSP is the Upper Midwest's link to the global marketplace, and its vital role in the economy and quality of life of this region is continually expanding.

As the Metropolitan Airports Commission's dual-track planning process moves toward its 1996 deadline on determining how best to meet our region's air service needs into the twenty-first century, the fate of MSP draws nearer: Will the airport be expanded at its present location, or will it be moved to a new site in Dakota County south of the Twin Cities?

The challenge is not a new one for the MAC; it has gone through similar exercises twice before in the early 1950s and early 1970s. Like today, those also were unpredictable times for an airline industry undergoing great change, conditions that liken aviation forecasting to aiming at a moving target.

Much of MSP's fate hinges on the future of Northwest Airlines, its home-base carrier. Northwest's fate is equally dependent on the health of the world's airline industry as a whole, and that raises a new set of issues: Can the world's airline industry fly above its current turbulent times and return to profitability? Will the industry weather the growing problems of noise, capacity, and an aging fleet? Do global alliances mean an industry dominated by a handful of megacarriers, and what will that mean for Minneapolis-St. Paul?

With the jury still out on the answers to those questions and more, the MAC must move ahead with one foot firmly planted on the ground and the other boldly stepping forward. That strategy has served MSP well in the past and allowed it to keep pace with the steady growth of Minneapolis-St. Paul's economy. MSP's passenger and cargo service are at record levels, and yet it remains one of the world's safest and most expeditious airports through which to pass.

Continuing to reach for the sky, America's North Coast Gateway has an even brighter future on the radar screen. Stay tuned.

Photo by Dan Halsey

Twin Cities Enterprises

CHAPTER SEVEN

THE AIRLINE INDUSTRY

Photo by Richard Hamilton Smith

Airlines, freight carriers, and companies specializing in aircraft sales and service play a vital role in the region's dynamic industrial scene.

Northwest Airlines, 106-107

KLM Royal Dutch Airlines, 108

Mesaba Aviation, Inc.
    A Wholly Owned Subsidiary of
    AirTran Corporation, 109

Northwest Airlines

Take a population nearly half the size of St. Paul, Minnesota. Lift those people 30,000 feet into the air. Wine them and dine them. Fluff their pillows. Arrange their vacations and help them conduct business back home as they fly or listen to classical or rock music as they nap. Deliver them safely—and punctually—all over the civilized world, from Bangkok to Amsterdam and from Anchorage to Orlando.

Impossible? Northwest Airlines does it every day.

In a year's time, 43 million passengers will fly Northwest. That's two and a half times the population of New York—the state, not just the city.

The human dramas and economic impacts achieved by these flights are monumental in scope, particularly so in Minnesota and the Upper Midwest where Northwest was born and where it still has its world headquarters.

The international carrier—fourth largest in the world—had its debut with a barnstorming pilot and a lone passenger from the present site of Minneapolis-St. Paul International Airport (then an auto racetrack) to Chicago.

The historic flight took place on July 5, 1927, just weeks after another Minnesota legend, young Charles Lindbergh of Little Falls, soloed the Atlantic. Byron Webster of St. Paul was the first passenger, with stunt pilot Charles "Speed" Holman at the controls of the two-seat Stinson Detroiter biplane. The flight took 12 1/2 hours, including a forced landing in a farm field for repairs.

This was Northwest's first venture into the passenger business. For nine months beforehand it had flown the U.S. mail to Chicago as a pioneering airline headed by Harold H. Emmons, who, with other investors, founded Northwest Airways in 1926 as a Detroit-based enterprise flying out of Minneapolis-St. Paul.

The fledgling airline flexed its wings westward toward the Pacific right from the outset, helped fight World War II with flights to Alaska and then to the Orient, and established itself as a global player in the relatively new realm of airborne transportation.

It had first reached the West Coast with a promotional flight in 1933 that starred no less a personage than aviatrix Amelia Earhart, who helped to sell the idea that Northwest could conquer the Rockies and

serve Seattle and, prophetically, perhaps one day go beyond to the Pacific Rim. It was not until the final weeks of World War II, in June 1945, that Northwest became the fourth transcontinental airline in the United States with flights from Seattle to New York, by way of Minneapolis-St. Paul. The company had become a publicly held corporation in 1941.

Northwest underwent a period of unparalleled growth under the leadership of president Donald Nyrop, beginning in

1954, succeeded by M.J. Lapensky in 1976, and by Steven G. Rothmeier in 1985. The following year, 1986, Northwest purchased Twin Cities-based Republic Airlines.

Today Northwest Airlines is Minnesota's premier economic "air force." Its 20,000 Minnesota employees (out of 45,000 worldwide) are at the summit of the state's job market. And that tells but a portion of the story. It is estimated that the airline's presence pumps an annual $2 bil-

ly improved Northwest's ranking in preference among business and leisure travelers. Most notable is Northwest's ascension to number one in on-time performance among the nation's seven largest airlines. Currently with major hubs in Minneapolis-St. Paul, Detroit, and Tokyo, Northwest has ranked consistently near the top of the industry in the U.S. Transportation Department's statistics on the least number of customer complaints.

In the past three years Northwest has made substantial investments in employee customer service training, new in-flight amenities and food service, new employee uniforms, and technological advances such as WorldLink, the airline's state-of-the-art passenger video, audio, and communications system. The cumulative effect of these improvements has been to thrust Northwest to the top of many airline passenger satisfaction surveys.

Northwest also has improved its size and scope since 1989, including the inauguration of service to several key international destinations in Asia and the South Pacific. In 1992 Northwest and its partner, KLM Royal Dutch Airlines, began to coordinate their services in an effort to improve passenger options and customer service, and to gain greater operating efficiencies. The two airlines operate joint service between KLM's hub at Amsterdam and Northwest's U.S. destinations. The two airlines also coordinate passenger handling on flights to many KLM destinations in Europe.

An open-skies agreement between the United States and the Netherlands is now allowing Northwest and KLM to further integrate their operations through coordinated schedules and pricing. As the two airlines assess their future plans, more dramatic undertakings are being considered. Eventually, the two airlines plan to operate as one, offering passengers the first truly global airline system.

While the 1990s so far have been a turbulent and financially difficult period for all airlines, Northwest has taken strong measures to secure its long-term profitability.

lion into Minnesota, according to studies by the Metropolitan Airports Commission.

Even more important, perhaps, is the unique abundance of air service provided to the region because of the airline's headquarters hub here. As the airport's dominant carrier, Northwest quite literally places the world at the doorstep of the Upper Midwest, and particularly Minnesota and the Twin Cities. With its regional airline partners, Northwest flies passengers to more than 240 cities throughout the

United States, Canada, Mexico, the Caribbean, Europe, Asia, and Australia.

Northwest became a privately held corporation once again in August 1989, when it was purchased by Wings Holdings, a partnership that included Al Checchi and Gary Wilson, KLM Royal Dutch Airlines, Bankers Trust, and others. Subsequently, John Dasburg was named president and chief executive officer.

A variety of major product and service improvements since 1989 have dramatical-

KLM Royal Dutch Airlines

A global transportation opportunity was launched at the doorstep of the Upper Midwest when KLM Royal Dutch Airlines synchronized its route system with that of the hometown Northwest Airlines in 1991.

As a result of that history-making agreement, daily service between Minneapolis-St. Paul and Amsterdam, Holland, is a reality that will connect passengers with any continent on the face of the planet save Antarctica.

The daily service on the "Skyway Across the Atlantic" allows passengers to fly non-stop from Minneapolis-St. Paul International Airport to Amsterdam with connections in Europe, the Middle East, Africa, South America, Asia, and even join up with Northwest in Australia or Japan to circumnavigate the globe. When passengers and cargo fly with KLM they use the most experienced airline service on earth. KLM,

RIGHT: The KLM-Northwest global partnership literally links the world for all Minnesotans at Minneapolis-St. Paul International Airport.

BELOW: KLM Royal Dutch Airlines has 25,000 employees and a fleet of approximately 90 airplanes.

after all, was founded in October 1919 and is the world's oldest scheduled airline with continuous service.

Today KLM carries more than eight million passengers and some half-million tons of cargo and mail each year. The Dutch-based carrier serves more than 157 cities in 81 countries on the six continents. The KLM-Northwest global partnership literally links the world for all Minnesotans at MSP, be it for business or vacation travel year round.

KLM Royal Dutch Airlines has 25,000 employees and a fleet of approximately 90

airplanes. While the airline itself dates back 74 years, its fleet of planes is among the youngest, with an average age of 5.3 years.

There is something distinctively intercontinental about service aboard KLM's royal, business, and economy classes. The in-flight cuisine may start with Dutch smoked eel, include grilled Norwegian salmon, and finish with Indonesian cakes. Mementos of the flight in Delft chinaware are presented in first class. Passengers may track their trip on a video map that charts each flight across the globe.

KLM passengers transferring at Amsterdam will experience a whole new age of airport convenience in Schiphol Airport, which was voted the world's best for nine years in a row. It is an international hub and a tax-free shopping center all under one roof, serving as the most advanced gateway into a unified Europe and to the world beyond.

Mesaba Aviation, Inc.
A WHOLLY OWNED SUBSIDIARY OF AIRTRAN CORPORATION

Of the 800 U.S. airports served by scheduled air carriers, there are 500 airports that realize both a convenience and an economic benefit from the scheduled air service they receive only from regional airlines. Mesaba is one of the nation's top 15 regional airlines and is dedicated to reinforcing that vital connection, according to Robert D. Swenson, president and chief executive officer of the Minneapolis-St. Paul International Airport-based carrier. Swenson says, "Many small and medium-size communities count on the regional airline industry to meet their travel needs and assist in their economic vitality."

Mesaba began to grow like the drifts in a Minnesota blizzard.

In 1983 Mesaba was one of the first regional airlines to go public and raise equity. Then, in 1984, it moved its headquarters to Minneapolis-St. Paul and signed a code-sharing agreement with Northwest Airlines. That same year Mesaba also became a "Part 121" air carrier, a classification that allowed it to begin flying Fokker F27 48-seat aircraft, a big jump over the 15-seat Beechcraft 99s it had been flying.

Code-sharing now made the firm a Northwest "Airlink," providing smaller-

to grow on. The commission has never lost sight of the Minneapolis-St. Paul International Airport's role as our regional gateway to the world, and that the regional airlines comprise the only transportation system that millions of Americans can rely on," says Swenson, acknowledging the Metropolitan Airports Commission's longtime support in the company's incremental growth.

Mesaba and its parent, AirTran Corporation, have grown profitably over the years. AirTran has reported a nearly fourfold increase in net income over the past half-decade, to $5.8 million in fiscal 1992. Further, it was rated the nation's 49th best-managed growth company, for companies with sales under $350 million, by *Forbes* magazine in 1992, up 30 places from the year before.

In reiterating Mesaba's commitment to help create a more prosperous Middle America, Rob Swenson cites the company's motto: "Safety, Reliability, Profitability, and People. With this foundation in place, Mesaba will continue to expand in regional airline service, the only form of fast, dependable, public transportation left for many cities."

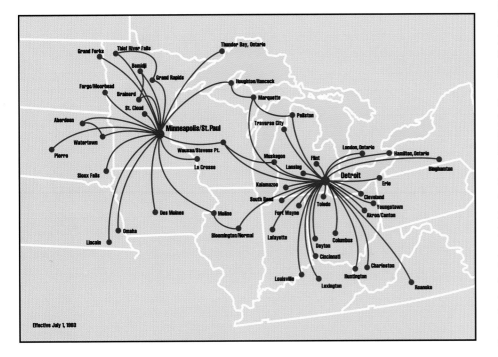

Mesaba celebrated its 20th anniversary as a scheduled airline in 1993. During the past 18 months Mesaba has added 25 new 37-passenger Dash 8 turboprop aircraft to its fleet and extended its service into 18 new markets, bringing to approximately 48 the number of cities served. Mesaba currently employs more than 1,300 people, generates annual revenues in excess of $125 million, and boards over 1.4 million passengers on its route system each year.

The original aviation business was founded in Grand Rapids, Minnesota, in 1944 with one war-surplus Piper J3 Cub. In 1978 the carrier was purchased by the Swenson family from Thief River Falls. The company was serving only one route with 25 employees, but it was the beginning of airline deregulation and

city travelers with "major carrier" service. Passengers could now call reservations worldwide, buy a computer-confirmed ticket, make convenient connections both domestically and internationally, check their baggage through to their final destination, and earn credits on Northwest's World Perk's frequent-flyer program.

Mesaba took another giant step in 1988, when it was selected to provide Northwest's Airlink service out of Detroit. Opening that major Michigan market added 325 employees, 15 new aircraft, and 10 new markets (including Cleveland, Dayton, and Akron, Ohio) during the first year of this new service.

Also in 1988, Mesaba built a major 80,000-square-foot maintenance facility and corporate headquarters at Minneapolis-St. Paul. "This has been a great airport

ABOVE: One of the deHavilland Dash 8 turboprop aircraft in Mesaba's fleet. The Dash 8 is ideal to provide comfortable, efficient travel for medium-size commercial traffic.

ABOVE LEFT: The Mesaba network, serving 48 cities in 15 states and 3 Canadian locations.

CHAPTER EIGHT

NETWORKS

Photo by Greg Ryan/Sally Beyer

 ourier services, ground transportation firms, communication businesses, utilities, and companies that provide aviation fuel link carriers to national and international markets.

InterNatural Designs, Inc., 112-116

National Interrent, 117

Northern States Power Company, 118-119

Hubbard Broadcasting, 120-121

AT&T, 122

Naegele Outdoor Advertising Company, 123

InterNatural Designs, Inc.

Two messages define the dream for Leah and Jon Miner in their melange of bustling family enterprises along busy Highway 169 in the Twin Cities suburb of New Hope, Minnesota.

One, a sign, says, "Mello Smello, Where Fun Is Serious Business™."

The second is pure Jon Miner. At 52, he is head coach and cofounder (with his wife, Leah, the president) of this promotional marketing firm, formally known as InterNatural Designs, Inc./Mello Smello®. With a primary focus to help its clients win lifetime customers, the company has created innovative children's and sports marketing programs.

According to Jon Miner, "We believe the ability to win lifetime customers is the ultimate competitive advantage for our retail and brand clients. Winning the respect and loyalty of a child can mean that child will commit his or her parents to you for years, and together will grow into a family of lifetime customers."

But the Miners also play with the Very Big Kids. With annual revenues approaching $75 million, their rate of growth is substantially faster than kiddie-car speed.

"Volume is vanity. Profit is prosperity," Jon Miner says with a certain abruptness, down-shifting during a recitation of rosy company prospects. "We're able to sustain a solid return on equity, with which we'll do as much as we can, for the good of kids and their families everywhere, and for the employee-family of our company and clients."

ABOVE: Jon Miner, chief executive officer, and his partner, wife Leah, president, greet guests at a recent company function.

MIDDLE: Parents Barbara and Morey Miner.

TOP: Brothers Doug and Jon Miner in the early days at Camp Wa-Ga-Tha-Ka.

It truly *is* a family business. Mark Miner, son of Leah and Jon, is vice president of marketing with a strong hand in product development and promotion. His wife, Kim, is director of "Mission Nutrition®" and school food service marketing for the firm. Their child, Shelby, is one of the youngest members of the Mello Smello "advisory board of directors."

Jon's brother and lifelong working partner, Doug Miner, is vice president of operations, with special responsibilities for international trade and administration. A graduate of Michigan State University's famous institutional management school and master of education, he's long on experience in restaurant and hotel operations, including a tour as director of corporate training for Curt Carlson's Radisson Corporation.

"Yes, Curt and my brother *do* have similarities," Doug says in reply to the inevitable question. "All highly creative people have their eccentricities. Jon is a big picture person. My responsibilities include details and follow-up. We have always been a productive, hard-hitting team."

Because the past is essential to understanding the Miner Companies—a vertically integrated organization supporting nearly 1,100 family members skilled in ideation, graphics, marketing, even mouthguard making and polymer chemistry—it is well to go back to the roots.

Leah and Jon Miner were raised on opposite ends of Minnesota's Mesabi Iron Range. It can be a demanding, hardscrabble place, where the work ethic often does more to steel the character than the many religions that reflect the region's ethnic makeup. Both had entrepreneurial upbringings: Leah, in the hamlet of Cook, toiled in the family's Miller's IGA Grocery with her parents, Walter and Marge, and two siblings, older brother Harlan and younger sister Maxine. "It was unusual in those days to have both parents working," she says. "But it taught us responsibility and the need to make something of our lives."

Jon and his brother, Doug, both orphans, found a loving but challenging home in Grand Rapids, with schoolteachers Barbara and Morey Miner. (Grandfather Harvey Stark was a prominent Grand Rapids attorney.)

The Miners also operated a family-oriented summer camp founded in 1926. Jon

Pictured above is just a sampling of the many stickers produced by Mello Smello and printed by AWT and NorthPrint.

and Doug became resorters early on, working their way up from bussers of dishes and dock boys to the demanding position of camp director. It was truly a precursor upbringing, the start of the path that led, with a few providential jogs, to today's task of motivating children via the sense of joy. Fun *is* serious business.

Significantly, the camp, called Wa-Ga-Tha-Ka, Ojibwa for "dwelling place among the birch trees," on Lake Wabana ("lake of many bays"), remains in the corporate structure. It's now a summer refuge to which the Miners bring children and their parents from all over the world to savor the Minnesota summer ("Big bass and bigger mosquitoes," says Jon), and to encourage self-reliance via rigorous aquatic and woodsy sports. "Wa-Ga-Tha-Ka is one of life's wonderful experiences," says Jon Miner. "I wish everyone could enjoy it."

Miner tells of a busy, Tom Sawyer boyhood: Of finding a second home in the Boy Scouts, where his dad and mom were leaders and to which the son remains devoted as a proud holder of the highest, Eagle, rank. Also of attending church, but being far less interested in the homily than helping to look after small fry in Sunday School; and of serving as a volunteer reader for C.K. Blandin (his eyesight was failing), the legendary papermill magnate whose namesake foundation has given tens of millions to good works in Minnesota through most of the twentieth century.

"Mr. Blandin was a hero and role model," says Miner. "Because of my connection, I was deputized by the school to learn if he might contribute to our new band uniforms. 'How much do you need, Jonny?' he asked. 'Almost $18,000, sir,' I replied. 'I've got $9,000, Jonny. Have you got $9,000?' 'Yes, sir,' I said. 'Thank you very much.'" (Miner explains that although the school lacked that much cash at the moment, students quickly raised it in a team effort.)

Leah and Jon graduated from different colleges in the Twin Cities, she from the Minneapolis School of Business, he from Macalester College, before going on to night school at St. Paul's William Mitchell College of Law. They met while working together at the First National Bank of Minneapolis.

The years 1968 and 1969 were auspicious ones: The two were married and, together with the senior Miners, bought a stake in a St. Paul printing business, Impressions, Inc., which they still own, together with stockholders Mark and Evelyn Jorgensen. "Mark and Ev were strong inspirations during our formative years," says Jon.

The Miners gained invaluable expertise in various innovative industrial technologies during the era, and began an enduring quarter-century relationship with the 3M Company. "How lucky we are," remarks Miner, "to have in Minnesota such leading international firms as 3M, Medtronic, Deluxe Check, Cargill, Cray, Dayton's, Pillsbury, and Honeywell."

The bond was 3M's discovery of microencapsulation, a means of coating miniscule, odor-holding cells upon paper, pores that break when compressed and release their scent into the air. The Miners soon confirmed that the "flavors" available (anything from attar of roses to the musky essence of skunk, a balm to most young male noses) create a powerful, multisensory promotional medium. They had found a major product niche in Mello Smello.

The Mello Smello "factory," one of

rants, service companies, and brands to best market themselves and attract targeted lifetime customers—children—to their enterprises. These innovative, child-oriented, continuity programs do motivate children to eat at a particular fast-food chain or buy their favorite foods from such clients as Taco Bell, Jack in the Box, Dairy Queen, the Marriott Corporation, General Mills, and Kellogg's.

To help IDI/Mello Smello position itself for the 1990s and catapult the company as a major force in the marketing and promotional arena, the IDI Strategy Group was formed. It is headed by Debra Pryor, a former senior executive at W.B. Doner, the world's largest retail advertising agency. With such broad experience in marketing and advertising, she instantly recognized

about a dozen Miner subsidiary companies (and growing), manufactures "millions and millions and millions" (quoting astrophysicist Carl Sagan) of stickers and other promotional items annually, for both the retail and promotional markets, and for third-party firms whose catchy messages the stick-tights carry. With kid appeal akin to baseball cards, the stickers are saved and avidly traded, to the extended benefit of the brands for which they bridge the gap between shelf and shopper. AWT (Advanced Web Technologies), the company that manufactures the odorous little articles, is near IDI/Mello Smello headquarters.

Twin City-based General Mills is another valuable partner that the Miner Companies have long served. It recently mounted the effective roll-out of its new pop-flavored "Soda-Licious" fruit chewables, offering in-pack stickers, odor-keyed to the product, as an incentive to purchase. The Mello Smello stickers are likewise produced in such "consumable" flavors as lemonade, peanut butter, Teenage Mutant Ninja Turtle pizza, even three-to-one Tanqueray dry martinis (definitely not for the kids)! Variations of these applications are endless and account for a significant share of company revenue and earnings.

Mello Smello is simultaneously a leading licenser to industry of many top film, cartoon, and product brand characters:

ABOVE: Camp Wa-Ga-Tha-Ka today, with a few friends on the new floating hot-tub— "Ja Cruzzee."

RIGHT: The Boy Scouts "Jamborall," held in the Twin Cities in 1992, featured a whole set of cards like this one. They were sponsored and produced by Mello Smello and NorthPrint.

The Ninja Turtles, Nintendo, Batman, Barbie, Disney, the Flintstones, Chipmunks, and the Jetsons, plus more. The company is careful to offer a wide selection of stars and heroes, someone for every bracket of kinder demographics.

Mello Smello retail stickers and related activities are also widely appealing: "To kids from three to 93," says Jon Miner. Printed on surgeon's tape that adheres to skin or clothing, they carry the names and logos of such organizations as the Minnesota Vikings, plus "pretend" tattoos and pretty fashion accents. Similar are "Make-A-Face" kits, which let youngsters disguise themselves as Count Chocula or Frankenburger, this impressing on wearers both an enduring brand awareness and a scary visage, in full color for Halloween.

Growing segments of IDI/Mello Smello are its Retail and Promotions groups. Established in the early 1980s, the two were created to address the growing need of retailers, fast-food chains, family restau-

the uniqueness of IDI and its endless opportunities.

"There is no other company in the world like IDI," enthusiastically states Pryor. "Not only can we provide our clients with strategic marketing and promotional planning, but we can execute each and every program, all in-house, from creative development to actual production to getting the message to children in schools. IDI is truly a family of fully integrated companies with seamless execution."

The IDI Strategy Group provides clients with an extensive profile of their targeted customers and develops a strategic marketing and promotional plan that "triggers" that customer to choose a particular store, fast-food restaurant, or brand.

According to Pryor, "What we've developed at IDI is a form of 'Trigger Marketing.' We identify for our customers those emotional triggers that overcome rational barriers to buying, and design a promotional program to trip those emotional triggers and motivate customers to choose our client's store or brand over other options."

The IDI/Mello Smello magazine, *Surprises*, is full of games, puzzles, and activities to heighten interaction between children and parents. The firm is committed to the idea that family values are vitally important to the future of the country. "Improved school nutrition is also high on our agenda," says Leah Miner. "We work with legions of schools to encourage participation in the educational 'Happy Meal' program." She explains that in this "Mission Nutrition," students receive brightly decorated lunch bags containing solid health information in an eating experience akin to a fast-food restaurant. Program adjuncts include stickers, rulers, and pencils, all imprinted with wellness messages.

One of the high-tech products at the Miner Companies has emerged from an alliance with E-Z GARD Industries, Inc., a young firm with a scarcely older president, already established as an impact player in the emerging sports health and safety industry.

Founder Jon Kittelsen has received developmental financing from the Miners in the congenial neighborhood of $1.5 million over the past three years. In return, his advanced mouth protectors have strengthened the Miners' stance as a firm staking its growth on kids, garnering additional goodwill together with the rewards that always seem to follow.

Ancillary to E-Z GARD is the "International Sports Safety Foundation" (ISSF), founded by the Miners to actively promote the safety and well-being of children and adolescents participating in sports. "With over 50 percent of all school-age children involved," says Jon Miner, "that's 22 million kids taking part in at least one organized sport. It's important to encourage kids to take preventive actions and reduce their chances of being seriously injured. For those reasons we founded the ISSF."

Just as Mission Nutrition encourages kids to eat more wisely, ISSF carries its

"Surprise!" Grand Rapids' own Judy Garland.

message via attention-getting printed material, aided by star pro athletes whose own personal foundations will benefit from the relationship as the product matures.

E-Z GARD inventor Kittelsen, 26, is a business wunderkind. While playing high school hockey at age 15 he lost his mouthguard in a mid-ice melee. When he couldn't find it, he kept skating until whistled into a penalty for an equipment violation that allowed the foe to score the winning goal. The infraction motivated the youngster to do some serious thinking about a better mouthguard.

What emerged was a far safer device in all respects, one that has been adopted by many Olympic and professional teams and has won the coveted blessing of NFL Properties, the licensing arm of the National Football League. Today many NFL players wear E-Z GARD protectors.

Waiting in the wings is a singular advancement in sports health, even performance: "Steroid-free and inherent in our proprietary design." Kittelsen tells how kinesiologists (specialists in the science of human musculature) have long been aware of the curious role of the "TM" joint. Located just ahead of the ear, it can actually reduce athletic performance by impeding the vital flow of oxygen-rich blood to the muscles, even block the transmission of nerve impulses, when the jaws are clenched tightly shut.

E-Z GARD's solution is "SHOCK

DOCTOR™," a customized mouthpiece that keeps the jaw fixed in the slightly separated "power position," (a matter of millimeters) during moments of peak endeavor. Maintaining the space significantly improves power, performance, and protection, says the company, citing reams of supportive test data.

E-Z GARD's marquee sports hero is U.S. 1992 Olympic Greco-Roman Wrestling silver-medal winner Dennis Koslowski of Golden Valley. Repeated tests on the kinesiometer before his Barcelona triumph proved that SHOCK DOCTOR™ increased his total body strength by almost 14 percent. "With our equilibrated mouthpiece, he enhanced his bench press by more than 16 percent, to 350 pounds," says a proud Kittelsen.

Viking All-Pro defensive lineman Chris Doleman is a big fan of, and spokesman for, E-Z GARD. His boss, Vikings' head coach Dennis Green, is also a big booster, supporting the mission of the Miner companies:

"Sports safety is all important," says the leader of the Purple. "One reason my team plays hard is that the members are all well protected. I insisted on the best mouthguard available. That's why I made the decision to have my team fitted with official NFL Pro Line E-Z GARD mouthguard system. Kids can play it safe with E-Z GARD, too."

Ideas flow from Jon Miner so swiftly that it is sometimes hard to track them, but four primary concerns stand out: He is strongly pro-kids, pro-roots (in the regional and familial sense), pro-trade, and pro-travel. All, he feels, are bridges that help span the distance between nations, peoples, and generations.

"And my abiding attitude is W.I.N.," says Miner, explaining that the acronym comes from the words "With Intensity Now." "It's an idea I credit to our own Lou Raiola, who got it from the great John Gagliardi, coach of the perennial small college football power, St. John's University of Collegeville, Minnesota. The coach motivates his kids with the slogan 'With Intensity Now! With Intensity Now! With Intensity Now! WIN! WIN! WIN!'"

Raiola, a college All American at St. John's, heads up the sports licensing division of IDI/Mello Smello, Line-Up Productions. One of its premier products is "The PlayMakers," limited-edition collector prints of sports and entertainment superstars from around the world. Those unique, vividly colored prints are neither trading cards nor posters, but rather a new niche category, positioned as affordable sports and entertainment art.

Line-Up was created to help corporate sponsors leverage their return on investment in sponsoring sports teams and entertainers and in promoting special events, also to assist professional sports teams in marketing their programs directed to children, families, and potential lifetime fans.

"We have more than 467,000 kids on our Mello Smello associate board of directors,'" Jon Miner says. "If that isn't corporate democracy I don't know what is," explaining that opinions and new product

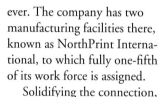

ABOVE: Next time you see a rainbow, you'll understand it starts—and ends—in Grand Rapids, Minnesota.

TOP: Frances Gumm (Judy Garland) and the Judy Garland Museum have always held a special place in the Miners' hearts. This photo shows the youthful Gumm sisters, with Judy in the middle, as they performed at Grand Rapids' own Rialto Theatre.

ideas are actively solicited from those junior consumers. When a 12-year-old terminally ill California girl was offered a chance to travel anywhere in the United States by the Make-A-Wish Foundation, she chose a visit to IDI/Mello Smello headquarters.

"The main thrust," adds Leah Miner, "is using our various media to teach children to do what is right: the importance of performance in family and school, the lifelong value of good nutrition, and, now, the practice of sports safety."

Miner roots reaching back to Grand Rapids and Lake Wabana are as strong as

ever. The company has two manufacturing facilities there, known as NorthPrint International, to which fully one-fifth of its work force is assigned.

Solidifying the connection, son Jay Miner makes his home in Grand Rapids, working in offices there as director of corporate sales for the family business. He also serves as waterfront director at Camp Wa-Ga-Tha-Ka, carrying the tradition into the 1990s.

The Miners—including Doug and his wife JoEllen, and friends Jerry and Shirley Miner, owners of Miner's Megamart and Central Square Mall in Grand Rapids—recently secured the childhood home of late movie star Judy Garland (born Frances Ethel Gumm) for the Itasca County Historical Society. It was both a sentimental and practical gesture. Jon's parents, Morey and Barbara Miner, were longtime active members of the society, both serving as officers in the late 1970s. In the future the home will become a centerpiece of Grand Rapids tourism.

The Gumm (Garland) family lived in the home, a typical two-story midwestern style white-frame house, for nearly 12 years before moving to California in 1926, when Judy was but a tyke. It will be refurbished as a museum and focus added attention on

the city's annual Judy Garland Festival, under the aegis of the history group.

The Miner family also had personal ties with the Gumms. Grandma Stark, Barbara Miner's mother, would babysit for the infant Judy, while brothers Jon and Doug later delivered papers there and attended scout meetings at the residence.

Laughing, Jon recalls how the Miners helped bring 13 of the surviving Munchkin actors from Garland's classic film, *The Wizard of Oz* to the star's namesake celebration several years ago. "Those wonderful people felt everyone had forgotten them, so they were especially grateful to be recognized," he recalls.

"We are also pleased to help in the upgrading of Northern Minnesota Community Colleges to four-year, degree-granting institutions," says Leah Miner. "It's nearly 300 miles from some Iron Range points to the Twin Cities, and coming to school down here is often out of the question. Jon and I also assist community college students with academic scholarships in areas where we do business: It's the best investment in both northern Minnesota and our companies."

A fiscal conservative, Jon Miner advocates public policy that assures a level playing field for private industry, and he's a strong advocate of international trade and the free exchange of ideas between people.

"We've been flying to Pacific Rim countries since the late 1960s—Taiwan, Mainland China, Hong Kong, South Korea, Thailand, and Indonesia; more than 30 business trips, all on Northwest Airlines, we're proud to say. We have friends, now into the third generation, all over the world. They stay in our house on visits to the United States. We help their families and friends find educational opportunities here."

Miner is convinced that a capacious airport, conveniently located, is essential to the continued economic vigor of the Upper Midwest. "A first-class airport is the region's essential portal to the new 'single,' global economy. We've long been blessed with unsurpassed airline service. I'm sure that remains essential in planning for the region's future."

National Interrent

Founded nearly 50 years ago as the first truly nationwide auto rental firm, Edina-based National Car Rental System, Inc., remains driven by the aim of unsurpassed customer service. It is now making that ideal as tangible as its fleet of sleek General Motors cars by aggressive, long-term investment in a number of exclusive, high-tech renter conveniences:

Newest and most visible is its exclusive "Smart Key," which brings the swift efficiency of today's automated teller machines to National locations across the domestic system. This interactive electronic technology permits customers to swiftly complete their own rental and return transactions at computer stations,

With 7,500 employees nationwide (1,000 in Minnesota, making it an important factor in the state economy), National is one of the "Big Three" in the U.S. car rental industry. Closely held, the firm does not disclose its financial figures. *Forbes* magazine, noted for tracking such things, estimated its 1991 sales near $950 million.

Not unlike Northwest and KLM Royal Dutch Airlines, National has entered into an agreement for the benefit of travelers all over the globe. Called Interrent, it is a worldwide network of more than 4,900 locations in 29 countries, all offering the duality of instantaneous communication backed up by the know-how of the local marketplace.

"Now," says Corbett, "you can get off a plane almost any place in the world and look for the green Interrent color. It means that Europcar across the Atlantic, Tilden of Canada, or Nippon Rent a Car in the Pacific will provide the same consistent service you get from National here in the United States. And we've all adopted the Interrent name for further differentiation.

"The reality is that we live in a business climate that has become global in every sense. It's essential to be part of an international system to market your product everywhere—even at home."

Corbett sees being based in Minnesota as an advantage for National. "Minnesota-based corporations have a nationally recognized reputation for good, honest service," he explains. "We've been told more than once that we're perceived as 'the nice people in the industry.'"

Corbett also finds strong reciprocal loyalty among Minnesota companies. "There's a heightened awareness of the advantages of mutual support. The fact that you live in the same community as a Dayton's Cargill, or Honeywell is a definite plus: It is good to be seen as a customer-driven local firm, determined to deliver maximum satisfaction."

then be off about their business.

Smart Key is an extension of "Emerald Aisle," the industry's first hassle-free venue for getting into, or out of, a rental car. Another National first, it takes full advantage of National's exhaustive computerized customer data base—the industry's most complete.

National's "QSRP" (Quality Service Recovery Program) is a less visible but equally vital system to further ensure customer satisfaction. Assuring that all renter concerns are addressed before a return is completed, it mandates a complete examination of possibly unsatisfactory transactions. Coupled with new levels of agent empowerment, QSRP permits numerous adjustments directly at the rental counter, followed up by satisfaction-confirming telephone calls from National service supervisors or management, if necessary.

All of these advances come under the

ABOVE: National's worldwide headquarters is located in Edina, just minutes from the Minneapolis-St. Paul Airport.

TOP: National's revolutionary Smart Key technology makes renting a car as easy and fast as using an ATM machine.

aegis of National's "Continuous Improvement Process." Six years in the making, it is paying off in growing customer loyalty and increased rental transactions for National.

"It's all too easy for car rentals to slip into a commodity frame of mind," says Geoff Corbett, National's executive vice president of sales and marketing. "Nothing enhances customer satisfaction like high technology, properly applied. Each renter is always addressed as the *person* she or he really is."

Northern States Power Company

When Edison's miracle of electricity revolutionized American life in the late 1800s, small utility companies sprang up across the country. Maverick operators frantically competed to build generating plants and transmission lines, wire homes and businesses, answer trouble calls, read meters, and sell light bulbs. Under-financed, under-sized, and poorly managed, countless small companies went bankrupt or were absorbed by their larger competitors.

The Upper Midwest was no exception. Across Minnesota, the Dakotas, and Wisconsin, electric light and power production was enthusiastically pursued by scores of small, inefficient operators. The growth

Just as the Minneapolis-St. Paul International Airport has grown to meet the expanding needs of the region and state, NSP has steadily evolved to become a major utility. The fragmented, fledgling company that Byllesby crafted now serves customers in Minnesota, North Dakota, South Dakota, Upper Michigan, and Wisconsin. NSP generates, transmits, and distributes electricity to about 1.3 million customers and distributes natural gas to about 370,000 customers. The Minneapolis-based, investor-owned utility

NSP is continually working to extend the operating lives of its power plants and to upgrade its transmission system. It invests heavily in programs to encourage efficient energy use, and works closely with its customers to promote and implement them.

A wide range of energy-management programs encourage customers to both modify and reduce the amount of electricity they use each day. These changes help customers reduce their cost of doing business and be more competitive. They also mean that NSP can postpone the need to build new power plants and can continue to meet customers' needs in an environmentally sound manner.

By working together with residential and business customers to help them analyze, manage, and lower their energy costs, NSP is able to control production expenses, reduce peak demand for electricity, and move toward meeting aggressive conservation goals.

NSP's programs include cash rebates, expert consultation, financing, and special rates to encourage energy conservation. Load management programs offer substantially lower rates to customers who shift their electric use to non-business hours.

One of NSP's long-standing energy partners is Northwest Airlines (NWA), based at the Minneapolis-St. Paul International Airport. In the Twin Cities metro area, NWA has more than 3 million square feet of facilities, including hangars, office space, shops, warehouses, and more. A substantial portion of the buildings' total annual operating budget is spent on electricity, so reducing energy costs is a high priority. Through a software program tying directly into NSP's computer, the airline is able to get immediate, ongoing information from NSP, providing invaluable data for projecting, planning, and implementing cost-saving programs.

NSP consultants and NWA managers work closely to track the airline's energy use and identify cost-savings opportunities. Consequently, the airline has realized substantial cost reductions through utilizing peak-controlled rate programs, energy-effi-

potential for someone with business acumen, personal worth, and access to investor dollars was enormous.

Henry M. Byllesby, a colleague of Thomas Edison, had the vision, technical expertise, and resources to grasp the opportunity and build an empire. In 1902 he began acquiring struggling electric and gas enterprises and injecting cash and engineering skill. By 1916 he had organized his burgeoning enterprise under the name Northern States Power Company (NSP).

In spite of the exploding growth of Byllesby's utility holdings, he gained an impressive reputation for exacting high standards from his new company. He insisted on quality, dependability, and exemplary customer service—the same values NSP stresses today, more than 75 years later.

ABOVE: NSP transmits electricity to 1.3 million customers in five states.

TOP: The changing Minneapolis skyline reflects NSP's steady growth.

employs about 7,100 people.

NSP's commitment to providing its customers with reliable, economic energy has been unwavering throughout its history. Its electric rates for commercial and industrial customers are among the lowest one-fourth in the nation. The company's carefully planned balance of coal, nuclear, and hydropower generation should ensure that its electric rates remain competitive well into the future. In addition, the present electric and gas transmission systems are fully capable of providing for both short- and long-term power needs.

Northwest Airlines has more than 3 million square feet of facilities in the Twin Cities metro area. Courtesy, Alvis Upitis

cient chillers, energy rebate programs, and energy-efficient lighting and equipment improvements.

Similarly, NSP has used a team approach to meet the energy needs of the Metropolitan Airports Commission (MAC) during years of rapid airport expansion and renovation. MAC members and the NSP account team meet quarterly to review facilities projects, assess changing needs, and undertake critical long-range planning.

Economic development is a top priority at NSP as the company's future success is clearly tied to the economic strength and vitality of the area it serves. Consequently, it has increased its emphasis on working with existing customers and their communities to promote a healthy business environment.

Among the many services offered are confidential location site assistance, utility rate comparisons, new construction design assistance, a savings-by-geographical-zone program called Project Gemini, networking opportunities with economic development allies in city and state government, and

access to SBIR-SEARCH, a federally funded research grant program for small business. NSP's Economic Development Department also publishes *The Rite Site Guide*, a handbook for businesses considering expansion or relocation, and the *Business Resource Directory*, a comprehensive listing of informational resources located in NSP's service area. Both publications are available free of charge.

NSP supports more than 35 economic development organizations with funding, in-kind services, and marketing support. In addition, NSP works with Advantage Minnesota, a nonprofit, public-private partnership charged with marketing Minnesota within the state and attracting businesses nationally and internationally.

Helping customers prosper and succeed means making a commitment to their communities. NSP sponsors and participates in a variety of programs and investments to revitalize the core areas of its service territory. The company recently invested in two venture capital funds: the Milestone Growth Fund, a small business investment company specializing in minority-owned enterprises, and the St. Paul Growth Ventures Fund I, a venture capital partnership that focuses on opportunities in the Metro East area.

Neighborhood and community develop-

ment organizations are not forgotten; they are supported through financial, consulting, and marketing communications assistance. The company recently committed to a $2-million investment in the National Equity Fund, a subsidiary of the Local Initiatives Support Corporation, an organization dedicated to transforming distressed neighborhoods into healthy communities. The funding will support projects producing low- and moderate-income housing units in Minneapolis and St. Paul.

In late 1992 NSP senior management approved implementation of the Affordable Housing Investment Program, a direct investment program using the federal Low Income Housing Tax Credit. NSP will invest up to $1.8 million each year in new affordable housing projects located throughout its service territory and will seek to leverage an equal investment level from other Upper Midwest corporations.

Throughout the 1990s NSP will continue to look for ways to enhance the range of services it provides. Working in partnership with its customers and the communities it serves, NSP will apply its creative energy to strengthen the business community and ensure a bright and promising future for the region.

Hubbard Broadcasting

Coming 50 years apart, separate communications involving two Stanley Hubbards help compress into several pages the immense role that one family has played in the business and technological growth of the Upper Midwest.

The first, a 1943 letter signed by then-Governor Harold E. Stassen, tells how recipient Stanley E. Hubbard was "one of the very first" to alert the governor to the need for a "Metropolitan Airway authority," now the Metropolitan Airports Commission (MAC). Stassen saluted the role of the late broadcasting pioneer by enclosing one of the pens used to sign the enabling legislation.

The second is a recent editorial in *Broadcasting* magazine, bible of the industry. It hails Stanley S. Hubbard for the "triumph of one man over insuperable odds" upon becoming licensee for the world's first direct broadcast satellite (DBS).

When launched early in 1994, Hubbard's United States Satellite Broadcasting (USSB) bird will bring 120 new TV channels to 100 million U.S. households via small 18-inch dishes—directly from space and without an inch of wire in between—making possible a depth and breadth of programming not attainable before.

"TV will never be the same again, thanks to the vision and courage of Stan Hubbard," wrote *Broadcasting*. "Both the medium and the country are in his debt."

The younger Hubbard relates that his late father—also an early aviator who spotted Prohibition-era rumrunners off Florida for Uncle Sam from Navy seaplanes—felt deeply

ABOVE: The Conus Communications control room, where satellite feeds are managed to and from more than 150 member stations.

BELOW LEFT: DBS reception equipment includes a decoder box and dish antenna measuring just 18 inches across.

about aviation safety.

"Although abhorring unwanted intrusions of government, he felt that human life was more important," says Stanley S., explaining that barnstormers often flew their joyriding passengers in planes that were literally deathtraps. "My dear dad also felt that a state authority was needed to regulate air traffic around the Twin Cities. He urged the creation of both today's MAC and a state department of aeronautics."

The senior Hubbard's concern was not amiss: Northwest Airways (the carrier's original name) operated early on from the main airports of both Minneapolis and St. Paul, even *between* the two—a practice marred by the fatal 1929 crash of a Ford Tri-Motor onto Dayton's Bluff in St. Paul.

Press clippings tell how the senior Hubbard came back from the Army Signal Corps of World War I to establish Hubbard Field in Louisville, then organized the first commercial airline in the United States—the Ohio Valley Aero Transport company—before engaging in derring-do that fed the legend that was to surround him.

For much of 1922 the *Miami Daily Metropolis* regaled its readers with accounts of federal efforts to stop the flow of bootleg booze into the United States from nearby British islands. In one, "Captain Stanley Hubbard, chief of the internal revenue flying service in Florida," managed to foil a saboteur who had drilled a hole in the hull of his flying boat.

Another time, Hubbard and a dozen aviators he commanded cornered a rogue schooner and its contraband of 11,500 cases of fine Canadian whiskey. Costing $5 a case in Montreal, the cargo would have fetched millions in thirsty South Florida.

Hubbard made national headlines in 1924 by flying over New York City the night of the national elections, shooting off variegated flares to show the course of President Coolidge's victory over Democratic challenger John W. Davis.

Hubbard then turned his promotional flair to advantage by returning to his native Minnesota and getting into the thick of radio, the hottest fad of the Roaring Twenties. He soon made his mark: His radio station WAMD ("Where all Minneapolis Dances," now KSTP) was first in the nation to survive on advertising revenue alone. (Other earlybird stations were subsidized by department stores, newspaper owners, and other sponsoring companies.)

KSTP-TV became the Twin Cities initial television station, going on the dial in April 1948, fully 10 years after company engineers had experimentally telecast an

ABOVE: Hubbard Broadcasting headquarters, located exactly upon the Minneapolis-St. Paul border.

TOP: Stanley E. Hubbard—aviation pioneer and founder of Hubbard Broadcasting.

American Legion parade in Minneapolis. Also the nation's first all-color station, Channel 5 broke vast areas of new ground in news, public affairs, and educational programming.

All the while, Stanley S. Hubbard, a varsity hockey player at the University of Minnesota, was growing up in the family business. Assuming its presidency in 1967 at the age of 34, he became chairman in 1981. His father died peacefully in late 1992, the legator of a broadcasting empire consisting of 11 stations in three states and a cluster of cutting-edge enterprises that have long enhanced the way America benefits from the public airwaves.

The younger Hubbard is also a chip off the old block.

Success, magazine for entrepreneurs, recently cited him in its annual Renegades (the Makers of Tomorrow) issue. "When Stanley Hubbard said he wanted to beat the cable kings by firing his own satellite into the air, they told him it was impossible. He's doing it, and he'll deliver three times as many channels as any cable system in the country."

Recognizing the limitations of conventional broadcasting—a multitude of fragmented regional audiences served by a plethora of stations that could never come close to delivering a truly national audience—Hubbard looked to the skies for direction.

A substantial first step was the creation of Conus Communications, parent of Hubbard's 24-hour All News Channel. Conus is driven by a satellite-linked network of 150 regional TV stations, many among the largest network affiliates in the country. Innovative keys to the system are an overhead signal relayer linked to a fleet of Conus "Newstars"—compact, easy-to-operate satellite vans that permit live and immediate national coverage of news wherever it happens.

Simultaneously, electronic advances were opening up whole new communication opportunities via direct broadcast satellite (DBS) technology: a single synchronous satellite capable of beaming a multitude of TV programs to all of the United States and much of Canada and Mexico.

"It came to me like a vision," Hubbard says, "that DBS was nothing less than a truly national broadcast license." Acting on the insight, he applied for a DBS license and a dozen years later became first in line to realize his dream.

That dream could well become a huge competitive challenge for U.S. television networks and cable companies—but a boon for consumers. DBS makes possible "niche" programming, offered to "affinity groups" of people linked by a common interest. Because Hubbard's DBS will embrace the entire country, millons of those scattered viewers

can tune in at once, a capability that will dilute audiences of cable and network broadcasters. Broadcasters are already hurting from dwindling watchers and pinched rate cards.

The USSB venture will broadcast from a high-powered satellite jointly owned by USSB and Hughes Communications, Inc. Hubbard and several co-investors have put up an additional $100 million-plus, in addition to untold hours of research, plannings, and market surveys.

"To receive USSB programming, all you'll need is a decoder box and an 18-inch disc antenna (someday to be reduced to 9.9 inches) to point out the window," says Hubbard. Initial cost will be $700, whittled down to an expected $300 within a few years, due to anticipated purchases in the millions. The elements are portable and can be taken to a summer cabin or winter ice fishing house and there is no monthly access fee, as with cable.

Viewers will be able to choose from free, advertiser-supported channels as well as subscription and pay-per-view channels offering feature films, top sporting events, and mass entertainment programming custom-created for DBS. All will be presented with pictures of laser-disc clarity and CD-quality stereo sound. Included is capability for high-definition television (HDTV).

USSB scored a major coup within a year of targeted startup by signing agreements with two leading entertainment networks, programs of which were formerly seen only on cable TV. The contracts—with Viacom and Time Warner—mean that USSB viewers will be able to tune to such stellar attractions as HBO, Showtime, MTV, and other premium services.

Economic implications of USSB are huge, especially for the home community of Hubbard Broadcasting, Inc. Its research estimates that there is initial demand for at least eight million dish-decoder units. "We expect to have our investment back in a year and a half," he adds, a good portent that the Twin Cities might soon be home to still another world-class business enterprise.

Even competitors are impressed, some awed. Says John Hillis, head of a cable news firm: "Hubbard is one of the first to recognize that the days of the big, all-powerful network broadcasters are over. Broadcasting in the future will be more like a supermarket, where you offer viewers a huge assortment of products and services and live on a margin of around 5 percent."

AT&T

Incorporated in 1885, AT&T traces its history to Alexander Graham Bell and his invention of the telephone in 1876. As parent company of the Bell System, AT&T's primary mission was to provide universal telephone service—service to virtually everyone in the United States.

In its first 50 years AT&T established subsidiaries and allied companies in more than a dozen other countries. It sold those interests in 1925 and focused on achieving its mission in the United States. It did, however, continue to provide international long-distance service.

The Bell System was dissolved at the end of 1983 with AT&T's divestiture of the Bell telephone companies.

Today AT&T operates worldwide in competitive, high-technology markets, with only its long-distance operation remaining under government regulation. With 2.4 million registered shareowners, AT&T's is the most widely held stock in America.

ABOVE: The AT&T VideoPhone 2500™, the world's first full-color motion videophone that works over regular phone lines.

BELOW: New computers are part of an AT&T gift of $750,000 in cash and equipment for Gallaudet University in Washington, D.C., the world's only four-year liberal arts university for deaf and hard-of-hearing students.

AT&T is optimistic about the future. It is also committed to growth in revenues, improved productivity, and better value for its customers. And its objective remains average annual earnings growth of at least 10 percent.

This optimism is based on AT&T's unique strength: its global networking capabilities. AT&T's strategy is to continuously enhance both its own global network and the networks of other service providers, such as telephone companies around the world, in order to make communications more useful to customers. AT&T will build on that strength through innovative products and systems that, profitable in their own right, add value to its network services. This, in turn, will generate greater and more profitable network usage, whether AT&T is serving consumers, small businesses, or large organizations that require integrated, end-to-end network solutions.

AT&T's worldwide intelligent network carries more than 150 million voice, data, video, and facsimile messages every business day. AT&T Bell Laboratories engages in basic research as well as product and service development. In addition, AT&T offers a general-purpose credit card, as well as financial and leasing services. AT&T has people in almost 100 nations around the world.

In Minnesota, AT&T has about 2,600 employees, most of whom work in the Twin Cities metropolitan area. AT&T purchases more than $137 million annually in goods and services from Minnesota suppliers, and pays about $48 million in Minnesota taxes each year.

The new AT&T Tower in downtown Minneapolis serves as AT&T's Upper Midwest headquarters for a six-state area. AT&T has two long-distance switching centers in downtown Minneapolis and two operator conference centers. In addition, AT&T has a long-distance operator center in Duluth and a small business sales division in Bloomington.

AT&T is ready as never before to face a future that was never brighter. And the company's confidence is based on the talent, the diversity, the enthusiasm, and the energy of AT&T people.

AT&T has come a long way since 1885. Today it is a global company that provides communications services and products, as well as network equipment and computer systems to businesses, consumers, telecommunications service providers, and government agencies.

In 1992 AT&T had a banner year, with record earnings of $2.86 per share and solid growth in revenue despite a worldwide economic slump. And its stock traded at post-divestiture highs, increasing AT&T's market value by more than $17 billion.

Naegele Outdoor Advertising Company

The Richfield mansion that dominates the intersection of highways I-494 and 35W is two things: both an imposing corporate headquarters and a stunning advertisement for the business served by the building's owner.

As a billboard showcasing its own medium, the Colonial Williamsburg home of Naegele Outdoor Advertising fits all the qualifications of the "spectacular" outdoor displays it exemplifies. Strikingly large, it's also eye-catching in design and insists upon being seen. (It's historically on target, too. Outdoor signs are the world's oldest form of advertising.)

Naegele's freeway location is similarly inspired. Billboards boomed along with automobiles, stimulated both by development around airports and new shopping areas away from city centers. As founder of the region's first outdoor company, Robert O. Naegele read those trends with great accuracy.

A bona fide innovator, he was in good company with outdoor legends like 3M's William McKnight, Carlson Companies' Curt Carlson (another world-class citizen), plus a lively Minneapolis advertising community that sparked the growth of the entire region.

Today's Naegele Outdoor is very much a business of the future. A wholly owned

ABOVE: The Colonial Williamsburg home of Naegele Outdoor Advertising fits all the qualifications of the "spectacular" outdoor displays it exemplifies.

BELOW: Then and now: examples of Naegele's billboard displays.

year, Depression-bound 1935, and grew solidly until the austerities of World War II.

With money tight after VJ Day, Naegele would sell his outdoor advertising contracts to the finance company at a discount to gain operating capital. (Between the discounted contracts and interest rates of 18 percent, there was scarcely enough money left for labor and materials.) The turning point came

subsidiary of (Brian) McCarty Holding Company, Inc., it purchased the historic Naegele billboard markets in Minneapolis-St. Paul, Jacksonville, Florida, Memphis, Tennessee, and Youngstown, Ohio, in 1991, making the firm eighth in size among the nation's outdoor companies.

A graduate of Minneapolis' Smaby School of Advertising, Naegele opened his first show card plant in a dirt floor garage rented for $12.50 a month. It made money in its first

in 1947, when First National Bank of St. Paul inked a lengthy contract, lending Naegele $30,000 on his paper, but without discount, thereby saving him $20,000 in charges that would have gone to a stricter lender.

By 1953 Naegele had added neon, fiber-

glass, posters, and painted bulletins. Naegele's former outdoor division led to a partnership with 3M board chairman William McKnight, whose firm was an early manufacturer of reflective sign material. He would buy outdoor companies and have Naegele manage them, with later options to buy.

A new holding company called Naegele Advertising was formed in 1957. Major shareholders were Bob Naegele, with 60 percent, and McKnight a 25 percent holder. A major coup was the acquisition of a Detroit outdoor company that brought lucrative automobile accounts.

In 1962 Naegele and Curt Carlson, just entering the hotel business, purchased outdoor firms in Jacksonville and all major markets in North Carolina. Carlson also retained Naegele to operate the hotelier's outdoor holdings in Indianapolis and Youngstown.

By acquiring the local branch of General Outdoor Advertising Company, Naegele in 1963 became the second-largest billboard company in the United States. The decade also marked the opening of Naegele's striking national headquarters building in the Minneapolis suburb of Richfield.

In 1970 Naegele disbanded his public company and board of directors and formed a partnership with Carlson. The new firm, Major Media Management Corporation, held 23 big-city markets in 12 states, and remained the parent company until the Naegele holdings were acquired by Morris Communications Corporation of Augusta, Georgia, in 1985.

Dorothy Schaeffer, the retired longtime assistant director of MSP Airport, recalls Bob Naegele with great affection: "He was always easy to work with and gave generously of his displays to worthwhile civic causes." She also speaks well of the new ownership's support of the 10-year-old Metropolitan Public Airport Foundation's beautification and charitable efforts on behalf of MSP and the many people who work there.

AIRPORT AND AIRLINE SERVICES

ravel agencies, ticketing services, retail shops, food and beverage services, as well as luggage, parking, security, weather, and maintenance services keep airports and airlines humming.

Host Marriott, 126-127

Calhoun Maintenance Company/ St. Paul Flight Center, 128

American Amusement Arcades, 129

Smarte Carte, Inc., 130

Host Marriott

A pair of life-size robotic regular customers, "Hank and Bob," trade recorded quips at the Cheers Bar, causing many a passenger to do a double-take as they pause for refreshments at the Twin Cities airport lounge.

The Cheers Bar hits a responsive note. No matter how far away from home a traveler is, he or she can step into the familiar setting of the popular television sitcom and even share in a few one-liners. The *Cheers* theme erases some of the solitude of traveling, and Host Marriott likes to make its guests feel at ease, even in this busiest of environments.

Some real-life celebrities have joined the boys at Cheers during its first two years—singer Helen Reddy, Minnesota Twins hurler Scott Erickson, Larry Drake of *L.A. Law,* Peter Arnett of *CNN News,*

ABOVE: As an international hub concessionaire, Host Marriott operates one of the newest and most complete duty-free shops in the nation at Minneapolis-St. Paul International Airport's Gold Concourse.

LEFT: Host Marriott's nine gift and news shops stock a wide selection of items for tourists and business travelers.

and Kelsey Grammer of *Cheers,* to name a few. Oh, yes. Bill Marriott, chairman of Marriott International, has stopped by, too. Of course, he owns Host Marriott Corporation.

It is indicative of the way Host Marriott has pumped new excitement into the food, beverage, and merchandising opportunities that await passengers and airport employees here and throughout the United States and in foreign lands. The *Cheers*-themed bar was an instant smash success with the clientele, part of a whole new way Host Marriott appeals to its millions of customers from all over the world. Once the domain of standard convenience foods and

gift-news stands, MSP International in the past two years has led the way in transforming its concourse concessions into a "Main Street of the World." Today familiar brand names (at competitive prices) welcome passengers to such restaurants as Burger King, Pizza Hut, Taco Bell, Nathan's Famous Hot Dogs, TCBY Yogurt, and Mrs. Fields Cookies. A Premium Stock brand in the bars features only the top-of-the-line liquors and beer that Host Marriott has found its customers prefer. The utilization of a branded concept for food service developed in the late 1980s, giving customers a selection of familiar food and beverage choices for a fair value.

Host Marriott can also move quickly to seize an opportunity. People are still amazed that the final score of the 1991 Super Bowl in Minneapolis was emblazoned on souvenir sweatshirts already on sale at the airport's gift stores as delighted fans boarded planes to head home the day after the game. A whole new look of merchandising—with a decidedly strong emphasis on Minnesota and regional products—has taken place at the airport, according to Karla Artz, Host Marriott's general manager in the Twin Cities.

"Visitors want to take home a gift or memento that will remind them of their trip to Minnesota," she explains. "That is why we have added so many specialties with a Minnesota identity—everything from professional sports logos to loons, and gift packets of wild rice." Visitors will find gifts bearing the logos of the Minnesota Twins, the Minnesota Vikings, the Minnesota Timberwolves, and the University of Minnesota.

While these regional themes carry over into the news and bookstore outlets, with familiar authors and local themes, there is a strong emphasis on business information and self-improvement books and tapes designed for the business traveler. The nine gift and news shops can outfit visitors with handcrafted gifts, jewelry, toys, souvenirs, sundries, travel accessories, film, snacks, glassware, and casual clothing items. "We have experienced dramatic gains in customer satisfaction during the past year, in food and beverage service as well as in our merchandise shops," marketing manager David St. Germain reveals.

As an international hub concessionaire, Host Marriott operates one of the newest and most complete duty-free shops in the nation at Minneapolis-St. Paul International Airport. Situated on the Gold Concourse, it features duty-free liquor, cigarettes, fragrances, leather goods, jewelry, and other gift merchandise available to travelers on international flights only. A fine selection of tax-paid gift merchandise is also available to all domestic and international customers.

The challenge of catering to the tastes of the entire world is matched only by the complexity of service that is demanded of such huge volumes of food and beverage in truly unique rushes of business. Blizzard conditions can cause flight delays that create unanticipated crowds of patrons throughout the airport's lounge and retail areas. A fare war in summer 1992 filled the airports with bargain-seekers in record proportions for three months in a row. Furthermore, special events literally put the world at Host Marriott's doorstep in the past few years, with the 1987 and 1991 World Series, the Super Bowl, the Special Olympics, the NCAA Final Four, and the Stanley Cup Playoffs all coming in rapid succession.

Artz recalls the phenomenal Super Bowl week in January 1991. Burger King sold 10,000 Whoppers and 4,000 pounds of French fries; Taco Bell dispensed 1,000 pounds of taco meat; Mrs. Fields baked 2,500 cookies; the snack bars served up 3,000 hot dogs; and Cheers pumped out 3,000 gallons of beer, while the jukebox ran nonstop with 2,000 spins of the records! The gift shops sold more than 10,000 Super Bowl T-shirts the day after the game alone.

Yet at the Twin Cities airport, patrons can dine in style at the Garden Restaurant, selecting from a menu of steaks, pastas, seafoods, salads, and specialties for dinner, as well as a complete variety of choices for breakfast and lunch. The dining room

peers out over the Blue and Red Concourse docking areas as jets taxi to and fro as part of the meal's entertainment.

Host Marriott is concessionaire at 69 domestic and 4 international airports, and it has 23,000 employees who are trained in quality service. With 2,900 associates on staff in the Twin Cities, 500 of them at MSP, Marriott is a major player in the economy of the Upper Midwest.

Host Marriott has relied on MSP as a key test-marketing location. Innovations in food, beverage, and merchandise products are often experienced by Minneapolis-St. Paul patrons long before they are witnessed in airports nationwide.

Host Marriott has also been at the forefront of an enlightened program to bring minorities and disadvantaged entrepreneurs into the business world. Working

closely with the Metropolitan Airports Commission, Host Marriott has worked with the owners of the Touch the Earth stores, the TCBY Yogurt shop, the Estes News Stand, the Pizza Express Snack Shop on the Blue Concourse, and the Flyers Bar & Deli in the charter terminal. It also has an active program of equal opportunity hiring for all its outlets.

Host Marriott does not limit itself to airports any longer. The Washington, D.C.-based company also provides food and beverage and gift merchandise service to airports, sports arenas, Travel Plazas, and amusement park gift shops.

Host Marriott has pumped new excitement into the airport concessions—with its *Cheers*-themed bar and other well-known brand-name restaurants.

Calhoun Maintenance Company / St. Paul Flight Center

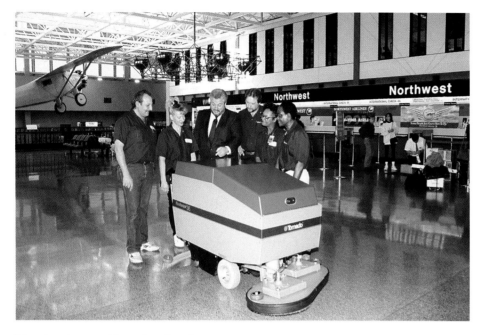

The gleaming good housekeeping that makes the Lindbergh Terminal at Minneapolis-St. Paul International Airport a singular metropolitan gateway is the proud achievement of a little-known Minneapolis mini-conglomerate, a firm that also operates the St. Paul Flight Center at St. Paul's Holman Field, hard under the sandstone bluffs of Minnesota's capital city.

The conglomerate is Short Companies of Minneapolis, headed by Brian Short, son of the late Robert E. Short of Minnesota trucking, DFL political, major league sports, and hospitality fame.

"My father set the service standard we strive for in all of our business lines," says Brian Short. "Although we operate in the transportation, contract cleaning, parking management, finance, and real estate management sectors, we maintain in each the detailed, personalized level of service necessary to meet the demands of the hospitality industry."

One of those divisions, Calhoun Maintenance Company, employs more than 130 people who work around the clock, 365 days a year, cleaning the Lindbergh and Humphrey terminals—keeping them up to the standards of a first-class hotel. Many seasoned travelers agree that they are the best-maintained facilities of their kind in the world.

Brian Short tells how Calhoun's beginnings at MSP coincided with one of the many Minnesota "blizzards of the century," in March 1985. He recalls that on the company's first day of operation, "Many of our supervisors and employees couldn't

Calhoun Maintenance Company employees and their latest equipment keep the famous mirror-like finish on the floors of the vast, main ticketing area of Minneapolis-St. Paul International Airport's Lindbergh Terminal.

make it in. I found myself pressed into service sweeping and emptying trash containers for 14 straight hours. When someone suggested that I move on to the restrooms, I excused myself, pointing out that my front-wheel-drive car was needed to shuttle supplies to the Humphrey Terminal. But we overcame the additional challenge imposed by the weather and gained great respect in the process for the task of maintaining the buildings."

St. Paul Flight Center is ideally located at the city's Downtown Airport to provide the full range of fixed-base operator services and to assure an easy, 15-minute driving commute to any part of the Twin Cities.

The ensuing years have been easier and the standard of service has been of great satisfaction to the Metropolitan Airports Commission. "I'm proud of our association with this airport and those responsible for its management. I'm also proud of our employees. They are true professionals who have worked at this airport for years. Because we are headquartered here, we can respond immediately to the needs of the airport community."

Ten miles downriver, Short's St. Paul Flight Center has been a fixture at the city's Downtown Airport for more than a dozen years. A full-service fixed-base operator ("a filling station of the air," says Short), it offers heated hangar storage, 24-hour line service, charter limousines, and gourmet catering, in addition to a relaxing pilots' lounge and 24-hour weather information.

St. Paul Flight is proud to be the base for many corporate flight departments and organizations such as the Minnesota Department of Transportation and the State Patrol Division. It also serves as the home and service base for the celebrated Life Link III, one of the nation's largest and finest air medical emergency services.

The Short FBO recently inaugurated a new maintenance division, specializing in the service of such turboprop and jet aircraft as the King Air, Cheyenne, and Cessna Citation, in addition to piston aircraft. The director of maintenance, who has more than two decades of experience, comes to Holman from a large maintenance facility at MSP.

Like many members of the Minnesota aviation community, Short is convinced that St. Paul Downtown Airport is *the* corporate facility for the region. "You get to and from your destination much quicker and with less hassle," he explains. "You eliminate long air traffic and ground delays. Any part of the metro area is within a 15-minute drive.

"We are blessed with two outstanding airports here," he continues. "We feel privileged to be a part of the community of each and in serving the general traveling public."

American Amusement Arcades

The bustling game room on the main concourse of Lindbergh Terminal has long been a magnet for many of the 20 million people who pass through Minneapolis-St. Paul International Airport (MSP) each year.

The place is irresistible, not only to kids of all ages, dressed-for-success business travelers, and smartly uniformed airline personnel, but also to moguls of the "coin-controlled" business: operators of amusement and vending machines and phonographs. Their visits are for the purpose of keeping up with the trade by checking out what's new at the trend-setting American Amusement Arcades location.

The company is among the oldest and largest firms of its kind in the United States. Employing more than 400 people, it operates "Piccadilly Circus" mall arcades over much of the five-state Upper Midwest. Its six "Circus Pizza" restaurants brighten the Twin City urban landscape, offering great

food, wholesome fun, and entertainment for individuals and families alike—places with great appeal for all types of parties, groups, and organization meetings.

AAA also provides total coin-operated equipment and maintenance services for hundreds of hospitality locations in the greater Minneapolis-St. Paul area.

Roots of the company, which go back more than 80 years, are entwined with two historic Minnesota entrepreneurial names: the Liebermans, probably the most senior, continuously held family enterprise in the U.S. coin-machine sector; and the Heilichers, a parallel business and only a few years younger. Both have also been longtime players in the recorded music and distribution industry.

American Amusement Arcades was formed in 1986, with the merger of Lieberman's Twin City Novelty and Advance

ABOVE: America Live Sports Bar in the Mall of America, Bloomington.

LEFT: American Amusements Arcades' Piccadilly Circus in the Ridgedale Shopping Center.

Carter Co., a closely held Heilicher firm. The friendly competitors had at last become one. "Our company operated the machines across the airfield, at the old MSP terminal," says AAA president Norman Pink. "I can remember changing film and chemicals in the quarter photo machine there."

The company moved to the current terminal in 1962, occupying its present location since day one. It continues to mesmerize generations of pinball wizards with state-of-the-art machines.

Airline cockpit crews gather there, tending to "fly" computerized jet fighters, even helicopter gun ships, that approach genuine flight simulators in their challenging complexity.

AAA executive vice president Gene Winstead finds notable the cooperation between the Metropolitan Airports Commission and its tenants: "The companies here are a cohesive group, making MSP an exceptionally strong point of entry to the region." His firm reciprocates by its involvement in the Metropolitan Public Airport Foundation, which Winstead serves as first vice president.

In addition to the airport tradition, its

family-fun-and-food Circus Pizza restaurants and Piccadilly Circus mall arcades, the firm has other solid points of connection with its home community.

American Amusements Arcades has operated the "Playland" and "Funland" centers at the Minnesota State Fair since the days of penny pinball and fortune scales. It is also the vendor of choice for coin arcades at other top spots: Valleyfair, America's Original Sports Bar and Arcade at the Mall of America, "Mississippi Live" at Riverplace, plus hundreds of "street arcades," hotel recreation centers, bowling alleys, restaurants, taverns, and other regional hospitality establishments.

AAA was a "natural" for its central role in two major league sporting events in the Twin Cities in 1992. Its attractions got big-time play in corporate hospitality centers at both the NFL Superbowl and NCAA Final Four. Says Gene Winstead: "We provided machines for the Anheuser-Busch Hospitality Tent, the Bud Bowl, the fan-oriented 'Superbowl Experience,' Coca-Cola's entertainment and promotional extravaganza, as well as several other corporate and party events."

To Winstead and Pink, the future of coin-controlled devices looks as bright as the lights that dazzle on the latest pinball machines. Technology is the key, bringing new games to the market and more customers into arcades—good prospects indeed for American Amusement Arcades.

Smarte Carte, Inc.

As a boy in St. Paul, Jim Muellner pressed industrial aprons in his mother's laundry. His modest pay, a penny a piece, was limited by the need to tediously untangle every apron string before ironing it flat.

As a budding inventor, the boy saw a better way. Why not, he asked, replace the strings with clasps, which could be sold to the customer? "When you're in business," was the motherly reply, "you can cut them off. But *I'm* in business, so please do it my way."

Since the late 1960s, when Muellner's Smarte Carte, Inc., evolved at Minneapolis-St. Paul International Airport (MSP), he has found a better way—the customer's way.

Today the White Bear Lake, Minnesota-based firm leads the international rental baggage cart business with more than 100 airport locations worldwide. There, more than 20 million grateful travelers help themselves with Smarte Carte® baggage carts annually.

After aprons, Muellner went on to gain a degree in engineering at the University of Minnesota, class of 1965, before setting out to design a better baggage cart in the family garage. However, the first models had hardly gone into MSP and airports at Los Angeles and Salt Lake City before the young company fell on desperate times.

As inventor-engineer, Muellner was able to rescue the firm from bankruptcy and, by stint of hard and seemingly endless work, see it through to today's viable enterprise, with 500 domestic and foreign employees—while never losing sight of his goal to help others help themselves.

Always the global market leader, Smarte

ABOVE: The firm's latest cart management unit allows travelers to purchase a baggage cart with a major credit card. Smarte Carte is currently using MSP Airport as a test site for this new technology.

TOP: Smarte Carte baggage carts in use in the baggage claim area at Minneapolis-St. Paul International Airport.

Carte has occasionally used MSP as its testing site. Travelers there are already using the company's newest cart, one that is pushed rather than pulled, as were prior models. The familiar push design is more familiar to those whose primary experience has been with carts used in supermarkets.

"Everyone at the Metropolitan Airports Commission (MAC) has been highly supportive of our efforts from day one," says

Muellner. "Without their solid support I'm sure we wouldn't be where we are today."

MSP also employs Muellner's cart management unit of the future, into which travelers can deposit cash or a major credit card for added convenience. The unit features an LCD instructional display that gives step-by-step directions and is programmable in multiple languages.

"Because airports are often noisy, we strive to design our equipment to be as quiet as possible. We chose a silent instructional display in the interest of a better environment," says Muellner.

Recently, Smarte Carte successfully introduced an international currency exchange machine able to receive 16 currencies and make change in the coinage of the local country.

An affiliated company, Smarte Locke, Inc., was formed in 1992 to provide electronic baggage lockers to airports.

Jim Muellner's achievements have not gone unnoticed. Smarte Carte received the 1992 Deubener Award for innovation and outstanding growth issued by the St. Paul Chamber of Commerce and named in honor of the St. Paulites who invented the paper shopping bag. Muellner has also been honored by his alma mater's Institute of Technology as one of Minnesota's "Top 101 Entrepreneurs."

On the public service side of the ledger, Smarte Carte has given back to communities in which airports and travelers participate in the firm's "Ring the Bell for Charity" program. Both Jim and Marilyn Muellner, the founder's wife and president of the Smarte Locke subsidiary, have been enthusiastic fund-raisers for "JFKids Port," the pathfinding on-site day care facility for employees of New York's John F. Kennedy International Airport.

Muellner and his firm have always been responsible corporate citizens, focusing on youth, education, health, and the arts and sciences as special areas in an employee-organized company giving program. Through those many efforts Smarte Carte hopes to improve the quality of life and help build a better world.

Mesaba Aviation maintains its fleet of turboprop Fokker and Fairchild aircraft at MSP International. The regional carrier has been consistently profitable since it started operations there in 1973. Courtesy, Mesaba Aviation, Inc./Brady T. Willette

THE PROFESSIONALS

A

rchitects, engineers, and contractors; insurance firms; and educational, medical, and legal services provide essential support to airports, airlines, and related industries.

Kraus-Anderson Companies, 134-135

HealthSpan Health Systems Corporation, 136-137

Oppenheimer Wolff & Donnelly, 138-139

Mayo Foundation, 140-141

RFA/Minnesota Engineering, 142

Courage Center, 143

Robins, Kaplan, Miller & Ciresi, 144-145

HNTB
  Architects Engineers Planners, 146

Minnesota Community College System, 147

Central Engineering Company, 148

Wenck Associates, Inc., 149

Woodward-Clyde Consultants, 150

Bruce A. Liesch Associates, Inc., 151

Kraus-Anderson Companies

With almost a century of experience in construction, Kraus-Anderson Construction Company is one of the oldest and most respected contractors in the United States.

The firm's history dates back to the turn of the century, when it operated as the J.L. Robinson Company. In 1929 Matthew N. Kraus and Amos Anderson gave their names to the business. But it was their young employee, Lloyd Engelsma, who gave the company a vision.

A Hinckley, Minnesota, native, Engelsma came to Minneapolis to study engineer-

To address the Twin Cities' growing construction needs, Kraus-Anderson opened a second office in St. Paul in 1949 and hired Iowa State University graduate Bill Jaeger as its estimator and engineer.

Today, as Kraus-Anderson Construction Company president and chief operating officer, Bill Jaeger oversees operations with a total of five Minnesota construction divisions: Minneapolis, St. Paul, Building, Midwest, and North. Each operates with its own officers and staff, yet each is able to draw on the immense resources of the total company, which today ranks among the

ing at the University of Minnesota and law at the Minneapolis College of Law (now William Mitchell College of Law in St. Paul). In 1933 he joined Kraus-Anderson as an office manager, estimator, and field supervisor. At the time, the firm primarily built gas stations. But Engelsma sensed silver linings in the Depression-clouded construction industry, and in 1938 he purchased his bosses' interest in the company and became an entrepreneur.

Engelsma's instincts proved sound. World War II put an end to the Depression, and Kraus-Anderson soon was taking on defense contracts. After the war the domestic construction boom continued. With public works projects such as St. Paul Junior High School and business projects such as KSTP radio and television facilities in St. Paul, Kraus-Anderson's revenues more than doubled between 1946 and 1950, from $1.1 million to $2.8 million.

ABOVE: Macy's, Mall of America, Bloomington.

RIGHT: Dain Tower, Minneapolis.

TOP RIGHT: The Minneapolis Hilton.

nation's top 100 building contractors. In this way, Kraus-Anderson is able to carry out a broad spectrum of projects from small remodelings to major complexes such as the 1.8-million-square-foot 3M Research and Development Center in Austin, Texas, and the 800-room Hilton Convention Center Hotel in Minneapolis.

Always looking for new opportunities to expand his company's service, in the late 1950s and throughout the 1960s Engelsma ventured into a new area—the ownership and operation of shopping centers. Once again taking a leadership role, Kraus-Anderson acquired ownership of two of the

Twin Cities' first shopping centers, Bloomington's Clover Shopping Center and Southtown Shopping Center. Today Kraus-Anderson, Incorporated, under president and chief operating officer Burt Dahlberg and executive vice president Dan Engelsma, owns and manages more than five million square feet of commercial and residential property from Florida to

Hawaii, including shopping centers, apartments, office buildings, medical offices, office/service facilities, bowling centers, and restaurants.

Today Kraus-Anderson is a diversified company comprised of a variety of separate enterprises, including Kraus-Anderson Insurance Agency, Kraus-Anderson Mortgage Company, Kraus-Anderson Development and Finance Company, Trans-Pacific Finance Limited, Key Group Advertising, Inc., and the Kraus-Anderson Bowling & Entertainment Centers, Inc. These enterprises are guided by vice chairman Bruce Engelsma.

Kraus-Anderson Construction Company's versatility is exemplified in its long-term relationship with the Metropolitan Airports Commission and the Minneapolis-St. Paul International Airport. Since 1980 Kraus-Anderson has completed more than 75 contracts at the airport, ranging from small remodeling to major projects such as the Republic Airlines Hangar (1980), Marriott Food Service Kitchens (1984 and 1987), and the twin skyways linking the main terminal building and the parking ramp (1992).

Current projects include a basement-level Ground Transportation Center, replacement of the upper-level roadway system that was completed in 1957 at the terminal building, and an automatic people-mover system to transport passengers from the terminal to the

car rental building.

In addition, Kraus-Anderson and the MAC have teamed on projects at other airport locations in Crystal and downtown St. Paul, and on projects such as the sound-abatement program in area schools. In 1990 Kraus-Anderson was awarded construction management for all work done at the airport. "Our responsibility is to see that construction projects, regardless of size, are completed on time and at the right price," explains Kraus-Anderson Construction Company project manager Craig Francois.

Under the continuous leadership of chairman Lloyd Engelsma for more than a half-century, Kraus-Anderson's activities

TOP: Mesaba Aviation Hangar, Minneapolis-St. Paul International Airport.

ABOVE: Marriott Food Service Kitchens, Minneapolis-St. Paul International Airport.

BELOW: Skyway to terminal, Minneapolis-St. Paul International Airport.

have grown to encompass an ever-expanding geographic and client base. But the philosophy that characterizes the firm remains the same:

To produce, on time, on budget, and to the customer's highest satisfaction.

HealthSpan Health Systems Corporation

HealthSpan has embarked on its second century as a leading source of integrated health services for the people of the Upper Midwest.

Formed in 1992 by the consolidation of Health One Corporation and Life Span, Inc., HealthSpan continues to refine its traditional strengths to meet head-on the overriding challenge to American health care: How best to extend the benefits of high-tech care, while containing costs and maintaining concern for people of all resource levels, in the countryside or city.

"We are committed to delivering the highest-quality care at affordable costs," says Gordon Sprenger, HealthSpan executive officer. "And our affiliated physicians are committed to this philosophy, as well as to strong patient relationships that go back several generations at several of our medical centers."

HealthSpan also enjoys a long relationship with the Metropolitan Airports Commission (MAC), operator of Minneapolis-St. Paul International Airport (MSP), where HealthSpan's Transportation Services has provided emergency medical services for more than 10 years. "It's often been said by area medical personnel that if you're going to have a heart attack, MSP is probably the best public place to have one," says MAC executive director Jeff Hamiel, reflecting on the tightly meshed

president of medical affairs at United Hospital, echoes the spirit of that judgment. "Like its snow-removal crews, the MAC's public safety services are widely recognized as second to none among U.S. airports. We are pleased to have achieved a strong working relationship with those professionals. We will always strive to keep a fine edge on emergency medical services at MSP."

HealthSpan provides high-quality, affordable health care to people living within a wide geographic area, primarily Minnesota. But it also helps to deliver care to persons in portions of Wisconsin, Iowa, South Dakota, and Michigan. HealthSpan is very active in helping to recruit physicians for affiliated clinics and hospitals in communities in those states and in helping to shape appropriate care according to local needs.

"We look upon the range and sophistication of our health services as a community trust," adds HealthSpan's Sprenger, summarizing the organization's operating philosophy. "The care and service we provide are an asset of the community in the broadest sense. Part of our mission is to determine the most appropriate manner in which this care should and can be delivered. Our stewardship of these assets requires that we act in this way."

Within the Minneapolis-St. Paul metropolitan area are these HealthSpan hospitals: Abbott Northwestern Hospital, United Hospital, Mercy & Unity Hospitals, and the Phillips Eye Institute.

ABOVE: Emergency medical care is provided at the MSP Airport by HealthSpan Transportation Services.

LEFT: State-of-the-art care at one of HealthSpan's hospitals in the Twin Cities metro area.

In its facilities approximately 15,600 employees, HealthSpan's invaluable human capital, provide care to some 2,600 licensed, acute-care bedsides in 13 hospitals and nursing homes, plus nearly three dozen affiliated medical groups.

Physicians are central to the success of HealthSpan. More than 3,200 in virtually every specialty area are affiliated with the organization. Representative M.D.s also play a role in shaping the policies of HealthSpan by participating in serving as hospital trustees, and in an assortment of medical advisory groups to management.

HealthSpan is also an important provider of health information to the community. Medformation provides valuable health information and physician referrals. A consumer information line enables people to speak directly with a registered nurse 24 hours a day. A cancer information line helps cancer patients and their families with the many complicated

lifesaving emergency services rendered by MSP's Police and Fire departments and the highly trained crews of HealthSpan's Transportation Services.

HealthSpan's Dan Foley, M.D., vice

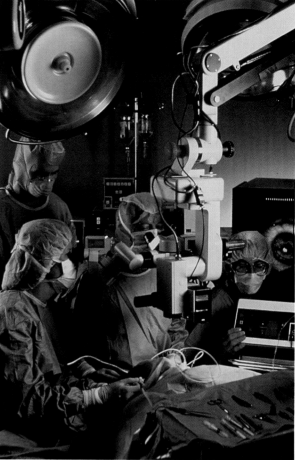

ment program.

Regarding the community's economic interests, HealthSpan is a leader in helping to reduce medical costs through the ongoing shift away from inpatient care to medical services in various outpatient settings. Current estimates are that by the year 2000, fewer than one-third of health care dollars will be spent on acute, inpatient care.

A parallel movement, toward containing costs without diminishing the quality of care, is to reduce the costly duplication of special services and the underutilization of costly medical equipment. A positive alternative to a hospital's having "one of everything" is the HealthSpan concept of selected "Centers of Excellence," where the finest of resources are focused on the best health care for the community.

Thanks to more than a century of planned growth to meet patient needs according to traditionally high regional health expectations and in line with the economic realities of its operating areas, HealthSpan has succeeded in becoming a truly "vertically integrated" care provider. The responsibility entails a fine blend of "value-added" quality and cost-effectiveness, accomplished best by a caring, experienced organization.

ABOVE: Rehabilitation at the Sister Kenny Institute involves relearning practical skills in a "high-touch" setting.

TOP RIGHT: Eye surgery is the ultimate in high technology at the internationally known Phillips Eye Institute.

questions springing from the disease. HealthSpan's sponsorship of Health Fair 11 (along with KARE-TV) provides screening and information to some 100,000 persons in Minnesota and western Wisconsin each year.

Outreach into communities via mobile vans and community health clinics are valuable methods by which HealthSpan brings care to people throughout the region. Still other dimensions of HealthSpan's far-ranging continuum of care come through a home care service, the region's largest medical transportation service, and an extensive home medical equip-

Oppenheimer Wolff & Donnelly

Founded in 1886 in Minnesota, Oppenheimer Wolff & Donnelly is a full-service law firm with an outstanding reputation for providing reliable, efficient solutions to legal challenges.

With more than 200 attorneys practicing in eight major cities, Oppenheimer is well positioned to serve its clients' legal needs. Oppenheimer attorneys are unique in their distinct ability to tap into the experience and talent of all attorneys throughout all offices. This team approach to legal solutions has been extremely well received by clients, particularly those with diversified businesses in the United States and abroad. The firm has offices in Brussels, Chicago, London, Minneapolis, New York, Paris, St. Paul, Washington, D.C., and an affiliated office in Amsterdam.

Oppenheimer is committed to the Twin Cities community in which it has its roots. Longstanding relationships with clients whose businesses have helped the Twin Cities to flourish reflect the firm's commitment to the area. Oppenheimer is proud to have served as legal counsel for the Metropolitan Airports Commission since its inception in 1943.

Beyond providing legal services for clients, Oppenheimer attorneys are actively involved in the community, serving as members of nonprofit boards, community volunteers, and pro bono legal advisors. The firm has received numerous awards for its involvement and willingness to support the Twin Cities community both financially and with volunteers. Oppenheimer is a significant supporter of major educational institutions, including the University of Minnesota, Hamline University, William Mitchell College of Law, and the University of St. Thomas. Oppenheimer's involvement as a part of a community network of sharing has influenced the firm since its beginnings. The firm is a member of the Minnesota Keystone Program, which recognizes businesses that contribute five percent of annual earnings to the community and state.

Oppenheimer is a member of Minnesota Meeting, a group that invites speakers from a variety of nations and backgrounds to come to the Twin Cities. This lecture series is important for the role it plays in identifying key current issues that affect the community. As part of its commitment to global concerns, Oppenheimer cosponsored Boris Yeltsin's 1989 tour of the United States. In 1990 the firm sponsored an education/work program for a group of Polish attorneys, and also cosponsored a speaking tour in Minnesota by Lech Walesa, leader of the Polish Solidarity Union.

Oppenheimer attorneys practice in five major areas of law—Business Litigation, Commercial, Corporate, General Litigation, and International. Within each of these departments, more defined business groups allow attorneys to focus their specific skills and experience on a variety of legal issues. Many attorneys participate in several business groups, bringing diverse skills, interests, and experience to a variety of areas.

■ Business Litigation: The Business Litigation Group includes business technology, ERISA and tax controversy, labor and employment, marketing and competition, professional liability, and securities.

■ Commercial: The Commercial Law Group includes banking and finance, commercial lending, real estate development and finance, and real estate remedies.

■ Corporate: The Corporate Law Group includes corporate finance transactions, employee benefits, tax trust and estates, and international corporate.

ABOVE: Claus Oldenburg's distinctive *Spoonbridge and Cherry* at the Walker Art Center Sculpture Garden, located on the edge of downtown Minneapolis. Courtesy, The Image Bank

LEFT: Ordway Music Theatre with the historic Landmark Center in the background, downtown St. Paul. Courtesy, George Heinrich

■ General Litigation: The General Litigation Group includes environmental law, toxic torts, insurance, products liability, and transportation law.

■ International: The International Law Group includes antitrust/competition law, East-West trade and investment, European Community (EC) law, foreign investment, international tax, and international employment issues.

Oppenheimer's European offices offer clients the benefits of a long-standing and respected EC presence. Attorneys residing in the Brussels office, for instance, are not only well versed in EC policy and its ramifications, but were part of the policy-making exercise itself. This experiential participation in the legal aspects of the single European market is invaluable to European and American clients alike.

The firm's legal practice evolves along with the ever-changing business climate, and its attorneys understand the critical importance of keeping clients updated on current activities in legislation and the business community, and how that activity may affect compliance and legal issues.

As a member of several professional associations, the firm is aware of changes in various industrial circles. For instance, its membership in Medical Alley, a Minnesota-based organization comprised of members of the medical device industry with common interests in government policy, helps Oppenheimer attorneys stay up to date on changes ranging from malpractice insurance to financing medical ventures to legislation's ultimate impact upon employee benefit plans. The firm believes its clients deserve well-informed attorneys who are in tune with the big picture of a specific industry.

Oppenheimer strives to keep its clients informed of current legal developments through seminars, conferences, and informative newsletters. The firm hosts several seminars throughout the year on subjects varying from changes in tax laws to sexual harassment policy reviews to EPA mandates of the Clean Air Act.

In 1992 Oppenheimer sponsored a conference on emissions trading, one of the first such forums on the idea of market-based incentives for environmental compliance. This type of attention to future developments in legal practice areas has helped the firm to assist clients in implementing preventive measures and ultimately saving resources. Attorneys are also involved as speakers and cosponsors of other conferences, and as authors of articles for external business, trade, and legal publications, as well as Oppenheimer's internal client newsletters.

A commitment to provide quality legal services to its clients, a dedication to the Twin Cities community, and a global view of business make Oppenheimer the premier legal choice.

Mayo Foundation

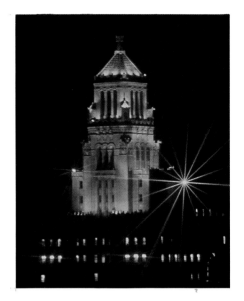

In 1928 Mayo Clinic opened its new building in Rochester, Minnesota—then the tallest structure between Chicago and the West Coast—to the peal of its 23-bell carillon and the beckoning lights of a powerful aircraft beacon atop the distinctive Plummer Building. The beams could be seen for more than 50 miles, even by the first scheduled Northwest Airways (NWA) passenger flights. Connecting the Twin Cities and Chicago, they had begun the year before, at $50 for the round trip.

Rochester—led by Drs. Charles H. and William J. Mayo, founders of the celebrated medical clinic pioneered by their father, William W. Mayo, M.D.—was already lobbying NWA to add their community to its brief list of intermediate stops. The persistence paid off. Chief pilot Charles Holman—the legendary "Speed," killed while stunting at an Omaha air show after setting Northwest on the course to success—was sent to Rochester with orders to help the community find a site and begin construction of its airport.

The Mayo brothers were men of remarkable vision. They foresaw the ultimate importance of aviation to their clinic even though NWA had carried only 126 passengers in all of 1927. Founded two decades before, the clinic was as innovative in its medical way as the new form of aerial transportation: a multipractice integration of highly specialized medicine with large programs of medical research and education. Then, as now, the focus at Mayo was on patient care, a combination of medical excellence and human kindness.

Taking the bull by the horns, the doctors optioned a site on Holman's recommendation; paid for the land, 285 acres in southeast Rochester; saw construction through to a swift completion; and officially dedicated the field in 1929 as Rochester Airport, resisting any temptation toward aggrandizing the family name.

Management of the airport, then as now, is by the Rochester Airport Company, a subsidiary of Mayo Foundation. In 1945, when privately owned airports became ineligible for U.S. aid, Mayo Foundation gave the facility to the city of Rochester with operational management continuing by the Rochester Airport Company under contract with the municipality. The arrangement exists to this day, after the facility's 1960 move to its present location and renaming as Rochester Municipal Airport.

Today's Metropolitan Airports Commission's Rochester representative is Mark (Jerry) Braatas, past president of the Rochester Airport Company. He was succeeded in that post by David W. Lawrence, a Mayo administrator who as part of his responsibilities serves as head of the management company.

"Our airport has always been inextricably linked with MSP and Northwest Airlines," says Lawrence, underscoring the importance of the facility for quick, comfortable transportation to the world-class clinic. "It's an airport in a city of 70,000 with second-level jet loaders and other amenities found in much larger terminals. We, like the clinic, care deeply about patients. By meeting their transportation needs we're able to keep our airport state-of-the-art."

Passenger counts there are understandably astonishing. The total in 1992 exceeded 300,000, bringing to some 9 million the number using the airport since 1960. Of the medical passengers, many are international patients. As former Metropolitan Council chair Steve Keefe suggests, "We give Minnesota another 'deep-water port on the world,'" says Lawrence. "It's a complement to and extension of MSP, through which a great number of our visitors pass twice."

Rochester Municipal Airport's and Mayo Clinic's long relationship with Northwest Airlines has resulted in many benefits, both tangible and almost incalculable (in terms of medicine and technology), for all who fly in modern jet aircraft.

Just before World War II NWA president Croil Hunter consulted Dr. Charles W. Mayo—son of one of the famous brothers and later a valued member of the carrier's board of directors—about the drowsiness of pilots flying over the Rockies on trips to the new station in Seattle.

Most likely hypoxia, said Mayo, and invited the company to send down some people to work with a blue-ribbon team the clinic would assign to the phenomenon of oxygen deprivation. At that time passenger flights were restricted to altitudes of less than 13,000 feet. The challenging solution was seen as a mask that would accomplish the tricky job of metering oxygen to the wearer in correct proportions, yet permit flight crews to use the radio, eat a meal, and move about the cabin.

In less than a year the clinic showed off

became the prototype for current suits.

A later NWA president, Donald Nyrop, chose Mayo Clinic over the airline's medical department to administer FAA physical examinations for "hard cases" among its pilots, believing that such a distancing would ensure more objective exams in the interest of the health and safety of everyone concerned.

Northwest today has another edge in the event of an in-flight medical emergency—wherever it might occur in the world. All a pilot need do is to call the Mayo Clinic in Rochester and talk directly to the on-call physician via a special single side-band high-frequency radio. Invaluable in helping flight crews decide what action to take, the service can also recommend alternate airports with the best medical facilities.

There's a long tradition of cooperation between Rochester Municipal Airport and its larger sibling in the Twin Cities. Until the advent of modern, do-it-all flight simulators for pilot training, Rochester lifted operational pressures off MSP by letting Northwest and other airlines practice touch-and-go landings and other maneuvers on its reinforced concrete runways.

"Although only 76 nautical miles apart, the two airports have never competed," says Lawrence. "That complementary relationship has helped both of us offer travelers a quality product." He finds no particular objections to growing sentiment for even closer ties between the two facilities, especially at a time of intensive long-range planning about the future of commercial aviation in all of the Upper Midwest.

"We need to think together, plan together, work together," says the Rochester Airport Company president.

The two major airports exist as a model of cooperation in a state singularly blessed with major commercial airline service to all parts of the world.

its new "BLB" (for Bulbulian, Lovelace, and Boothby, the Mayo physician/scientist developers) oxygen mask to an applauding world on a high-altitude demonstration flight to Los Angeles. On a later demonstration over Boston, a planeload of passengers ate chicken dinners at 23,000 feet while wearing the masks.

Northwest subsequently became the first U.S. airline to install oxygen outlets at each passenger seat, after the Mayo innovation had helped the Allies win the war by giving their aircrews the decisive advantage of workable high-altitude combat operations.

Mayo Foundation also contributed to the World War II effort by designing a pneumatic-pressure anti-blackout suit (G suit) enabling military pilots to withstand the increased gravitational forces encountered during combat. Using a specially built human centrifuge, Mayo aeromedical scientists developed the G suit that was mass-produced for military aviators and

RFA / Minnesota Engineering

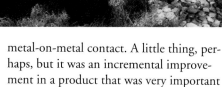

Leonardo da Vinci never had to wrestle with the complexities of an automatic card-shuffler for casino blackjack tables. Nor, near as we know, did he ever create a pair of rollerblades for the Renaissance or an improved valve for a heart implant. For 50 years now, a myriad of such daydreams as these have been forged into reality at RFA/Minnesota Engineering.

"But we don't call ourselves inventors," stresses president Ben Barnard, who joined the firm in 1973. "We're engineers." And,

he adds, "Economics is the ringmaster of this business."

RFA/Minnesota Engineering began in 1943 as Minnesota Engineering Co. and was purchased by Rogers, Freels & Associates, since shortened to RFA. We all celebrate the company's golden anniversary in the products that surround our daily lives. A John Deere lawn mower's innovative versatility will make weekend tasks a lot easier. A unique dam on the Zumbro River in Rochester, Minnesota, will save property and even lives from the ravages of flash-flooding. A rugged Ford Motor Co. tractor transmission will improve agricultural production

on medium-size to large farms.

The client list is impressive: Caterpillar, 3M, Maytag Corporation, Honeywell, St. Jude Medical Center, Data-Card Corporation, and The Trane Company are but a few of the 130 nationally known organizations that rely on objective analysis of a professional outsider.

Employing 70 people, RFA/Minnesota Engineering works on a wide range of consumer products, medical devices, heavy-equipment designs and machines, and, yes, even an automatic card-shuffler now employed at casinos throughout the United States.

Whether the firm's challenges include the mixing up of playing cards or the creation of a Rube Goldberg-looking machine that moves along a railroad track while it removes and replaces railroad ties, many of the same basic truths of engineering and mechanics apply.

The in-line plastic frame for rollerblade skates revolutionized summertime recreation with a fastening system that secured the wheels to the frame without washers or

metal-on-metal contact. A little thing, perhaps, but it was an incremental improvement in a product that was very important in the public's acceptance.

RFA often does for a company what it could do for itself, but staffing for 100 percent of need is poor business practice. A seasoned group of engineers able to work on a specific task or problem at the right time is a valuable resource. Clients simply buy time and talent at RFA/Minnesota Engineering to work on projects as needed. Occasionally, the results are negative, as well, and the engineering firm will advise that a project is impractical and should be altered or, indeed, cancelled.

"We work entirely for the client," Barnard emphasizes. RFA/Minnesota Engineering has no proprietary products of its own, nor does it intend to stray from that special and highly confidential relationship with its customers.

TOP RIGHT: NOMA's four-wheel steer riding lawn mower.

ABOVE: Caterpillar's 994 front-end loader. Its tires are 12 feet in diameter, and it weighs 370,000 pounds.

RIGHT: Shuffle Master's automatic card shuffler, widely used by the Las Vegas gaming industry.

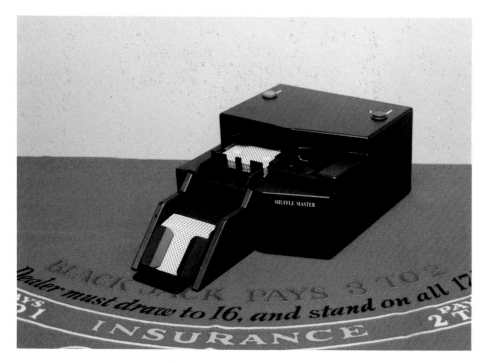

Courage Center

The story of Courage Center, in Golden Valley, a western suburb of Minneapolis, is one of helping to empower people with disabilities to become more independent in their communities. It is the story of a strong commitment to improving the lives of people with disabilities.

The concerned citizens who founded the organization in 1928 could hardly have foreseen the changes in today's society and the current scope of Courage Center services. They would be amazed at the integration of individuals with disabilities into society, at the barriers that have fallen through the years, and at how comprehensive the organization's services have become.

An early goal for Courage Center was to help rural disabled children get an education. Later goals embraced meaningful work for homebound disabled adults and provision of special equipment. Today's goal is to empower people with disabilities to achieve their full potential by providing excellence in comprehensive rehabilitation, enrichment, vocational, independent living, and educational services.

In carrying out its mission, Courage Center operates four major facilities in Minnesota and provides recreation and therapy services in other community settings.

■ Courage Center headquarters in Golden Valley houses Courage Residence, a transitional rehabilitation facility for adults, a therapeutic warm-water pool and gymnasium, administrative and support offices, education and conference facilities, outpatient therapy clinics, and a broad variety of programs and activities designed to meet the physical, social, and emotional needs of people with disabilities. Specialized services range from driver assessment and training to a lending library of adapted toys and software.

■ Camp Courage, about 50 miles west of the Twin Cities, has 35 buildings on 305 acres of woods, fields, and lakeshore. Camp Courage hosts campers with physical disabilities; vision, speech, and hearing impairments; and language disorders. Sessions include specialty camps such as an oncology camp for children with cancer and their siblings.

■ Courage North, a residential camp at Lake George, near Minnesota's Itasca State Park, has 95 acres of towering pines and shoreline. Programs stress outdoor adventures and leadership for hearing-impaired and physically disabled campers. Specialty

camps include Burn Camp and sessions for children with hemophilia.

■ Courage St. Croix, in Stillwater, is about 20 miles northeast of downtown St. Paul. The facility provides aquatic and therapy services in the east metropolitan area, western Wisconsin, and the St. Croix River Valley.

■ Other service sites include Courage Duluth, providing sports and recreation ser-

vices in the northeast area of Minnesota, more than 30 regional day camps, and therapy contracts with schools, day care centers, and nursing homes.

All together, Courage Center has more than 70 programs and services that benefit some 20,000 children and adults each year. Rehabilitation professionals and nearly 2,000 volunteers work to help meet the many individual needs of people with disabilities.

Throughout the organization's history, countless volunteers and community contributors have generously invested in Courage Center. This commitment has helped ensure that people with disabilities can continue to reach their full potential and increase their independence through the services of Courage Center.

Thank you to the contributor who made it possible for Courage Center to be part of this commemorative publication.

TOP: Youngsters enjoy outdoor activities at Camp Courage, about 50 miles west of the Twin Cities.

LEFT: In carrying out its mission, Courage Center provides recreation and therapy services, including occupational therapy.

Robins, Kaplan, Miller & Ciresi

In the spring of 1938, while the country was in the depths of the Depression, two young lawyers got together to share an office and an ambition to make their mark in the legal world. As great as their vision might have been, Solly Robins and Julius Davis could not have imagined the impact that the law firm they were founding would have in the Twin Cities, across the country, and around the world. Robins, Kaplan, Miller & Ciresi has grown from two lawyers and one small office into a national firm with eight offices across the United States.

The national system of offices that has developed over the years is a unique feature of the firm. Founded in St. Paul, the firm soon established its Minneapolis base in the early 1940s. As the needs of the firm's clients grew nationally during the 1970s, attorneys began moving from Minneapolis to Atlanta, Boston, Chicago, San Francisco, Southern California, and Washington, D.C., establishing offices and growing business for the firm in those metropolitan centers. This national network provides tremendous flexibility in shifting resources around the country to support client needs in the most effective manner possible.

Over the past 55 years attorneys for the firm from every office have litigated such high-profile cases as the Thanksgiving Day Norwest Bank fire in Minneapolis, the collapse of the Hyatt Hotel walkway in Kansas City, the First Interstate Bank fire in Los Angeles, the One Meridian Office Tower fire in Philadelphia, and lawsuits surrounding the Dalkon Shield and Copper-7 IUD cases.

In 1984, when thousands died in Bhopal, India, from a toxic gas leak at a Union Carbide plant, Robins, Kaplan, Miller & Ciresi was selected by the government of India to represent its citizens in the extraordinarily complex litigation. The firm assisted the government in designing and executing litigation strategy both in the United States and India.

During the 1990s the firm achieved remarkable success in intellectual property litigation. Representing Honeywell in its patent infringement suit against Minolta over the autofocus camera technology, the firm utilized innovative audiovisual techniques to present extremely technical and scientific data to a jury. With complex information made accessible and under-

RIGHT: The LaSalle Plaza is the Minneapolis home of Robins, Kaplan, Miller & Ciresi.

BELOW: The conference room on the 29th floor is one of many conference facilities used by and for firm clients.

standable, the jury came back with a precedent-setting verdict for Honeywell.

The firm is well known in the insurance industry as lawyers and staff investigators have successfully represented insurers in some of the most complex coverage and subrogation disputes in the industry. Often, key evidence at accident or disaster sites has been uncovered by the firm's knowledgeable investigation experts who were on site within 24 hours of the incident.

That litigation experience has transferred into all other areas of business as well. Intellectual property, communications, employment, antitrust, and industrial loss and catastrophe are only a few of the areas in which the firm's lawyers represent a broad client network of manufacturers, service providers, specialty retailers, corporate entities, and entrepreneurs.

The corporate and transactional group has the scope and depth of experience usually found in firms exclusively devoted to

corporate work. The firm's corporate lawyers are involved with deals that have national business implications and involve *Fortune* 500 companies, national banks and developers, and national retailing concerns.

Knowledge of the regulatory issues facing clients is important to offering a broad spectrum of service. Frequently, clients across the country face issues that can only be resolved through the bureaucracy in Washington. Firm attorneys who know their way around the federal agency system are able to expedite solutions, and act as a resource to clients in resolving their regulatory problems.

The tradition of handling complex issues that are often without precedent is also reflected in the plaintiff practice of the firm. Attorneys working in mass tort, personal injury, and medical malpractice areas often face significant logistical and jurisdictional difficulties in pursuing the best legal

TOP RIGHT: The library provides a comfortable setting for research on client matters.

RIGHT: The main lobby of Robins, Kaplan is a welcoming place for clients and attorneys.

solutions for all of the firm's clients, and have frequently broken new legal ground in the results they have achieved.

The attorneys at Robins, Kaplan, Miller & Ciresi are supported by a very sophisticated system of staff and technology that enables the firm to provide a high level of service to clients that is both efficient and cost effective. This includes computerized document-retrieval data bases and litigation management reports as well as skilled support staff who are highly trained in the execution of these systems.

In describing the firm, managing partner Thomas C. Kayser says, "Our special

skill is the melding of the creative with the credible. We assure our clients vigorous, informed advocacy, backed by attorneys and researchers who cover the whole waterfront of the law, thus providing total, cost-effective, and client-driven service."

Legal issues will change and become more complex as our society evolves, the needs of individuals and organizations will change as our world becomes more fragmented, and the process and language of the law will change as new ideas, industries, and information are incorporated into daily life. Robins, Kaplan, Miller & Ciresi, accustomed to growth through the management of change, will continue to address the issues of the future and will change and develop expertise to accommodate the new needs of clients.

In 1938 Solly Robins and Julius Davis knew that they had laid the foundation for a unique law firm. The vision of the founders continues today, and provides the momentum for the firm's expansion into the future.

HNTB Corporation
ARCHITECTS ENGINEERS PLANNERS

HNTB Corporation, a Howard Needles Tammen & Bergendoff company, is proud to help celebrate the 50th anniversary of the Metropolitan Airports Commission (MAC) and the rich history of the Minneapolis-St. Paul International Airport, America's North Coast Gateway. The firm is also pleased to be working with MAC and the Metropolitan Council in planning the future of Minnesota's air transporation system.

To help lay the groundwork for the continued development of the state's aviation facilities, an HNTB-managed dual-track airport planning process has been undertaken to assist in determining the future of MSP. The objective of this important study is to provide residents of Minnesota and surrounding areas with the best solution for meeting the area's long-term air service needs. To accomplish this objective, the study will identify the best options for expanding and improving MSP on its current site. It will also produce plans for the development of a possible replacement airport in the Minneapolis-St. Paul area.

One of the first steps in the process was the development of a long-term comprehensive plan for MSP. HNTB evaluated estimates for traffic and passenger demand at the airport through 2020 and assessed

HNTB has developed a long-term comprehensive plan for Minneapolis-St. Paul International Airport, evaluating estimates for traffic and passenger demand at the airport through 2020 and assessing the terminal and airfield upgrades necessary to meet these projections.

the terminal and airfield upgrades necessary to meet these projections. In addition, the plan addresses the compatibility of the airport with the surrounding land uses.

To investigate alternatives for the possible replacement airport, the HNTB

team developed conceptual plans that will meet the needs of air travelers in the next century. To maximize operational flexibility and efficiency, planners have proposed a six-runway facility with the main terminal building in the center of the airfield. The layout would generate maximum airfield capacity by providing a flow-through traffic pattern that would keep taxiing aircraft off active runways.

When the studies are complete, a decision document that includes preliminary engineering and an environmental assessment, both for expanding the existing airport and for the potential replacement facility, will be prepared. This document will enable the Minnesota legislature to confidently decide the future of MSP.

The winning combination of experience and expertise enables HNTB to plan and design the projects that move people and goods through America's air transportation system.

Minnesota Community College System

One of Minnesota's best-kept secrets is its state Community College System: 21 far-flung campuses, each attuned to the needs of its local area and each providing open-door access to students from 16 to 60.

Community colleges pride themselves on being user-friendly and responsive to each student's educational aspirations. That means challenging academic courses for students aiming to transfer for four-year university degrees and practical courses for those who want to mix academics with job preparation.

For taxpayers, the bottom line is a statewide network that prepares students at the lowest cost of any college or university system in the state.

Community colleges began more than 75 years ago as locally operated junior colleges—the newer name accurately suggests the much broader role they now play in keeping Minnesotans productive, economically competitive, and intellectually satisfied.

The community college system is headed by Dr. Geraldine Evans, herself an alumna of the system. Like thousands of others, she transferred her community college credits to the University of Minnesota where she earned bachelor's, master's and doctoral degrees.

Says Dr. Evans, "We adapt our college curriculum to the needs of each college community. Our colleges and area employers are constantly joining hands to improve the skills of the local work force—at the most affordable cost." Community college tuition is $37.50 per credit hour, or about $1,700 a year for full-time students.

Examples of college-employer cooperation include specialized training of security guards for Northwest Airlines at Inver Hills Community College, using the school's expertise in law enforcement. Inver Hills also provides flight training, used by some students as the foundation for four-year degrees at nearby state universities. Nursing is another strong career program, providing two-thirds of Minnesota's registered nurses in recent years.

Dr. Evans has pushed hard for quality assurance, quality management, and attention to individual needs of students. That means challenging honors programs for top students and remedial programs for those who have been out of high school for a time, or who enter college unprepared for tough college courses. "Our quality concern begins with the individual student," she says.

Community colleges without fanfare have built enrollment to 57,000, including about 37,000 students in the Twin Cities area. The system's mission lists the "best possible teaching" as a goal, using full-time teachers who need not pursue the research demanded at most universities. "Over 90

RIGHT: Dr. Geraldine Evans is chancellor of the Minnesota Community College System. She speaks from experience, having graduated from one of Minnesota's 21 community colleges. Dr. Evans transferred her credits to the University of Minnesota, a path followed by many community college graduates.

BELOW: Inver Hills, set in the rolling hills of Dakota County, is one of six community colleges in the Minneapolis-St. Paul metropolitan area. Many students prepare for jobs while others accumulate credits that can be transferred to four-year colleges and universities.

percent of our instructors have advanced degrees and we constantly strive to upgrade their skills," Dr. Evans says.

Students use community colleges for many reasons. About 28 percent transfer their credits to four-year baccalaureate programs, while others come for classes or even one class needed to fulfill career needs or personal goals. Thus, the user-friendly label. Community colleges like to say they provide "education for a changing world."

"A growing concern is to match our programs to the specific needs of local campuses and the surrounding community," Dr. Evans explains. She says that the global economy in which Minnesota finds itself is increasingly predicated on the management of information.

"That is not to say we can afford to ignore the 'general education' goal of being able to think, speak, and write well; in short, to be a good communicator," Dr. Evans continues. "In today's uncertain, fast-changing world, to be generally educated is an absolute necessity in keeping one's job and forging ahead. Our job is to provide that help for every Minnesotan who desires it."

Central Engineering Company

Founded in 1955 by Loren E. Swanson, Central Engineering Company has become recognized as a world-class authority in the field of aircraft engine test facilities. Known by its brand name of Cenco, the corporation employs a staff of mechanical, electrical, computer, and architectural engineers to design a wide variety of aircraft engine test equipment, including huge concrete-and-steel jet engine test buildings and intricate printed circuit boards.

"It's a far cry from the propeller-engine days, when airplane engines in the Twin Cities oftentimes were merely attached to a truck bed and revved up out-of-doors," Swanson recalls. "Today the testing equipment and sites are as complex and critical as the giant jet engines themselves—and they are continuing to grow in size and complexity."

ABOVE: Northwest Airlines' recently remodeled engine preparation area.

LEFT: Jet engine in a thrust stand built by Central Engineering.

But the 130 people who work for Cenco offer more than design expertise. The firm has a complete manufacturing facility at its suburban St. Anthony site, including machine, electrical, and assembly shops. The machinists, electrical technicians, welders, and assemblers work in concert with the engineering departments to achieve the highest degree of quality in workmanship.

Cenco engineers and technicians install their test facility equipment around the world—from Minneapolis to Argentina and from China to Kuwait—working with leaders of the aviation industry and with

governments on military installations. In fact, Cenco has engineered, manufactured, and installed more aircraft engine test facilities than any other company in the world. In 1991 it opened a sales office near Manchester, England, and Swanson foresees expansion to other parts of the world as well.

A fully instrumented jet test cell by Cenco is located at the Northwest Airlines engine overhaul facility at Minneapolis-St. Paul International Airport. In fact, Cenco has maintained a close relationship with Northwest since 1961. Cenco did a major rework of the NWA test cell in 1992, adding a new thrust stand, engine preparation area, and a monorail engine delivery

system to efficiently integrate engine preparation with testing.

Central Engineering continues to lead in industry innovations. In 1992 it delivered a new vibration-measurement system for jet engines, a critical test for massive engines eight feet in diameter that rotate at more than 3,000 revolutions per minute. Called the MPI-320, the system detects vibration levels at various points on an engine and computes how to balance the jet's rotating components to reduce vibrations to optimum levels.

New and growing technical fields—such as computational fluid dynamics, digital signal processing, touchscreen control and display panels, and the Open Software Foundation's software windowing user interface—play a major role in the systems developed and implemented at Cenco. At Central Engineering Company, the most recent developments in science and technology drive the design and development efforts.

Wenck Associates, Inc.

The success story of Wenck Associates, Inc., has long been entwined with the history of the Minneapolis-St. Paul International Airport.

Norm Wenck is the founder and president of this leading Minnesota professional environmental engineering consulting firm. Wenck cut his pollution-control teeth on the 1971 oil spill that sent 200,000 gallons of jet fuel into the Mississippi River. Wenck stayed on the job for 40 days and nights, until the spill was cleared up.

"You know you have a problem," he muses, "when a marina calls and says, 'Hey, your oil is sinking our dock by eating the buoyant plastic!'"

Later, he and his colleagues helped chart the Metropolitan Airports Commission's positive environmental path by pioneering a program for the safe handling of runway and apron runoff, by thwarting chemical encroachment on groundwater, and even by mounting an FAA study to mitigate the hazards of aircraft hydroplaning through a better understanding of runway friction.

Today some 50 Wenck employees labor in elegant, energy-efficient headquarters in the Minneapolis suburb of Maple Plain. Other offices are in St. Paul and Duluth, Minnesota, and Grand Rapids, Michigan. This group of specialists practices in many areas of environmental engineering, as well as geology, hydrogeology, chemistry, and the other earth sciences. They are frequently invited to speak at national and international forums.

Wenck has sizable contracts across the United States and overseas and, since its founding in 1985, the privately held firm has enjoyed an annual growth of 30 percent. Projects are as diverse as air pollution control, groundwater cleanup, landfill expansion, wastewater treatment, tank excavation, lake restoration, flood control, and wetland protection.

Wenck is a company honored by its peers for its swift reaction to environmental crises, using efficient measures that often erase those problems before they get out of hand—or budget. Here are just a few examples of Wenck responses:

■ Using a unique but affordable combination of powerful oxidants and ultraviolet light to destroy groundwater contaminants.

ABOVE: In an award-winning project, 99.9999 percent PCBs in soils were destroyed using infrared thermal treatment. Additionally, in-situ vacuum extraction systems have removed more than 100 tons of solvent. They are among the largest such systems in the country.

TOP: Wenck designed the $3.3-million restoration of a chain of seven Minnesota lakes. The company has repeatedly won recognition for its creative protection of water resources.

■ Adopting in-place vacuum extraction to remove subsurface contamination without costly excavation.

■ Instituting Minnesota's largest lake restoration project using 500 acres of wetlands for natural water filtration.

■ Expediting the complex cleanup of a Superfund chemical coatings site 33 months ahead of schedule and $3.5 million under anticipated costs.

The firm's 21 prestigious state and national environmental awards were fully deserved.

Looking ahead, Norm Wenck is bullish on America and its ability to counter the ravages of pollution. "U.S. industry is aggressive in pollution control, and other countries are stepping up their efforts in the same direction. By combining creativity with common sense, we're helping industry solve its environmental problems for good."

Woodward-Clyde Consultants

A recent major arrival on the Minnesota consulting engineering scene is Woodward-Clyde Consultants. Woodward-Clyde is an international consulting firm that has achieved prominence as a leader in geotechnical, environmental, and waste management services. Founded in 1950, the firm has grown to more than 60 offices throughout the United States and abroad. *Engineering News Record* has listed Woodward-Clyde in the top 50 U.S. design firms since that listing began in 1965.

Woodward-Clyde and its staff of 2,400 specialists have helped lead the fight against enduring damage from some of the world's major oil spills: the San Francisco Bay mishap of 1971 and the Amoco *Cadiz* spill off the French coast of Britanny seven years later, before serving as lead technical advisor to Exxon after the 1989 *Valdez* accident in Alaska.

Because its services also encompass planning, permitting, engineering, and construction phases, the firm was chosen to design the insulated, vertical supports that keep the Trans-Alaska Pipeline well above the frozen tundra. Woodward-Clyde won a major environmental award for the unique design aspects that prevented the melting of the frozen ground around the conduits carrying hot oil.

Since opening the firm's Minneapolis office in 1991, Woodward-Clyde has already been involved in several noteworthy projects in the Upper Midwest:

■ Design of Browning-Ferris Industries' Flying Cloud Landfill closure in Eden Prairie, close to the Metropolitan Airports Commission's Flying Cloud reliever airport. In addition to the design, monitoring, and construction quality control, the project also includes an important community relations dimension.

To that end, Woodward-Clyde brought in specialists to initiate a dialogue with the local community. Openness was maintained via news releases to the media, newsletters to area residents, informational meetings, and even an open house at a nearby mall. There, scientists and engineers presented the results of a site risk assessment and candidly fielded questions from the public.

■ A Minnesota-wide assignment involved environmental compliance audits at 98 Army National Guard facilities at 76

TOP: During investigations at Rocky Mountain Arsenal's Basin F near Denver, Woodward-Clyde did everything from preparing detailed safety plans and training personnel to design and construction management. The firm had the best safety record of any contractor at this No. 1 site on EPA's National Priorities List.

MIDDLE: Concrete was blasted from within inches of critical structural elements of this lock without causing any damage.

BOTTOM: For a proposed 2,000-megawatt coal-fired power plant, Woodward-Clyde developed methodology to evaluate how the plant's emissions would affect regional haze as far away as the Grand Canyon—some 300 miles away.

different locations. The Headquarters Department of the Army has tasked the U.S. Army Corps of Engineers to develop the Environmental Compliance Assessment System (ECAS) to conduct an assessment of every Army installation in the continental United States and overseas. Minnesota was selected as one of two test states for initiating the ECAS program. Woodward-Clyde was responsible for all aspects of the project, which included a 12-day intensive on-site survey and assessment period, and a three-month evaluation and report development period.

■ Design projects included the civil and structural design of a new storage facility for General Mills. And, on the flip side, vibration monitoring for the demolition of the University of Minnesota's famous old "brickyard," Memorial Stadium, to ensure the structural integrity of surrounding buildings.

■ In the interest of a more pristine environment, the Minneapolis office designed a municipal hydroelectric plant on the Mississippi River at St. Cloud. The existing dam at the facility was formerly owned by Northern States Power Company.

■ Woodward-Clyde was selected for its geotechnical expertise in an earlier design for removing concrete by blasting, as part of the rehabilitation of Lock Number 1 on the Mississippi River at the Twin City's Ford Dam. Much of the dynamiting was done underwater, within a few inches of, but without damaging, critical elements of the massive lock.

A reflection of the company at large, Woodward-Clyde's Minneapolis office has a staff of 28 engineers, scientists, and support people. The specialists are skilled in environmental, civil, structural, geotechnical, water resources, and hydraulic engineering.

The Minneapolis office regularly draws on the full range of talent and services available through Woodward-Clyde operations worldwide. The company also provides major economies of scale for its clients because it has long been a powerful, single-source supplier.

Minnesota is home to 17 of the *Fortune* 500 companies, and many of the state's major corporations have national and international operations. With 60 locations worldwide, Woodward-Clyde provides the convenience of a local firm with resources that reach worldwide.

Bruce A. Liesch Associates, Inc.

There's much more to Minneapolis-St. Paul International Airport than meets the eye, especially at the critical point where human safety, efficient flight operations, and the integrity of the natural environment come together.

A scientific gatekeeper at the intersection is Bruce A. Liesch Associates, Inc., the environmental consulting and engineering firm charged with assisting the Metropolitan Airports Commission (MAC) to address environmental issues ranging from hazardous materials handling to indoor air quality, and helping the MAC manage its impact on soils, and on ground and surface water resources: essentially all environmental issues from the earth's surface and down.

Liesch Associates is well-qualified for the task. Founded 25 years ago by principal geologist Bruce Liesch, a leading specialist in the field of groundwater, the firm expanded into site investigation and remediation in the early 1970s as the nation came fully to grips with the environment. "That's typical of our development," says managing principal Brian Liesch. "We've grown deliberately by responding to the needs of our clients."

Those needs led Liesch to develop expertise in stormwater and wastewater treatment. Now active in all aspects of environmental consulting—with special expertise in air quality, industrial wastewater, and environmental hygiene, over and above its core competencies—Liesch employs 70 specialists at its suburban Minneapolis headquarters and offices in Albert Lea, Minnesota, and Madison, Wisconsin.

Liesch manages several environmental projects for the MAC. A main one is helping to prevent liquid releases from contaminating the ground and surface water resources under and near the main airport.

"Few people know that MSP has more than 50 different storage tank installations, many with multiple tanks, most of them underground," says Harry Summitt, airport project director for Liesch. "Daily fuel throughput averages more than one million gallons." The largest tank installation is the seven-million-gallon fuel storage complex visible along Post Road, serving ramp areas via underground pipeline and hydrant systems.

That complex, like most other storage facilities there, is owned and/or operated by airport tenants. Holding everything

ABOVE: Environmental planning and construction is conducted with a vision for the natural environment.

BELOW: State-of-the-art computer-aided drafting design (CADD) assures increased proficiency in engineering specifications.

from oil to ethylene glycol, they are scrupulously inventoried and tested to prevent and detect leaks and spills. In the event of a mishap, the action plan developed by Liesch directs an immediate response to minimize effects of the spill. As a final safeguard, containment facilities between the airport and the receiving waters are designed to prevent spills from reaching the Minnesota River or nearby lakes.

Glycol, the antifreeze sprayed on aircraft surfaces to melt lift-impairing ice and snow, is another concern. While the substance had been routinely used at airports for years, its application was increased by a 1992 FAA order promulgated to reduce air mishaps due to ice buildup.

"The ideal approach to controlling glycol," says Summitt, "is dedicated deicing areas at the ends of runways, where planes can be deiced just prior to takeoff. Such facilities can be equipped with glycol recovery systems."

There's a strong financial incentive, too. Annual glycol usage at MSP had been approximately 500,000 gallons, until the FAA Winter Operations Guidance for Air Carriers resulted in even higher volumes. Spent glycol can be recylced for nonaviation uses, reducing the cost of wastewater treatment while creating a new revenue source.

Another Liesch project at MSP will result in a highly detailed geological profile of the airport's subterranean features. Based on the most thorough inventory ever done via current and historic well drillings and soil-boring data, the document will accurately show subsurface features and display the direction and velocity of groundwater migrations beneath the airport and outside its boundaries.

Other Liesch projects range from indoor air-quality investigations to environmental site assessments for newly acquired properties, from waste disposal to routine environmental monitoring. The Metropolitan Airports Commission has taken an aggressive, active approach to protect its neighboring resources. Bruce A. Liesch Associates is pleased to be able to assist the MAC in its efforts.

CHAPTER ELEVEN

FINANCE
AND
DEVELOPMENT

Photo by Greg Ryan/Sally Beyer

T he area's solid
financial base
provides a
dynamic envi-
ronment for economic
opportunity and
growth, while local
developers, contractors,
property management
firms, and real estate
professionals work to
revitalize and create the
urban landscapes of
today and tomorrow.

Adolfson & Peterson, Inc., 154-155

The API Group, 156-157

National Trade Trust, 158-159

MacQueen Equipment, Inc., 160-161

Dain Bosworth, 162-163

SBM Company, 164

Hotel Capital Group, 165

Miller & Schroeder Financial, Inc., 166

Bell Mortgage Company, 167

Adolfson & Peterson, Inc.

Wherever you go in life—to school or college, to the airport, to the hospital, to work, to church, to a shopping mall, or even to jail—you are likely to be surrounded by an environment created by Adolfson & Peterson, Inc.

In a very real sense this 47-year-old Minneapolis company has constructed a whole public way of life in Minnesota and beyond. It is a quiet giant that is building our future, and its motto, "Total Construction Services," is no idle mission statement.

For example, shoppers at Bloomingdale's, inside the world's largest indoor shopping complex, the Mall of America, find themselves amid a stunning retail Valhalla of imported marble, custom-fashioned by Adolfson & Peterson. More mundane, but of even greater importance, the entire concrete structure of the megamall itself, as well as the surrounding roadway, was constructed by Adolfson & Peterson—a complex that has

ABOVE: Some 214,000 square feet of structural steel and imported Italian marble make up the Bloomingdale's building at the Mall of America (the largest mall in North America) in Bloomington.

BELOW: Built for Northwest Airlines, the Gold Concourse at MSP features the first moving walkway at the airport.

brought tourists the world over to shop in Minnesota.

The privately held enterprise also was a major contractor in the new downtown Minneapolis Hilton Hotel.

Twin Citians at the Minneapolis-St. Paul International Airport have relied increasingly on Adolfson & Peterson in recent years. The firm constructed the Gold Concourse at the main terminal building and also erected the parking ramp towers that lead to the new skyways. It has retrofitted several carousel areas, reconstructed worn portions of the parking ramp itself, and was involved in the South Terminal expansion.

"And these facilities had to remain open 24 hours a day while the work was completed," notes Howard L. Rekstad, director of business development. More than 20 million passengers continued uninterrupted through the airport as the major construction churned onward in time for the Super Bowl deadline of January 1992. "We finished on time," he adds.

Time, budget, and a minimum amount of interruption are standards of performance that have given Adolfson & Peterson its deserved reputation in the industry. The firm works with clients on a flow of budget and deadline information from start to finish so there are no surprises en route.

More than 500 schools have been built by this innovator in public

works. For example, a new high school was recently completed in Stillwater, Minnesota. More renovations are under way in Edina, St. Louis Park, and elsewhere as public facilities comply with the Americans With Disabilities Act and are brought up to code with increasingly higher building standards. And the Community College in Cloquet is an outright inspiration for young Native Americans getting an education there.

Working with Hodne Architects of Minneapolis on the Cloquet project, Adolfson & Peterson built a facility for education that is designed around the mythical thunderbird, with a sky-blue dome and earth-green flagstones, its columns honed roughly from timbers taken from the property. The colors of the building relate to the directional colors of the compass that are a part of the Indian tradition.

By contrast, aerospace engineers at Honeywell, Inc., may be working in a "clean room" so isolated from the world that a cubic foot of space would yield no more than 10 particles so small you could fit thousands of them on the breadth of a human hair. AP Technology Management, a high-tech subsidiary headed by president Mark Houge, specializes in making some of the cleanest work spaces on earth—and beyond.

Houge explains that the growth of cleanroom environments is required when companies miniaturize the products they manufacture. Miniscule equipment in medicine and electronics circuitry, for example, must be manufactured in a sterile environment where a speck of dust is detrimental to the production process. Ultimate cleanliness is not an option: It is an absolute necessity. The industry has great potential in pharmaceuticals, medicine, electronics, aerospace,

and even food processing, where decay-causing organisms now can be screened out to preserve otherwise perishable foods indefinitely.

Adolfson & Peterson did $125 million in the general contracting business in 1992, while doing another $60 million in its Construction Management Division. Headed by Robert J. Coruzzi, vice president of construction management, this division expresses yet another creative extension into the future of construction. Construction management, a field in which the firm has held a leadership role since 1985, brings Adolfson & Peterson's decades of experience and expertise into a project at the very outset. Coruzzi explains that his division manages a project for the client, working in partnership with the owner, architect, and with other suppliers.

"I am convinced that this is an excellent way for an owner to construct a building," says company president David Adolfson. "They get our knowledge on the front end to help them meet the budget, rather than perhaps designing, going over budget, redesigning, and putting it out for bid again. That old process does not work as well as it did in the past."

There is a soft-spoken professionalism at Adolfson & Peterson that comes from a confident and steady growth, as well as a low turnover of key personnel. The years of experience have helped the firm develop the brawny world of heavy construction into a scientific art that allows little margin of error in delivering the desired results to its customers.

ABOVE: The Colonnade tower is located in Golden Valley between the western suburbs and downtown Minneapolis. A perfect alternative for those looking for a shorter commute, it offers the finest office space in the Twin Cities. The exterior features exquisite waterfalls and a reflecting pool, and the interior fountains and stonework are made with Minnesota stone.

BELOW: Coon Rapids Senior High School has one of the largest high school field houses in Minnesota (112,000 square feet) and features a number of gyms and an indoor running track.

Three other divisions complete the five sectors of Adolfson & Peterson:

The General Construction Division is headed by vice president John Palmquist. His group appoints a project manager for each building project, with individual supervisors on site who are responsible for masonry, con-

crete, and carpentry. Adolfson & Peterson's reputation in these fields is impeccable. Clients will often specify Adolfson & Peterson work crews as part of a project precondition because of their fine craftsmanship.

The Industrial Division is headed by vice president Clyde Terwey. This wing of the firm specializes in heavy industrial works for private enterprise and government entities. Much of its work has been devoted to building wastewater-treatment facilities, parking ramps (and their rehabilitation), and special industrial projects.

The Design-Build Division is headed by vice president Dick Nordick. Under it, Adolfson & Peterson works directly with clients from the outset to help design and build a structure, including the hiring of an architect. Using Adolfson & Peterson builders, the Design-Build concept is a quick way to get a building from start to finish. It is particularly popular with retail developers.

Overseeing the entire spectrum of company divisions and projects is Brook Adolfson, vice president of quality control. His office, as the name implies, checks on every one of the projects as they develop and are completed.

The Adolfson & Peterson office in Denver is headed by senior vice presidents Richard Weicht, Sr., and Mike Peterson. This office also supervises construction in Arizona.

It is no coincidence that the firm exhibits a Scandinavian mastery of structure and design. Its roots go back to George Adolfson, father of David and Brook, the current

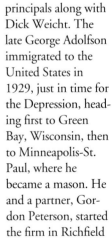

principals along with Dick Weicht. The late George Adolfson immigrated to the United States in 1929, just in time for the Depression, heading first to Green Bay, Wisconsin, then to Minneapolis-St. Paul, where he became a mason. He and a partner, Gordon Peterson, started the firm in Richfield in 1946.

The business grew steadily as a general construction firm. Peterson was bought out in 1980, the year the Denver office was opened. Today Adolfson & Peterson employs 250 and upwards, depending upon the season.

The API Group

A long-established but little-known Minnesota construction consortium is seen by industry experts as among the few major contractors best able to lead in the long-overdue restoration of America's aging public infrastructure: bridges, vital energy systems, mechanisms for environmental improvement and natural-resource extension, and other sinews of commerce left to rust in over a generation of not-so-benign neglect. The organization, the Roseville-based API Group, has flourished as competitors and others in related sectors have haltingly made their way through a long and unrelieved economic flatland.

As an example of its leadership, API's LeJeune Steel Company of Minneapolis recently entered into a partnership with

ABOVE: Some $400,000 in inventory movement is tracked daily by a state-of-the-art computer system linking the eight distribution centers of API Supply Company.

LEFT: Chairman of The API Group, Lee R. Anderson.

mass-merchandising giant Walmart Corporation to provide steel for the construction of 275 new retail stores nationwide in the next year.

"We are very positive on what we see in the crystal ball," says API's management team. "We've long known that the United States simply must rebuild its infrastructure. We're ideally positioned to help with efficient new modes of energy generation and conservation, plus the waste-management and -recycling systems acquired to bring America back to full speed."

API has been a factor in regional construction since 1926. It was founded by Reuben L. Anderson, Sr., a pioneer among the mostly Scandinavian Upper Midwest engineers whose companies toughed it out through the Great Depression, then helped win World War II with legendary feats of construction in support of U.S. troops

around the world.

For the past 20 years API's sales and service curves have soared reassuringly for group chairman Lee R. Anderson, son of the founder, as he oversees the carefully "layered" expansion of the now 14-member group. The aim has been to broaden the geographical coverage of its three basic businesses—construction, distribution, and manufacturing—while selectively adding new companies (vertically integrated with the old) that could leverage the unique "one-stop" services tendered a growing list of clients.

The strategy was to accumulate new companies either of strong regional backgrounds, or struggling, underutilized firms of good repute that could benefit from API's strong central core. An example of the former is Duluth's Jamar Company, a solid, 75-year veteran of many kinds of contracting,

acquired in 1985 for API's Construction Services Group.

The outcome has been a coherence of niche companies in several uncommon businesses. Their unique strengths are now maximized by a single-source headquarters that provides the benefits of computer-assisted-design (CAD), intensive employee cross training for higher productivity, and regional offices made stronger by dual service as headquarters for one or more API companies.

The firm operates plants and offices in 10 states, and at 30 facilities domiciled in one million square feet of building space. General business is conducted in all 48 contiguous United States. API Construction is licensed to operate in 33 states.

Privately held API sales are close to $250 million annually. Margins are near 15 percent; assets exceed $85 million. The company has more than 1,800 employees: 600 corporate workers plus another 1,200 highly skilled tradesmen, most of them union members, who work on exacting projects.

Example: A big paper mill or generating utility needs a new process boiler. Called "outages," because production must be shut down temporarily, such jobs require that

ABOVE: With almost 70 years in the commercial and industrial fire protection segment, API Group companies lead the nation in the design, installation, and maintenance of systems custom-made to the exacting needs of the facilities they protect.

RIGHT: Gleaming insulated, metal-jacketed piping testifies to API's leadership in the construction and engineering of thermal retention and conservation systems for the power industry, papermaking, and similar process enterprises. The group seems among the firms most able to lead in the restoration of the nation's long-neglected public infrastructure.

API bring in as many as 500 mechanics to complete the task in a minimal time, perhaps 20 days, and with no slippage, because continuous-process plants lose tens of thousands of dollars for every hour they are down.

Industrial Contractors of Bismarck, North Dakota, Pentecost Construction of Marquette, Michigan, and Sonneman Construction of Cloquet, Minnesota, are all API Construction Services Group members skilled in those complicated tasks.

But API is much, much more. It concentrates on the commercial and industrial areas of construction and engineering, in both application and distribution, with emphasis on generation and conservation for the power industry, papermaking, and similar processing enterprises. It is composed of three groups:

Construction Services: With eight locations in four states, this group ranks among the top industrial insulation contractors nationwide, and distributes all kinds of insulation building materials. With annual sales of more than $20 million, it also provides specialty thermal-retention systems. Its fire protection firms fabricate, install, and retrofit systems for institutional, commercial, and industrial customers, a segment of API that ranks among the top fire protection providers in the United States. One of these is 68-year-old Viking Automatic Sprinkler Company of St. Paul. It ranks number one in both size and reputation in the five Upper Midwest states.

Materials Distribution: This group, of which API Supply Company is the whole-

sale arm, serves a largely agricultural area embracing eight Upper Midwest states via as many centralized distribution depots. Sales by 3,200 lumber dealers and home centers generate revenues of some $90 million annually. A state-of-the-art computer center tracks $400,000 in daily inventory activities, helping to keep customer prices highly competitive—and better. The group also includes API Supply, Inc., which specializes in the leasing and rental of specialty construction equipment, and ASDCO of Duluth, wholesaler of construction materials to North County contractors.

Manufacturing: This entity is driven to maintain API's cutting edge in the creation of specialized construction products because it must also serve its own demanding construction group. This relationship has resulted in annual sales of more than $40 million, sparked by two notable API acquisitions:

■ Anco Products, Inc., of Elkhart, Indiana, acquired in 1972, is a leading national manufacturer and fabricator of flexible heating and cooling air ducts, plus innovative insulation material. Textrafine™, both high-tensile and cryogenic, is a proprietary product that has become the standard for designers and engineers.

■ Fifty-year-old LeJeune Steel Company of Minneapolis, acquired in 1989, is Minnesota's largest and one of the region's leading structural steel fabricators. Lately it has helped the Twin Cities meet an unprecedented demand for its products, assisting LeJeune attain revenues of more than $30 million, up 25 percent from 10 years ago.

Wisconsin Structural Steel of Barronett provides specialized high-tolerance welding services, mainly to LeJeune, in the fabrication of customer structural steel framework.

LeJeune fabricated the structural steel for the skyways connecting the parking ramp and Lindbergh Terminal at MSP. It also prepared 35,000 tons of girders and other members for three notable metro buildings: the neighboring Mall of America, the Minneapolis Convention Center, and the nearby 60-story Norwest Center.

In the energy field, API Construction provided the boiler and precipitator insulation for Hennepin County's refuse-to-steam plant near Target Center, and recently entered into a partnership to provide insulation for the Koch Refinery at Pine Bend.

API Construction has also been a 15-year supplier of insulation for piping and mechanical systems at MSP. Elsewhere in aviation, API's Western States Fire Protection Company has an office in Seattle to better serve Boeing Aircraft, a major supplier of Twin Cities-based Northwest Airlines.

In the larger picture, API sees its philosophy of acquisition according to both niche and geography as a guarantor of continued growth: When one market goes down, as has the local commercial sector lately, it tends to pick up business in the agricultural and industrial sectors.

Taken together, API is a design-construction-manufacturing-supply company that's prepared to help in retrofitting the nation's infrastructure.

National Trade Trust

A catalyst is an ingredient that is essential to make things happen. When present its effect can be instantaneous, can seem magical, and can be profound.

In the world of small business, National Trade Trust (NTT) is a catalyst, providing essential financial and management services to investors and to businesses with good products, creditworthy customers, and growing sales opportunities. Armed with an expanding list of loyal investors and a unique set of risk-management disciplines, the Trust has so far satisfied its founder's

creative programs, a client company assigns its purchase order to NTT. In exchange it receives the funding necessary to cover all the direct costs of producing that order. This program allows clients to produce additional orders or convert back orders to bottom-line profits, and devote more time and energy satisfying the management needs of growing the business. Other capital needs can be met from the assignment of the company's receivables.

Mark Muenzhuber, the Trust's director of marketing, says that "the key for

operations for about three months," says Kittler, "and became well satisfied with its ability." With financing supplied by the Trust, the company expanded its operations from Minnesota into Wisconsin and South Dakota, taking on several large contracts in competition with Waste Management, Inc., BFI, and other industry giants. By mid-1992 the firm had attracted new equity and was shipping tires to its South Dakota reduction facility and converting them to fuel. As this article is being written the company is contemplating acquisitions, mergers, and a public offering of its stock.

Muenzhuber believes that with imaginative marketing, NTT can grow indefinitely. He points out that enterprises that have relied on NTT are extremely varied. For example, MF Industries, Inc., of St. Croix Falls, Wisconsin, came to the Trust for help when a large order for its computer-controlled, hydraulic metal-forming and -shearing machines tapped out its bank line of credit. MF Industries, Inc., later became involved in the privatization of the ESPE metal-forming machin-

J. Patrick Kittler, NTT's founder and trustee.

vision of a profitable means to bridge the gap between start-up financing and bankable operations for promising growth companies.

In absence of this creative source, small and medium-size enterprises may not be able to market their products with any assurance that sales fulfillment financing is available to them if needed.

Upon qualification for one of NTT's

National Trade Trust is to work closely with companies that have histories of integrity, successful product delivery, effective cost control, and creditworthy customers." Growing sales and profits can rapidly make the client attractive to the rest of the financial industry.

A prime example is one particular company that became a client of the Trust when it was six months old and working on its third contract to clean up used tire dumps under state and county environmental programs. "We had watched its

ery works in Slovakia.

NTT's vice president of administration, Sherri Pesek, gives an example of how a seasonal business can benefit. "Marty Irving, president of Martin Sports International in Duluth, Minnesota, makes golf clubs and needs to ship them to market in the early spring in our part of the country, and we understand his urgency. Since most of Marty's club heads are made by third-party suppliers we helped him obtain letters of credit so Marty's custom clubs could be delivered to meet his deadline in February."

"Every transaction is different and each is treated with individual care," says J. Patrick Kittler, founder and trustee. "Working together, our personnel provide qualified companies with a tailor-made program to transform their purchase orders and current receivables into satisfied customers, good credit, and executives who are free to concentrate on growth." It has enabled Marty Irving and others like him to successfully manage growth until they desire equity investors or can obtain bank financing.

Another of the Trust's clients that came to it as a very early stage company is now in the midst of a rapidly growing demand for its aluminum guitar bodies. With large orders from Fender Guitar and with rock stars like Bon Jovi showcasing his company's product, Martin Schulte of Spruce Hill Machines is predicting a million-dollar market during his company's second year.

"We are not venture capitalists," Kittler declares. "We don't ask for an ownership position in the client's business. The mission of the Trust is to assemble financial resources and provide these to growth companies where it can secure its assets by focusing on the creditworthiness of its client's customers, bank letters of credit, insurance, and other security factors," continues Kittler, who founded the organization after working closely with the financial, legal, and operating needs of growing companies for 30 years.

"Traditional banking institutions often are not as readily able to provide this type of financial service for firms that have rapidly expanding or fluctuating money needs during periods of sales growth," Kittler explains. "These traditional means often may be faced with a lending limit, competing demands on available resources, regulatory inhibitions, or lack of risk management resources for this type of business. By cooperating with NTT, a bank comes out with a stronger customer and additional collateral."

Jean Bretz, who together with her husband, Randy, owns Bretellen Marketing in Milwaukee, Wisconsin, appreciates the personal side of working with NTT. Her firm designs and manufactures decorative indoor and outdoor lighting, as well as custom-designed heirloom trunks, selling through such major retailers as K mart, Walmart, American Drug, HomeBase, and Brookstone.

"In today's business climate," she notes, "banks are very reluctant to finance the capital for growth, so you have to look at alternative sources, and what's been wonderful about National Trade Trust is that they're problem solvers. I will sit down and tell them what I want to do and they will help me figure out how I can accomplish it. I don't know anyone else who does that."

Linda Alt, NTT's vice president of investor relations, notes that some of the "perks" of this kind of arrangement include faster financial support, which allows the client to make business decisions swiftly and openly; automatic credit adjustments, based on eligible sales orders and receivables; full funding for labor and materials; none of the costs and delays experienced in equity or long-term debt financing; no loss of ownership; no long-term or residual commitments; total flexibility for the client on how funds are used once an order is delivered; the assurance that, based on cash flow and sound business practices, the financing will be there when needed; and insurance against bad customer credit.

Operating under the guidance of its newly appointed executive vice president, Wayne Podratz, the securities group raises the capital needed for NTT's financing transactions by offering high-yield, short-term notes to individual and institutional investors. The notes, offered through selected brokerage firms, are fully collateralized. The notes can be redeemed at par upon 90 days' notice.

Professionalism and the teamwork approach, according to Kittler, has been the force behind the success of National Trade Trust. The company headquarters will remain in Minneapolis, where it has found quality people and created a solid base to support it as it continues to branch out nationally. "We have had a satisfyingly good record," Kittler notes.

Sherri Pesek, vice president of administration.

MacQueen Equipment, Inc.

Mountains of Minnesota snow can choke an airport to a standstill in a matter of minutes. For that reason, a whole armored division of immense snowplows and snowblowers stand ready to attack at the drop of a snowflake at Minneapolis-St. Paul International Airport and at other airports in the northern tier of states. The airport, indeed, has 3,000 acres of concrete and land that must be groomed and maintained throughout the changing seasons.

MacQueen Equipment, Inc., of St. Paul, Minnesota, provides the technological muscle that cleans up our environment. It may be a blizzard that dumps 30 inches of snow onto 1,000 acres of paved surface. Or it could be a flurry of litter that needs to be swept away from an 8,000-car parking ramp. These are the giants of the industry, too. Trucks and plows can cost $250,000 each, and sweepers can require an investment of up to $80,000 per unit. So it is critical that their performance be matched to the job at hand.

Representing heavy equipment from Oshkosh Trucks, Inc., and Elgin Sweeper Corporation, as well as other major lines, MacQueen can be relied upon day or night to speed parts during an emergency or to plan for deicing equipment for tomorrow's jumbo jets.

It is not uncommon for the company's service representatives to receive a call at 1 a.m. in the middle of a raging Minnesota

snowstorm to obtain parts or information to keep plows moving, to keep runways open, and to keep airliners landing safely. Millions of dollars and millions of lives rely on this kind of unsung dedication each winter.

"Service is the main theme of our business," explains Bill Garber, president of MacQueen Equipment. "The big thing an airport looks for is performance and service." He notes that if a piece of equipment falters an entire airport can be shut down, which can result in hundreds of thousands of dollars in direct losses and countless dramas of personal and professional inconvenience.

Therefore, MacQueen becomes involved in "whatever hits the pavement." The company even sells equipment to fill in cracks in paving, a preventive maintenance that Garber equates with a dentist filling a tooth, rather than replacing a whole set of teeth.

In addition to providing giant snowblowers and plows (with blades up to 27

ABOVE: The Oshkosh truck and snowblower in action on an MSP runway.

LEFT: The three-wheel Elgin Pelican street sweeper is located at MSP International Airport.

sales are devoted to the airport market. The major portion of the business is devoted to solid waste-disposal and -recycling systems for communities of all sizes. It even has vacuum systems to clean sand and debris from storm sewers.

"Cleanliness is what we're really selling," he explains. In the airport environment, an unwanted bit of debris can pose a genuine threat to the internal workings of a jet engine. Elgin sweeper equipment keeps the airport environment extremely clean, thus preventing costly mechanical problems, airline delays, and even hazards to navigation.

And what is good for an airport is good for a community as well. MacQueen Equipment supplies a variety of solid waste-hauling trucks and equipment for governmental customers throughout the region. Trucks outfitted with automated hydraulic pickup systems, for example, make rubbish hauling quicker, safer, and more efficient for communities and taxpayers.

Garber looks upon MacQueen as "recession proof" in a world that needs to clean up after itself. The recycling of waste is another important facet of the company's vital role.

MacQueen was founded in 1962 by John MacQueen, a former county engineer. The firm had its beginning in Duluth, but was moved to St. Paul in 1967 and is currently located in that city's Midway section.

ABOVE: This Eagle model, four-wheel Elgin street sweeper is moved to different airport areas in the seven-county metro area.

RIGHT: The Oshkosh snowblower can cast up to 150 feet and 3,000 tons an hour.

feet long), MacQueen Equipment keeps an extensive inventory of parts that can be delivered in minutes. The company also will customize its lines of equipment to meet the specific needs of customers.

Much of the massive equipment will log very few actual miles over the course of a decade. But the work the machines perform is grueling, and replacement usually comes after six to ten years. Metropolitan airports will usually then put the equipment into service at smaller airports or sell the machines to other regional airports.

A significant portion of MacQueen's

Dain Bosworth

A soaring tower in downtown Minneapolis stands as a monument to Twin Cities-bred Dain Bosworth, one of the nation's largest full-service regional securities firms. The company's move into the new Dain Bosworth Plaza in early 1992 marked a milestone in its history. "That speaks louder than words about our financial vigor and dedication to benefit the area by creating new sources of wealth and opportunities for growth," says Judy Gaviser, head of Dain Bosworth's marketing department.

In fact, Dain Bosworth was one of the first investment banking organizations that the Metropolitan Airports Commission (MAC) turned to for direction in structuring a $270-million, 1992 bond issue for new capital investment by Northwest Airlines. The tax-exempt financing was essential to keeping the carrier's headquarters, and its immeasurable transportation and economic benefits, in Minnesota.

Dain Bosworth presents a valuable mix of both the sophisticated and the deeply

rooted provincial. Long among the premier regional brokerage firms according to the revealing indicator of "return on average equity" (30 percent in its most recent fiscal year), it has solid, bedrock foundations in its home community. "Being a strong regional gives us the ability to stay close to our customers and focus on investment opportunities in our own backyard while offering the broad spectrum of products and services as well as the financial strength of a major New York Stock Exchange member firm," states Gaviser.

Kalman & Co., founded in St. Paul in 1909, was the original firm from which Dain Bosworth later emerged. J.M. Dain & Co. appeared in Minneapolis 20 years later, then Dain merged with Kalman, followed by the acquisition of Quail & Co., to form Dain, Kalman & Quail, Inc., in 1967. Ten years later, following several other acquisitions including the Denver firm of Bosworth Sullivan & Co., the firm's name was changed to Dain Bosworth Incorporated.

With nearly 1,800 employees in the 16 states generally west to the Pacific from the Great Lakes, and north of the far-southern Great Plains, Dain Bosworth had a banner year in fiscal 1992. Net revenues were $255 million, up almost 25 percent from the previous year. Pre-tax earnings grew to more than $39 million, a 49 percent increment versus 1991.

Most visible of DBI's three lines of business is the Retail Sales Group. With over 700 investment executives in more than 50 offices, it has historically been the firm's "bread and butter" division, lately sparking overall company performance by capitalizing on the twin opportunities of lower certificate of deposit rates, and consequent increased issuance of common and preferred stocks and bonds.

Two other groups play essential roles at the firm.

ABOVE: The many talents of Dain Bosworth's people are uniquely able to meet the diversity of client needs in a broad multiregional market.

LEFT: The firm's move into the new Dain Bosworth Plaza in early 1992 marked a milestone in its history.

And their fiscal impact is even greater in driving the financing of public and private organizations essential to the prosperity and quality of life in all of the areas touched by Dain Bosworth's presence.

The Corporate Capital Group is expert in the financing of new and established corporations, research germane to that

Such offerings make possible the construction and upkeep of hospitals and health clinics, schools, roads, bridges, and sewer and water systems; capital projects at public entities such as Minneapolis-St. Paul International Airport and the Minneapolis Convention Center; and the financing of sports stadiums such as the Hubert Humphrey Metrodome and Target Center.

Culminating a two-year project to maximize the cost-effectiveness of its computer systems, Dain Bosworth is currently rolling out an exclusive "Client Management System." This company-developed software gives individual investment executives automatically updated client account information on each individual customer. "CMS is really a client service tool," says David Sogge of the Retail Sales Group. "It facilitates portfolio reporting and offers word processing for improved communication with clients and increased efficiency and productivity inside the organization."

Philanthropic activity at the firm also keeps pace, a major vehicle being the Dain Bosworth Foundation, which donated more than $755,000 to nonprofit organizations and charitable causes during 1992. A conspicuously successful partnership exists with Anwatin Middle School, an inner-city middle school in Minneapolis. There, among other programs, student "Character Counts" rewards for high academic and/or social performance proved so popular and effective that a new DBI "Future Scholarship" has been created. It allows a high-achieving student to earn $10,000 in incremental grants for college studies by keeping up the good work during the remaining four years of high school.

This and other activities in the community have made Dain Bosworth a frequent recipient of the prestigious "Keystone Award," given by the Minneapolis Chamber of Commerce to companies that contribute between 2 and 5 percent of pre-tax profits to charitable organizations.

In examining the driving forces behind Dain Bosworth's performance, chief executive officer Irv Weiser stresses how the many talents of its people are uniquely able to meet the diversity of client needs in a broad multiregional market. "Our four strategic forces of quality, growth, information, and pride will sustain our continued strong financial performance through the 1990s."

function, the sale of equities to various institutions, and over-the-counter trading. The transactions it structures are both vital sinews of growth for business enterprises and their employees, and also creators of financial instruments for the prosperous investment of others.

In the past two years corporate finance completed 48 public offerings that provided a record $3.1 billion in new capital for its business clients, many of whom are headquarted here in the economically dynamic northwest quadrant. The Corporate Capital Group offers focused expertise over a vast spectrum of industries including health care, financial services, food and agribusiness, and retailing. It delivers a wide range of financial services, broad distribution of securities, and ongoing research coverage to its clients.

The Fixed Income Group provides three distinct services: the sales, trading, and underwriting of both taxable and tax-exempt securities as well as public finance investment banking. In 1991 and 1992 the group's public finance and municipal departments had management participation in 868 issues totaling $15 billion. These issues reflect the group's banking specialties in housing, health care, economic development, and infrastructure financing throughout a 19-state region.

SBM Company

Now managing approximately one billion dollars in assets, SBM Company understandably prides itself on an enviable record of financial accomplishment, according to Roman Schmid, its chairman, president, and chief executive officer.

Thriving through all of the periods of recession, inflation, depression, stagnation, war, and peace since 1914, SBM has anchored its philosophy in conservatism and innovation. The initials SBM, adopted in April 1992 as the corporate name, come from its former title of State Bond and Mortgage Company.

SBM has become an umbrella for a whole family of investment and financial services, including life insurance, tax-deferred annuities, mutual funds, investment certificates, and other securities.

The SBM Company is located at 8400 Normandale Lake Boulevard in Bloomington, Minnesota, yet still retains some roots in the old German community of New Ulm, Minnesota, where it was founded in 1914 by Theodore Schonlau and a group of local investors.

Today SBM oversees investments for approximately 70,000 clients in 33 states. It has discovered that its midwestern philosophy of financial soundness has found acceptance on both coasts and as far away as Hawaii. Yet the cautious underpinnings have not stifled its ability to innovate.

SBM's insurance subsidiary is one of very few life insurance companies that has an investment portfolio considered 100 percent socially responsible. "We are second to none in socially responsible investments," says Schmid of a program that has had increasing popularity with its clientele. He explains that it was a natural expansion of opportunity for the firm, which had already been deeply committed to U.S. government

Roman G. Schmid, chairman, president, and chief executive officer of SBM Company.

agency-backed securities in its life insurance company subsidiary.

"The key to our continued growth has been our innovativeness—the ability to find a niche—and our conservatism. We also have established a reputation of treating our clients with integrity," Schmid explains.

For example, the company has striven to minimize risk. "We were never into junk bonds," he continues. "We have always been very conservative." SBM has always dedicated itself to personal service to its agents, brokers, and customers. This has created a reputation for credibility and service that has become its hallmark in the industry.

The company itself is privately held, with approximately 30 percent of it employee-owned. Schmid himself is indicative of the firm's stability. He has been with SBM for 46 years, being appointed president and chief executive officer in 1970 and chairman of the board in 1978.

SBM moved to the Minneapolis-St. Paul area in 1988 to take advantage of the Twin Cities' reputation as a financial center and to make better use of the transportation hub through Minneapolis-St. Paul International Airport.

"It has brought us closer to the marketplace," concludes Schmid, a move that has coincided with substantial growth during the past five years.

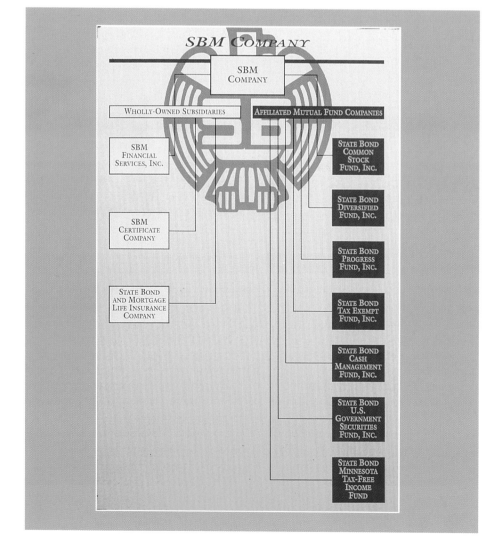

Hotel Capital Group

As denoted by its name, Hotel Capital Group is a fast-growing Twin Cities-based hospitality company that's hitched its star to the limited-service sector of the lodging industry: those affordable, no-frill hostelries bearing such logos as Super 8, Comfort Inn, and Best Western.

As its principals correctly predicted, the company's ceiling and visibility have been unlimited, thanks to their long experience in the core business involved and the emergent position of that segment of the lodging industry. The aviation analogy is appropriate. Hotel Capital Group is a tenant of the Metropolitan Airports Commission (MAC) reliever airport at Crystal, Minnesota, where it keeps in a company-owned hangar an aircraft for the regional business uses the firm considers essential to the fast, safe, and efficient operations of its motels.

Principals of the Twin Cities-based cor-

poration are the well-matched pair of Roger Hoy and Jim Cooper, both longtime players in the hotel industry. They have combined experience of more than 22 years in the placement of both debt and equity financing for hotels and motels, and the development and operation of their own lodging properties. Separately, each principal is also the owner of his own enterprise.

Hoy heads The Capital Companies, also of Minneapolis, which specializes in the equity placement and brokerage of lodging properties throughout the Midwest and Southwest. His primary career emphasis has been the securing of investors for, and ownership of, lodging properties. During the past 12 years Hoy has secured investors for hospitality properties valued in excess of $137 million. He also has had

ABOVE: Hotel Capital Group's Super 8 Motel in Espanola, New Mexico.

TOP: Roger Hoy and Jim Cooper (seated), principals of Hotel Capital Group.

ownership in nine hotel properties.

Cooper is a CPA and the chief executive officer of his own mortgage company, Specialty Mortgage of St. Paul. Over the past nine years he has secured more than $280 million of mortgage financings and has supervised the origination and completion of $70 million in construction financing for Super 8 Motels, Inc., during its period of high growth in the 1980s. He brings to the partnership detailed, hands-on experience in financial accounting, internal control disciplines, and the ownership/operation of eight hotels.

Currently, the company's properties consist of seven hotels. Operating in three states, Hotel Capital Group currently employs 76 people and has three additional properties in the development stage.

"In the 1980s construction of high-end, labor-intensive, full-service hotels boomed," says Jim Cooper, explaining: "Overbuilding and the recession have decimated the high-end segment of the industry, while recession has actually given the limited-service segment a big boost. Consumers have become more cost conscious and have flocked to limited-service motels. Even with the likelihood of heightened economic activity, we feel that the trend of consumer price discrimination is here to stay."

Roger Hoy is equally optimistic about the limited-service sector. "Operating a limited-service property takes about one-tenth the management effort of a full-service hotel. Our lenders like us because we have very simple operations, we stay focused on our core business, and we have experience in all aspects of the lodging business. We've successfully raised financing for more than $400 million in lodging properties and possess a thorough understanding of such operations.

"Being able to put it all together has given us an edge over our typical competition, which may have only one of the many talents needed to make a lodging deal work," continues Hoy. "Hotel Capital Group is a strong team that provides total management oversight, including operational training, daily financial monitoring, and regular consultation regarding all aspects of property operation."

Asked what separates Hotel Capital Group from its competition, both partners agree that the vital difference is their ability to establish business relationships marked by a high degree of trust and openness.

Says Hoy, "No one who has entered into a deal with us has ever been hurt." Adds Cooper, "We work constantly to make sure that our relationships are long term. That is why we have been successful."

Miller & Schroeder Financial, Inc.

Miller & Schroeder Financial, Inc. (M&S), is an investment banking firm specializing in publicly financed projects. Headquartered in Minneapolis, Miller & Schroeder is ranked as one of the nation's leading regional investment banking firms. Since its founding more than a quarter-century ago, M&S has arranged more than $22 billion in financing for some 2,300 projects in 42 states.

Miller & Schroeder's relationship with the Metropolitan Airports Commission began in the late 1970s. Since that time M&S is pleased to have been involved in $400 million in financing for Minneapolis-St. Paul International Airport. This is the type of long-term relationship with its clients that Miller & Schroeder values and works to foster. M&S understands that investment banking is much more than an exercise in numerical calculation. It's a business where a firm's commitment to its clients is the most valuable currency of all.

Clients who choose to work with Miller & Schroeder benefit not just from the firm's extensive in-house expertise; they also gain access to Miller & Schroeder's vast network of working relationships forged over the years. This network allows clients to profit from the considerable synergy and diversity of ideas that is at the heart of innovation.

Miller & Schroeder prides itself on straight talk. From the first exploratory steps to the final documentation, the firm's expertise truly becomes the client's expertise. M&S' broad base of clients includes municipalities and public entities of varying sizes, financing small and large projects nationwide.

In order to afford its clients every advantage, M&S responds quickly to the changing financial conditions experienced in today's market. Miller & Schroeder's experience with rating agencies and credit providers allows for the sound structuring of financing that affords the housing industry, governmental entities, businesses, and airports the opportunity to help create their own futures.

As the Metropolitan Airports Commission and Minneapolis-St. Paul International Airport move toward another 50 years of growth, Miller & Schroeder is proud to be a part of their continuing story of success.

Construction worker John Johnson and his daughter, Brianna, on the second level of the Mall of America. Miller & Schroeder was hired by the city of Bloomington to put together financing for the infrastructure portion of the world-class shopping center.

Bell Mortgage Company

"At Bell Mortgage we respect tradition, but we aren't driven by it. We work hard to maintain our reputation as the area's oldest and most prestigious mortgage banking firm, but that's not our major concern. Our major concern is to meet the needs of our clients and our community—to be progressive and service-oriented. That might not sound too glamorous, but perhaps it explains our continued growth, after 100 years in the industry," says chief executive officer Gary V. Kirt of this Minneapolis company founded in 1880.

With more than 100 full-time professionals who average a minimum of 10 years in the mortgage business, Bell's staff is second to none in product, production, processing, underwriting, and closing their clients' real estate transactions. Those professionals are firmly focused on today's and tomorrow's mortgage products and technology, but they remain cognizant that the future owes much to the past.

The company goes back to David C. Bell, a New Englander who arrived in the 1850s at a raw lumbering hamlet around St. Anthony Falls. He lived to leave an indelible mark on Minneapolis—as Hennepin County treasurer, cofounder of the YMCA, also the American Automobile Association, a linseed oil company, and several banks, as well as creator of the mortgage company bearing his name.

Bell pioneered the mortgage business as it is known today. As early as 1880 he was

Bell Mortgage's Brooklyn Center office is located in a 120-year-old barn at the authentically restored Earle Brown Heritage Center.

originating mortgages in Minnesota and selling them to banks in New York, a practice that brought significant capital to Minnesota and expedited the development of the area.

Kirt purchased David C. Bell in 1980 and was joined by Michael A. Fannon, the new firm's president, to form Bell Mortgage in 1990. It's a company committed to providing the home buyer with a much-needed alternative to the overly complex mortgage system. Offering a complete line of government and conventional products, the firm today is among the nation's largest independent mortgage bankers, having helped well over 100,000 families obtain financing for their homes.

In addition to administrative offices in Minnetonka, Bell has branch offices in Bloomington, Coon Rapids, St. Louis Park, and Brooklyn Center. Consistent with the firm's long role in regional history, Bell's Brooklyn Center office is located in a 120-year-old barn at the authentically restored Earle Brown Heritage Center.

Bell's continued growth stems from its ability to bring new and innovative mortgage products from all over the country to the metro area, also via its staff of experienced professionals and a state-of-the-art

computer system that make the mortgage process as stress-free as possible for borrowers.

"Even today," says Kirt, "we get new customers from families with three or four generations of experience with Bell—some going back to the early 1900s. That testifies to the value of enduring relationships, which are rare in an industry known for its start-up companies that last only a few years, or large national firms that open and close offices on a moment's notice."

Bell Mortgage is an ideal place for aspiring mortgage bankers to seek career advancement. "You'd be on the top team in town," Michael Fannon tells those looking for a premier employer. "It always raises the level of your performance to work with the best." He adds that although mortgage banking is challenging, its rewards can be considerable, and not just financial. Important values inhere in helping others to home ownership.

Bell Mortgage's commitment does not stop with the client, but continues in the footsteps of David C. Bell. The firm makes contributions to a variety of civic causes and supports its many employee-volunteers who work with more than 20 local community organizations.

"The dream of home ownership is alive and well in Minnesota," says Kirt, "and Bell is well into its second century of meeting the needs of its customers and the community."

CHAPTER TWELVE

CONVENTIONS AND VISITORS

Photo by Greg Ryan/Sally Beyer

 **W**orld-class convention centers, resorts, hotels and motels, restaurants, and cultural and sports attractions serve the important convention and tourism industries.

Residence Inn By Marriott Minneapolis/Eden Prairie, 170-171

Carlson Companies Carlson Travel Network ■ Carlson Hospitality/Radisson Hotels International, 172

Holiday Inn Airport #2, 173

Minneapolis-St. Paul Airport Hilton Hotel, 174

Cedars Edina Apartment Community, 175

Residence Inn By Marriott
MINNEAPOLIS / EDEN PRAIRIE

Whatever it takes!

It's not an official motto or fancy corporate advertising slogan. You won't find it on a banner over the fireplace in the Gatehouse, or stitched into the linens in your suite, or displayed on buttons and baseball caps.

But if you spend some time at the Residence Inn in Eden Prairie, just 10 minutes west of Minneapolis-St. Paul International Airport, you'll experience it in a style of away-from-home living that shows the combined influence of the legendary Marriott service philosophy and the skill and dedication of a home-grown staff of more than 40.

Since the Twin Cities' first Residence Inn (the first in the five-state area) opened in 1985, thousands of busy travelers have made it their home away from home for extended stays, some for as long as a year or more as well as for short-term trips. Whether working in the high-rise canyons of downtown Minneapolis and St. Paul, or heading out to the many commercial and industrial clusters scattered around the Twin Cities, they've found it a satisfying substitute for the comfortable homes they've had to leave behind.

The stories staffers tell reflect the neighborhood-style relationships that result. Past guests who have stayed while finding a home in the Twin Cities have invited their Residence Inn hosts to their housewarmings. Holiday seasons invariably bring cards and visits from former residents who still remember the names of the people who

took such good care of them. And it's always a pleasure to hear from those like the guest who felt ill one evening and accepted a staffer's offer of a short ride to nearby Fairview Southdale Hospital. It turned out he had suffered a mild heart attack—and without prompt attention might have suffered a second, more serious one.

Most people who spend time in

a Residence Inn spend a significant amount of time there: Five or more nights is the underlying design standard, but 14 nights is average for long-term guests, 26 nights for international visitors. That dictates the style and substance of the 128 units provided in Eden Prairie—32 two-level penthouses and 96 studio suites, most with wood-burning fireplaces. Rather than being stacked in a high rise or strung together in an endless chain, suites are combined, eight at a time, into a neighborhood of residential-style buildings.

Regardless of size or location, each suite is designed for the needs of longer-term guests, most of whom come to the Twin Cities for extended business engagements, short-term assignments, training activities, or corporate relocation. In contrast to a standard hotel room, a Residence Inn suite is spacious, yet packed end to end with amenities. There's **room** in these rooms—half again as much as the largest conventional hotel accommodations in the

studios, and about 850 square feet (the size of a comfortable apartment) in the penthouse configurations.

Studios offer full-size sofas and plush chairs in the living area and a full kitchen/breakfast bar in addition to the expected bed and bath. Penthouses have vaulted ceilings (with a private bed and bath) in an upstairs loft, overlooking the living room and kitchen below. A second bathroom and a large multipurpose room designed to serve as office, meeting room, or second bedroom (a full-size bed folds out of sight into the wall during the day) completes the penthouse.

The business activities of the typical guest—who, perhaps 90 percent of the time, arrives by way of Minneapolis-St. Paul International Airport—are supported by suite and staff alike. Guests working solo find the breakfast bar doubles nicely as a desk and the sofa makes for a relaxed reading lounge; for meetings, tables, chairs, and other necessities are available as need-ed. Multiple phones (with built-in jacks to accommodate computer modems) are standard, and private lines can be installed for those who want their calls direct. Staffers are accustomed to hosting international travelers, handling requests for hometown newspapers from around the world, recommending sources of ethnic foods, even finding translators for those who need them; the switchboard is hooked into AT&T's Language Line service.

Each suite's kitchen is fully stocked with microwave, stove, oven, and refrigerator plus dishes and cooking utensils. To fill up the cupboards and the refrigerator, the inn's shuttle will take guests anywhere from a conventional supermarket to a specialized ethnic grocer. Or drop off a shopping list at the front desk in the morning and you'll return to find the groceries neatly put away—at no additional charge. Housekeeping even does the dishes. To meet the "neighbors," guests in residence can take advantage of the inn's complimentary breakfast each morning, a hospitality hour in the evening, even a themed dinner once a week.

For families in transit, the Residence Inn offers a relaxed location, a swimming

ABOVE AND BOTTOM LEFT: The inn's 32 two-level penthouses offer a full kitchen, breakfast bar, wood-burning fireplace, vaulted ceilings, and an upstairs loft in about 850 square feet.

TOP LEFT: The Residence Inn in Eden Prairie is just 10 minutes from MSP International Airport.

pool and other fitness facilities, and perhaps a few amenities the kids would be happy to forgo temporarily—it's not uncommon for working guests leaving for their morning freeway journeys to encounter a school bus arriving to pick up its own commuters.

It's no secret that first impressions count. Guests arriving at the Residence Inn in Eden Prairie share a first impression that says a lot about the time to come: No matter what time of the day or night they turn the key to their room for the first time, they enter to find a light on and the radio softly playing. It's a little touch, something they might do before leaving home. It says they've found more than a place to stay—they've found a place to live for awhile.

A place where people will do "whatever it takes" to make sure they feel right at home.

Carlson Companies
CARLSON TRAVEL NETWORK ■ CARLSON HOSPITALITY / RADISSON HOTELS INTERNATIONAL

With a love for hotels nurtured by the legendary Golden Strings in the Flame Room of the original Radisson Hotel in downtown Minneapolis, Curtis L. Carlson has leveraged the natural synergy of hospitality and travel into twin bastions of his extended family of companies. That family has a nationwide work force of almost 100,000 and generates systemwide revenues of nearly $10 billion annually, making it one of the nation's largest privately owned corporations.

But size alone is not the Carlson Companies' consuming goal. The Minnesota entrepreneur says, "Our aim is to become the very best in the world in both the hotel and travel industries by always providing the highest-quality service to our business and leisure clients."

Emphasis on quality and service unites the Carlson Hospitality Group, a $2.8-billion arm that's become a major force in the global hotel, resort, and restaurant industries. Under the leadership of group president Juergen Bartels, the Radisson organization has catapulted from 89th position a decade ago (based on total rooms) to number seven in the current global ranking.

Adding hotels at the current rate of one every 5.5 days, the lodging operation of the group—which includes Radisson Hotels International, Country Lodging by Carlson, and Colony Hotels & Resorts—encompasses more than 339 locations in 28 countries worldwide.

Restaurant operations under the Carlson Hospitality Group include 230 T.G.I. Friday's Restaurants and 240 family-style

ABOVE: Radisson Hotels International, which traces its roots to Minneapolis, is aggressively expanding around the globe offering world-class locations such as the Radisson Sierra Plaza Hotel Manzanillo in Manzanillo, Mexico.

BELOW: Carlson Travel Network's first trademark office, with its innovative design, is located in the skyway system in downtown Minneapolis.

Country Kitchen locations.

The group is expanding worldwide, including Eastern Europe. One showcase project is the Radisson Slavjanskaya Hotel Moscow, the first U.S.-managed hotel in the Commonwealth of Independent States, the former USSR. Other Radisson hotel projects in Eastern Europe are located in Poland; former East Berlin; Riga, Latvia; and Budapest, Hungary.

Radisson has also recently expanded

into the cruise industry with the revolutionary designed *SSC Radisson Diamond*, the world's first twin-hull luxury cruise ship.

Carlson Travel Network is as much a presence in its segment of the travel industry as Carlson Hospitality is in its. Carlson Travel Network embraces more than 2,200 travel agencies in 21 countries, with more than $6 billion in systemwide revenues. One of the world's largest travel agency operations, Carlson Travel Network is also the nation's oldest, having acquired pathfinding Ask Mr. Foster in 1979.

Carlson Travel Network is a leader in providing travel management services to U.S. and multinational corporations, including many *Fortune* 500 companies. It boasts the most advanced travel management technologies in the travel industry, and its nationwide network of Corporate Business Centers and travel professionals are able to handle every reservation, ticketing, and travel information need for today's business travelers.

Carlson Travel Network also is a leader in the leisure segment, where its pacesetting "Associate," or franchise, approach allows smaller, local travel agencies to capitalize on the national buying and branding clout of the nationally known Carlson name. Tours, cruises, and escorted and independent travel for individuals and groups are sold by the retail division's travel agents in all 50 states.

Carlson Travel Network is truly a global force to reckon with. Its international division includes company-owned Carlson Travel Network-United Kingdom and A.T. Mays, the Travel Agents (Carlson Travel Network's Retail Division in the United Kingdom), and more than 300 independently owned Associate locations in Western Europe and the Pacific Rim.

The Minnesota-based Radisson Hotels International and Carlson Travel Network are twin sources of excellence in a monumentally large travel-and-tourism industry soon to top $2 trillion in annual gross output.

Holiday Inn Airport #2

The word "Airport" is attached to the end of the name of the Holiday Inn Airport #2 with good reason: Guests are shuttled between Minneapolis-St. Paul International Airport to the strategically located hotel approximately 15 minutes west on 494.

Situated at the southwest corner of Interstate 494 and Highway 100, the hotel is easily accessible to the most talked-about attraction in Bloomington—the Mall of America, just six minutes away! Holiday Inn Airport #2 is 20 minutes from downtown Minneapolis, so it attracts Twins and Viking fans alike.

The variety of customers is aided by the Holiday Inn's sophisticated international reservations network, which general manager Terry Dunlay says accounts for more than 30 percent of the business staying at a Holiday Inn in the United States.

Holiday Inn Airport #2 is a mini-vacation spot in itself. Its extraordinarily huge indoor pool is the largest in Bloomington. "It was once outdoors, but we soon discovered that an outdoor pool in Minnesota was impractical because of the brief summers and long winters," Dunlay explains. A sauna, whirlpool, and game room were added in the new area to create a relaxing atmosphere.

ABOVE: Holiday Inn's newly refurbished guest rooms offer a respite from a busy day of business or sightseeing.

TOP: Marti's Dining Room is known for its great food, especially the delicious homemade soups.

Marti's Dining Room and Coffee Shop have excellent reputations with hotel guests, nearby office workers, and residents of the surrounding communities and are known for their great food, especially the delicious homemade soups. Partners Lounge is a popular after-work getaway spot that features complimentary hors d'oeuvres. Holiday Inn Airport #2 can accommodate groups from 15 to 225 for meetings and banquets.

As a participant in the Holiday Inn Priority Club, patrons nationwide accumulate points that can be redeemed for everything from free vacation packages to quality appliances, luggage, and sports equipment. Northwest Worldperk points can also be achieved by staying at the hotel and flying Northwest Airlines.

Guests staying in the Holiday Inn Airport #2's Executive Wing enjoy a pantry that offers free continental breakfast, soft drinks, wine, hot and cold hors d'oeuvres, and several in-room amenities, including newspapers delivered to the door each morning.

The facility shows none of its 23 years, thanks to recent renovations and subsequent additions. In 1992 the hotel refurbished all guest rooms.

Minneapolis-St. Paul Airport Hilton Hotel

Cole Porter put it most eloquently when he wrote, "You'd Be So Nice To Come Home To." In those words lie the very existence of the Minneapolis-St. Paul Airport Hilton.

The hotel towers 12 stories over the lush Minnesota Valley Wildlife Refuge, set on a bluff, and just one mile from the new Mall of America—the nation's largest indoor shopping and entertainment complex.

"When you talk location, the Airport Hilton couldn't be in a better spot," notes director of sales Mark Israel. "The closest full-service hotel to the airport, around the corner from the mega-mall, and sitting in the tranquillity of the wildlife refuge, is really the best of all worlds," he says.

The Minneapolis-St. Paul Airport Hilton is located in the fashionable Bloomington area of the Twin Cities. With easy access to all major freeways, the Hilton is the closest full-service hotel to the Minneapolis-St. Paul International Airport. Yet

through 30-foot windows.

With 300 deluxe guest rooms and suites, the Hilton is truly in a class by itself. Each room features either a king or two double beds, remote-control cable television with feature movies, two computer modem-compatible telephones, and all of the bathroom amenities that go with the Hilton name. Nonsmoking and fully accessible rooms are also available. The penthouse level features continental breakfast each morning, hot and cold hors d'oeuvres and beverages each evening, as well as upgraded rooms and amenities (such as plush bathrobes), nightly turndown and snack service, and daily morning newspaper—Hilton, You'd Be So Nice To Come Home To!

There is a large, glass atrium indoor pool area, with two whirlpool spas, a redwood sauna, and complete exercise area with state-of-the-art equipment.

If quiet conversation over food and drink is your style, enjoy the relaxing Lobby Lounge or try Cafe Carabella for breakfast, lunch, or dinner. If high energy is more to your liking, the Flamingos nightclub should fit the bill; happy hour and hors d'oeuvres will give you the strength to dance the night away. And if you prefer the finer things in life, the Biscayne Bay is the place for you. This AAA Four Diamond Award-winning restaurant fea-

ABOVE: Conveniently located in Bloomington, the Hilton is just minutes from the new Mall of America.

LEFT: The Hilton's large, glass atrium pool area also contains two whirlpool spas and a redwood sauna.

despite its three-minute proximity to this major gateway, it enjoys relative tranquillity from air traffic due to restrictions placed on flight patterns by its neighbor, the Minnesota River Valley Wildlife Preserve.

Tranquillity indeed. From the moment you enter the hotel's atrium, tree-filled lobby, you are struck by the quiet flow of a two-story waterfall, and light colors all displayed in the rays of sunshine passing

tures the finest seafood, flown in daily from all three coasts and Canada, to please the most discriminating of palates. Bon appetit!

The Hilton has more than 17,000 square feet of flexible banquet and meeting space, including one of Minneapolis' only state-of-the-art audiovisual theaters, and a professional AAA Four Diamond catering and convention services staff that can make a

meeting for 5 to 2,500 the outstanding success that meeting goers have come to expect.

An interesting thing about the Hilton is its staff's commitment to the environment. They are proud to boast that they are one of the most environmentally conscious hotels in the entire country! Situated directly next to the Minnesota Valley Wildlife Refuge, the hotel conducts a comprehensive recycling program. From paper, glass, cardboard, and cans, the Hilton even recycles its food waste for animal feed.

The Hilton is also the only hotel in Minneapolis to offer "Green Rooms." The environmentally designed rooms include individual-osmosis water purifiers, shower head mineral and compound extractors, state-of-the-art in-room air purifiers, and oxygenating plant life. These rooms are offered at a modest premium. At the Airport Hilton you can not only enjoy a significantly cleaner environmental surrounding, but also enjoy the satisfaction of knowing that you are staying with a hotel that takes the extra steps to leave a cleaner world for our posterity.

Just minutes away, and easily accessible via a large network of user-friendly freeways, are downtown Minneapolis and St. Paul, the Minnesota Zoo, Canterbury Downs, Valleyfair Amusement Park, the Metrodome, and the Met Center, located next to the Mall of America.

It appears that Mr. Porter might have been describing the Minneapolis-St. Paul Airport Hilton—"So Nice To Come Home To!"

Cedars Edina Apartment Community

For more than 10 years corporate relocation directors have made Cedars Edina Apartment Community their first choice as a home away from home for employees being transferred to the Twin Cities area or sent there on temporary duty.

"We are distinguished for spacious, full-size apartments in a resortlike environment at the center of the Twin Cities metropolitan area," says Sandra Lattu, property manager of the 25-acre community.

Longtime corporate customers are legion. Among them are AT&T, Control Data, Cray Research, Honeywell, General Mills, National Car Rental, Northwest Airlines, Sperry, Toro, and the Minnesota North Stars professional hockey team.

Even the location is inspired. Only one-half block west of Edina's "main street," France Avenue South, it's but a short distance from such Twin Cities institutions as Byerly's, Southdale Mall, and the Galleria. A seven-screen movie theater is another nearby amenity.

Nearby thoroughfares permit guests to drive to Minneapolis-St. Paul International Airport (MSP) and close-by Mall of America in about 10 minutes. Downtown Minneapolis takes only 15 minutes, and there is direct bus service into the city's center.

"We're especially proud of the size, luxury, and economical cost of our large apartments," says Lattu. "One-bedroom, one-bath units are a full 800 square feet. The two-bedroom apartments, all with two baths, are a little over 1,000 square feet."

Because Cedars Edina rentals are for a minimum period of one month, the per-night cost of any apartment is well under

ABOVE: Every Cedars Edina apartment is spacious and luxuriously furnished.

TOP: The parklike grounds are well manicured and landscaped with colorful flowers and trees.

that of similar space in top area hotels. "Savings can come to one-third," she adds. "Comparables show that our prices are always the most advantageous for people on corporate stay in the Twin Cities."

All apartments are fully furnished. Fixtures include china, silver, linens (for both bedroom and bath), new GE kitchen appliances, garbage disposal, and every required cooking utensil—also comforters, pillows, and other homelike amenities.

Maid service is offered, and there is daily laundry and dry cleaning pickup and delivery at each guest's door. Late-night check-in is another convenience. Apartment parking is underground and all of the

buildings are connected by warm, subsurface walkways.

For fitness' sake, there are complete indoor recreational facilities. The exercise room is a serious one, with treadmill, stair climber, exercise bike and "lat" pull, bench press, and leg extension and leg curl machines. There is also a racquetball court and a tanning bed.

The full-size indoor swimming pool has a whirlpool and sauna. Outside are two tennis courts, a double basketball court, volleyball court, and an outdoor pool with whirlpool. For golf enthusiasts, nearby Braemar Park is home to both the all-weather Edina Golf Dome and a fine 18-hole municipal golf course.

The parklike grounds are full of pleasant surprises: well-manicured green areas with comfortable benches for conversation or reading, a reflecting pool with wooden bridge, and colorful flowers and trees to make summer complete.

Cedars Edina has several public rooms for the use of its guests. In the screening room a large color TV is linked to both community cable and videocassette player. The latest feature films are shown there every Tuesday night, accompanied by complimentary soft drinks and popcorn. Down the hall is a spacious conference room that can be used as a training center.

In the Fireplace Lounge coffee service begins at 6 a.m. every day and guests can meet or be picked up there by social and business acquaintances. A party room, available for short-term entertainment, is popular among visitors with families.

Concierge servies are wide and accommodating: Office, postage, delivery, limousine, and other transporation services are offered. Door delivery of the *Minneapolis Star-Tribune* and *The Wall Street Journal* may be arranged, and catering service is available through the office.

No detail is too small for the responsive staff and facilities at Cedars Edina, the centrally located, resortlike apartment community catering to corporate relocation and temporary residential needs in amenity-surrounded Edina, Minnesota.

CHAPTER THIRTEEN

MANUFACTURERS, HIGH-TECH, AND IMPORT/EXPORT

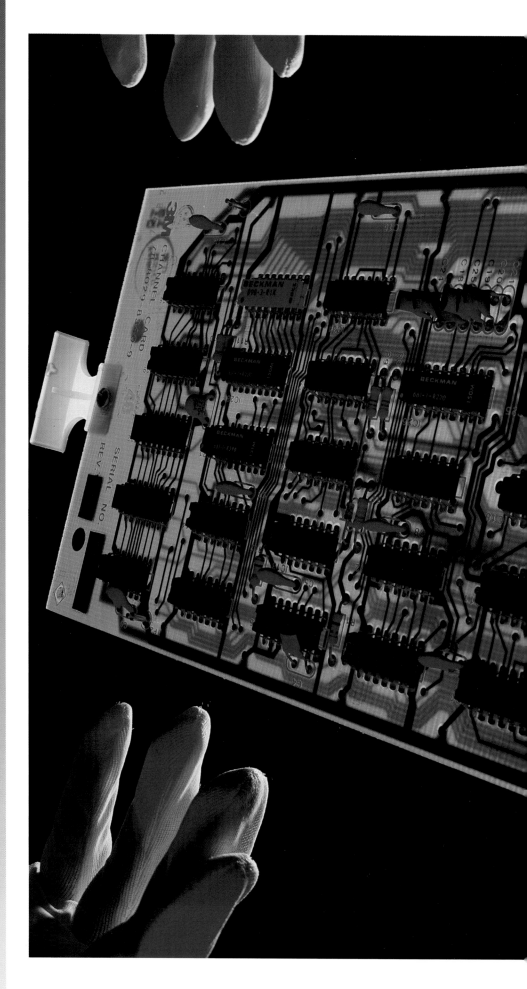

Photo by Greg Ryan/Sally Beyer

he Twin Cities' location and qualified work force draw manufacturers, high-tech industries, and import/export businesses to the region.

Diversified Dynamics Corporation, 178-179

Ceridian Corporation, 180-181

Control Data Systems, 182-183

Jostens, Inc., 184-185

Hypro Corporation, 186

Dri-Steem Humidifier Company, 187

Advantek Incorporated, 188-189

Horton Holding, Inc., 190

The Bergquist Company, 191

Dotronix, Inc., 192

Paramax, A Unisys Company, 193

Foley-Belsaw Company, 194-195

Minntech Corporation, 196

DataCard Corporation, 197

Metal-Matic, Inc., 198-199

Dresser-Rand Electric Machinery, 200

McLaughlin Gormley King Company, 201

Precision Associates, Inc., 202-203

Diversified Dynamics Corporation

In just a couple of seconds an unusual force will pare the meat cleanly from the bone in preparation for all those chicken morsels that are sold nationwide through fast-food eateries.

The unusual force is water—and the company behind that force (and a myriad of other modern-day miracles) is Diversified Dynamics Corporation of Blaine, Minnesota. Whether the task is as mundane as a do-it-yourselfer painting the living room or as sophisticated as suppressing the dust in a South African diamond mine, this organization lives up to the Hemingway definition of courage: "Grace under pressure."

Its ability to make and adapt pumping equipment for an entire range of industrial, commercial, and consumer uses is testimony to Diversified Dynamics founder William Bruggeman's corporate objective: "We are not 'selling' anything. Our whole purpose

here is to simplify the lives of people."

Diversified Dynamics pumps are wresting the salt from seawater in a portable system that supplies ample fresh water for commercial and naval vessels at sea. Cat Pump-powered reverse-osmosis systems were employed to provide much-needed water supplies to our troops and allies during Desert Storm.

The pumping equipment can provide lifesaving deicing solvents for the wings of aircraft to assure safe takeoffs during the winter months. And they can inject chemicals into the ground for fertilizing and pest control rather than surface spray to help

protect the environment. Furthermore, Diversified builds pumps that can clean runways at airports, wash jumbo jets, and blast away deteriorating concrete. Special machinery even cleans the huge parking facilities, trash bins, and grounds transport equipment serving the passengers at Minneapolis-St. Paul International Airport.

The applications are as diverse and dynamic as the firm's name. The pumps help force along the processes for making everything from margarine to catsup. Indeed, the firm cuts the meat off poultry with "water knives" and wet-sandblasts building surfaces in a process that is six times faster and much more environmentally safe than traditional sandblasting with air pressure.

Reverse-osmosis systems help remove hazardous liquids from industrial waste and homogenizers blend seemingly incompatible components such as oils and water for the manufacture of household products such as face creams and lotions.

"We are a customer service-oriented company," emphasizes Bruggeman, a mechanical engineering graduate of Hamline and the University of Minnesota. After working for other firms, Bruggeman foresaw a need for customized pump applications, but he could find no local supplier that met his own specifications.

"I had been in Japan twice, once with the Navy and once with the Marines," he recalls. "I noticed the Japanese utilizing a lot of pumps in the postwar cleanup and many ag spraying applications, and I assumed somebody there was manufacturing them."

With no hesitation and with no leads to go on, Bruggeman flew to Japan and spent two weeks there. The first few days were occupied finding a pump manufacturer (Maruyama of Tokyo). Within two weeks the Japanese entrepreneurs had created a prototype that he could take back to Minnesota with him.

The two companies have continued to work together in a successful, long-term business relationship. Bruggeman estimates he has traveled to Japan more than 60 times.

Although there are several sub-businesses within the corporation, Diversified Dynamics has two major subsidiaries and four international branches. The Power Flo Division manufactures an entire family of paint-applicating products for consumer

ABOVE: Corporate headquarters in Minneapolis is the hub for Cat Pumps design engineers, quality-control managers, sales representatives, applications specialists, and an international sales and service distributor network.

LEFT: The Original Paint Stick is twice as fast as a regular roller, and there's no messy paint tray, no more bending, and no more ladders!

BELOW: Advanced manufacturing techniques and extensive use of high-quality materials contribute to Cat Pumps' long-life performance and reputation for dependability.

giants such as Sears and Montgomery Ward. It makes sprayers and roller equipment for painting, and the high-pressure Power Klean water systems for washing cars and garden and household equipment. It also manufactures the Quick Mask product for masking surfaces prior to painting,

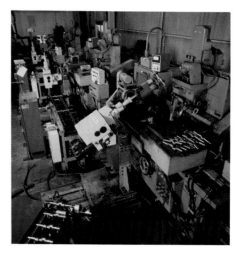

through a steel rod. This is more than a gimmick, and he cites an example: "When you are dismantling an oil refinery, you don't want to do it with a flame. High-pressure water cutting is the answer."

He explains that Cat Pumps' "water

required the worldwide availability of service kits minimizes down time.

There is more than a family of products serving the public at Diversified Dynamics. There is the Bruggeman family itself. Ruth Bruggeman works with the Consumer Prod-

LEFT: Cat Pumps makes every effort to fulfill emergency orders and service needs—even if the service requires helicoptering a technician to a site that cannot be reached quickly by any other means.

BELOW: The Power Klean blasts away dirt, removes grease, and even washes and waxes your car. It has 20 times more pressure than water from your garden hose, yet requires 75 percent less water. It's easy to use, versatile, and cleans almost everything around the house.

and a Power Flo Heat Gun and other paint-stripping equipment for professionals and do-it-yourselfers. The Original Paint Stick is a refreshingly simple device for painters using a roller or paint pad on a long handle. The paint is drawn into the sturdy, transparent handle with a plunger action. The painter gradually feeds the paint into the perforated roller head by simply pushing the handle forward periodically while rolling on the paint. It can be used for walls, ceilings, and floors, either indoors or outdoors, with virtually no mess and fast, easy cleanup.

The industrial muscle comes from the other subsidiary, Cat Pumps. There are more than 350 models of these pumps, with capacities ranging from 100 to 7,000 pounds of pressure per square inch. One of its newest innovations is the Tuff Cat Cleaning System, a versatile high-pressure water system with a whole panorama of attachments. It comes standard with adjustable vari-nozzle, safety GFCI power cord, high-pressure hose, gun, lance, chemical injector, American motor, and SF Cat Pump. (Optional accessories such as sandblaster, agitator nozzles, rotating brush, wet or dry vacuum system, drain-pipe cleaner, and wet-sandblaster expand the cleaning options.) This system can be used to clean boats, cars, small aircraft, and lawn and garden equipment, as well as floors and virtually any other building surface, interior or exterior. It can even be used for misting and humidification systems.

Bruggeman notes that intensifier attachments to the firm's pumps can produce a jet of water so powerful that it can cut

knife" technology is employed to actually cut paper and corrugated box materials with such a fine, fast bead that they do not even get wet in the process! These miracle-working technologies have a guaranteed future in terms of their safety and environmental soundness, and they have produced a new generation of quality workmanship at affordable costs.

Cat Pumps prides itself on having devoted 25 years to the design, manufacture, and application of compact, portable high-pressure triplex pumps, a commitment unique in the industry. The product line rarely needs major servicing, but when maintenance is

ucts Division, filling 90 percent of the Power Flo aftermarket orders within an astonishing eight hours upon receipt of the order.

Five Bruggeman sons of William and Ruth run the company, which celebrated its 26th anniversary in January 1993. Steve Bruggeman is president and general manager of Cat Pumps; Tom Bruggeman is president and general manager of Power Flo; William Bruggeman III is product manager of Cat Pumps; Dan Bruggeman is marketing manager of Power Flo and European outlet manager; and Jon Bruggeman is manager of the technical engineering staff that serves both divisions.

Ceridian Corporation

Ceridian Corporation is an information management and employer services company. It is among the nation's largest providers of payroll processing and human resources management services, audience measurement and market research, and financial transaction processing, as well as a preferred supplier of technology and technology-based services to defense and civil government agencies worldwide.

Ceridian's businesses bring their customers decades of experience, as well as a commitment to outstanding service, quality, and technology. Each is known in its markets for technical expertise, market knowledge, customer focus, high-quality products, and service excellence. Ceridian is also known for the expertise and dedication of its employees. The businesses of Ceridian include:

Ceridian Employer Services. As the nation's second-largest provider of employer services, Ceridian Employer Services provides business customers with high-quality, flexible payroll processing, tax filing, and human resources management services. Best known for its payroll processing (approximately one of every 40 U.S. paychecks), Ceridian offers the widest range of employer services in the industry. Ceridian Employer Services, for example, administers employee-assistance programs for approximately one million workers and their families. The organization's commitment to service excellence is backed by more than 60 years of service industry experience.

The Arbitron Company. Arbitron ranks as the world's largest syndicated audience measurement service and the second-largest market research firm. The full-service media and marketing information firm's services are used by nearly 4,000 radio and television stations, advertising agencies, and advertisers to maximize the efficiency and impact of advertising purchases and sales. Those clients benefit from Arbitron's four decades of media measurement and market research experience. Arbitron is also involved in both broadcast and print advertising expenditure tracking and monitoring through Com-

petitive Media Services, a joint venture.

Ceridian Network Services. For nearly two decades Ceridian Network Services has provided business and government customers with value-added information services based on computer and network technologies. The businesses of Ceridian Network Services include TeleMoney Services, which ranks among the nation's top providers of credit card and check authorization services; Business Information Services, which provides industry-specific computer applications and tools to address the information management needs of government, financial institutions, and corporations; and Enterprise Network Solutions, which serves the network inte-

gration and management services market. In addition, Ceridian Network Services provides services for users of CASE (computer-aided software engineering) tools.

Computing Devices International. This business is a preferred supplier of electronic systems, systems integration, and services to defense and civil government

Ceridian Corporation is an information management and employer services company. Broadcasters and advertisers use its audience-measurement services to buy and sell advertising time on television programs such as the popular *Northern Exposure,* and defense and civil government customers use its electronic systems. Ceridian helps toy stores and other employers manage their relationships with employees through services such as payroll-processing and employee-assistance programs.

agencies. Computing Devices International has a 35-year tradition of providing high-value, high-quality solutions to customer needs. Its customer base includes not only the U.S. defense and civil gov-

ernment agencies, but also major contractors at home and abroad, and government agencies from more than a dozen nations. Computing Devices International also serves NASA through Barrios Technology, a business unit that provides information systems, systems integration services, and computer applications to the space community.

Ceridian and its businesses have long been major contributors to Minnesota's reputation as a leader in the development and delivery of technology and technology-based services. The experience, expertise, and initiative that Ceridian—its businesses and its people—continues to bring to the technology-based services market will help Minnesota maintain and build upon that reputation in the future.

Control Data Systems

Towing a skid full of refrigerator-size crates, the freight tractor eases up to the cargo bay of a Northwest 747 jumbo jet. It's a bright October morning at Minneapolis-St. Paul International Airport, as another shipment of Control Data Systems computers is loaded for an overseas destination.

The airport has been a critical transportation hub for Control Data throughout its 35 years of operation in the Twin Cities. From the massive mainframes it pioneered in the 1960s to the sleek integrated desktop solutions that it sells today, Control Data ships to customers in more than 40 countries.

Today's payload is a powerful computer server bound for Bangkok, Thailand. It will anchor a new regional processing center for the government's Ministry of the Interior. A nationwide network of Control Data computers enables the ministry to maintain one of the most sophisticated population data bases in the world.

Whether the challenge is managing housing and demographic data for 22 million Thais or designing a French bullet train that goes 250 miles per hour, Control Data focuses its expertise on integrating computer solutions to business-specific problems in data base management, network communications, and maufacturing design. It assists customers in technical, government, and commercial markets worldwide.

To meet the changing needs of its customers, Control Data is shifting resources from the manufacturing and development of computer systems to the integration and application arena. Through software joint ventures with companies such as Structural Dynamics Research Corporation and Intergraph Corporation and manufacturing agreements with hardware suppliers like Silicon Graphics, Inc., and NEC Corporation, Control Data is able to acquire products and resell them as well as expand distribution channels for its own products.

"Control Data's integration strategy requires that we provide the best hardware and software available to meet our customers' needs," says Jim Ousley, Control Data president and chief executive officer. "Our third-party relationships represent a powerful force in providing open systems platforms and solutions."

Today's open systems are based on a standard operating system that accepts a broad variety of applications that can run on a wide range of computer platforms. This compatibility enables users to customize their solutions with the best technology available. Control Data brings its rich heritage of high-performance computing to the realm of open systems, offering platforms, operating systems, networking, integration, and storage-management capabilities.

Control Data Systems was established in

ABOVE: The U.S. Army Corps of Engineers employs Control Data's expertise to integrate a worldwide network of computer users.

LEFT: Minneapolis-St. Paul International Airport enables the Twin Cities-based Control Data to serve its customers around the world.

RIGHT: Control Data technology aids engineers at illustrious Lamborghini in the design and production of sports cars like the sleek Diablo Roadster.

1992 as a spin-off of Ceridian Corporation (formerly Control Data Corporation). Founded in 1957 by William Norris, CDC emerged as the premier computer company for engineering and scientific markets. Its high-performance computers were among the fastest and most powerful in the industry from that time until the 1980s. During this period, the firm diversified into other businesses, including financial services, pay-

roll processing, and broadcast ratings measurement.

In order to unlock the value of the businesses within this diversified information services corporation and enable them to grow faster, CDC reorganized and restructured. The "new" Control Data consists of CDC's Computer Products business, which has competed prominently in the international arena for more than two decades. It is focused solely on the computer marketplace. CDC's remaining information services businesses are now Ceridian Corporation.

"We have a great heritage to build on, but we have to look and move forward," Ousley says. "The new Control Data is in a much better position to penetrate new markets and excel at new technologies."

More than 3,000 employees comprise Control Data's worldwide operations, with service and support available in some 40 countries. Locally, corporate headquarters in Arden Hills and sales and service offices in Bloomington employ 900 workers. Systems analysts, engineers, and consultants install and maintain products, integrate computer systems, and assist customers in analyzing and refining application solutions.

"Our computer professionals are the living heritage of Control Data's 35 years of leadership in high-performance computing," Ousley says. "Their Brainware™ represents collected wisdom that spans the history of the computer industry." The company has trademarked the term to emphasize its unique blend of expertise and experience in solving customer problems. It is based on the assumption that the people who put the solutions together are the most important factor influencing the suc-

cess of those solutions.

More than 1,600 customers around the world employ Control Data's services. They represent a wide variety of industries from both the public and private sectors but fall into two main categories: manufacturing design and information management. In these areas, the company works with customers to integrate computing solutions that fit their unique environments.

Control Data's ICEM suite of integrated design, manufacturing, and engineering software is designed to help discrete manufacturing companies improve the quality of their products while concurrently speeding up their product life cycles.

Lamborghini, the prestigious manufac-

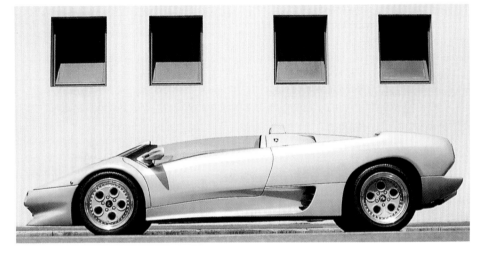

turer of high-performance sports cars and Formula One racers, uses Control Data's ICEM suite to design and produce automobiles. In fact, around 70 percent of all the design and construction of the cars is carried out on this system.

Control Data's EDL is another valuable integration tool in design engineering. Canadair, a designer and manufacturer of fire-fighting aircraft, uses EDL to manage the release process in the design and manufacture of its water bombers. EDL also aids Chrysler Technologies Airborne Systems in its engineering environment to refurbish military and civilian aircraft.

Control Data's CYBER workstations offer one of the industry's most powerful graphics and numeric-intensive computing capabilities. This technology allowed Technoforme to develop the innovative design of France's high-speed "bullet trains."

In information management, Control Data concentrates on helping customers

"re-engineer" their computing environments using data base servers and storage servers so they can take advantage of open-systems technology and client-server computing.

Data stored on CYBER high-end mainframes aid engineers at Aerospatiale in France in the design and manufacture of its Airbus passenger aircraft. These high-performance mainframes are critical for the organization, management, and recovery of large amounts of sensitive data.

At the University of Minnesota's Health Sciences Computing Services, the combination of Control Data's high-speed connection, EXPRESS Link, and the UNIX-based 4680 InfoServer enables users to analyze data files for the more than 800 health sciences projects currently residing on a CYBER mainframe.

The U.S. Army Corps of Engineers uses Control Data 4000 InfoServers, Oracle (a data base management system), and CYBER mainframes to integrate a worldwide network of 10,000 computer users and 13 hubs. Among other chores, this technology enables the Corps to monitor river traffic on the Mississippi and its tributaries.

People, products, processes, and partnerships: These are the quality building blocks that enable Control Data to manage today's complex information technology. With a culture in which individuals are self-motivated to do the job right and a corporate goal of defect-free products and services, Control Data is committed to continuous quality improvement. This commitment teamed with a leading edge of computing technology since its inception will carry the company as a forerunner of industry trends into the twenty-first century.

Jostens, Inc.

Begun almost a century ago as a small-town Minnesota watch repair shop, Jostens has grown into one of the world's largest suppliers of products and services for the education, youth, sports award, and recognition markets.

Today Jostens is a diversified *Fortune* 500 company with 46 plant and office facilities nationwide, employing more than 8,000 service-oriented people. The company prides itself on its quality products, community involvement, and concern for people.

In 1897 Otto Josten opened his jewelry and watch repair shop upstairs over the opera house in Owatonna, Minnesota. The company found a secure niche within the decade by crafting high school class rings. The pace quickened in 1922, when teacher-coach-motivator Daniel C. Gainey was hired as the first full-time ring salesperson.

In less than a year Gainey had written so many orders, nearly $20,000, that he was called back to the shop to help meet the production challenge his sales coup had prompted. It was the first of many big orders from the "master" salesman. Gainey was named Jostens board chairman and chief executive officer in 1933 as Jostens' sales rose to nearly $500,000 a year.

As the leading class ring company in the country, Jostens diversified in the 1960s by adding graduation diplomas and announcements, high school yearbooks, crested jewel-

ABOVE: Jostens proudly displays its championship sports awards at Minneapolis-St. Paul International Airport in the Lindbergh Terminal. © Doug Baartman Photography, Minneapolis

TOP: Jostens products make special events like graduation important and memorable. © Doug Baartman Photography, Minneapolis

ry, and school photography in Canada.

In 1969 the firm moved its headquarters from Owatonna to a site across from the Minneapolis-St. Paul International Airport (MSP) to facilitate transportation for the fast-growing $70-million-plus company. By now Jostens had become a dominant player in the national school market and was traded over the New York Stock Exchange.

Gainey, the charismatic architect of growth, retired in 1968, after 33 years at the helm. He was soon succeeded by H. William Lurton, Jostens' second long-term leader. Lurton began his career as a yearbook sales representative in 1955, progressing through key executive positions in the Yearbook Division to become president in 1971, chief executive officer one year later, and board chairman in 1975.

Under Lurton's leadership Jostens expanded into five divisions and broadened its mission of preserving memories and celebrating group and individual achievements. The firm has been a *Fortune* 500 company since 1985 and its fiscal year 1992 sales exceeded $900 million.

In anticipation of declining school enroll-

ment in the 1970s, Jostens expanded the company's core School Products Group and sharpened the skills of its sales force. Sales representatives were trained as counselor salespersons, expert problem-solvers in every detail of their business to provide heightened customer service—in everything from the layout of yearbooks to organizing school fund-raisers.

In addition to its position as the world's largest yearbook supplier, Jostens also produces textbooks, yearbook and school photography, desktop publishing services, plus commercial and custom printing. Wayneco, another School Products unit, specializes in the direct marketing of customized products to collegiate, alumni, and other special interest groups.

Jostens' Recognition Division, begun in 1970, helps businesses and professional sports teams celebrate peak performance with customized trophies, jewelry, watches, and other awards denoting achievements.

During its two decades, Recognition has become the preferred vendor for celebrating the achievement of an astonishing number of sports champions—crafting 19 Super Bowl rings (more than all other competitors combined); 21 NFL conference championship rings; medals for two Olympic Games, as well as U.S. Olympic Festivals and Special Olympics; also rings for World Series, Stanley Cup, and NBA champions, and the men's and women's NCAA Final Four basketball teams.

Proud of both its leadership in sports

Not only a top financial performer, Jostens has a long tradition of making qualitative internal improvements, always seeking to become a better corporate citizen for its employees, customers, and the global business community.

The firm takes pride in its commitment to diversity in the marketplace, seeking to "recruit, train, hire, promote, and retain people from various backgrounds, cultures, abilities, and disabilities," in the words of chief executive officer Lurton.

of the nonprofit Renaissance Education Foundation. Dedicated to keeping students in school by generating deeper involvement in education, it rewards classroom achievement with imaginative perks for students and teachers alike.

Chief executive officer Lurton sets the example for community involvement. He is deeply engaged in numerous national, regional, and local volunteer causes, ranging from the U.S. Chamber of Commerce, where he served as chairman from 1992 to 1993, to the Minnesota Business partnership and the Minneapolis YMCA. Every employee is strongly encouraged to show the same caring spirit. Many respond by giving gener-

awards and its home airport, the company has chosen the main retail concourse of the Lindbergh Terminal as the location of a kiosk displaying the craft and quality of its prized award items.

Another facet of Jostens' businesses, Jostens Sportswear manufactures custom-imprinted clothing with popular professional team logos, college insignias, cartoons, and other graphics for sale in upscale and discount stores, college bookstores, military exchanges, and theme parks.

The creation of Jostens Learning Corporation was another result of the firm's proactive response to declining school populations in the 1970s.

Jostens began by acquiring such high-tech firms as Prescription Learning, the Borg-Warner units of Systems 280, Hartley Courseware, and Educational Systems Corporation, which were all merged in 1989 to form Jostens Learning. In 1992 the company acquired Wicat Systems Inc., a world leader in courseware for flight simulation programs (22 of the top 30 international airlines are users, including Northwest Airlines). It was the largest acquisition in Jostens history.

Jostens is the nation's leading provider of integrated educational systems for grades K-12 (where a large percentage of U.S. schools are still without computer-based curricula), as well as for institutions such as the U.S. military, the telecommunications industry, and public utilities.

Jostens is the leading supplier of custom products for the Canadian education, business and sports markets, an achievement parallel to the company's dominant position in the United States. Jostens also has European operations with offices and sales forces in Great Britain, France, and Spain.

Similarly, its Total Quality Management (TQM) program is implemented to encourage problem-solving teamwork for the delivery of higher customer satisfaction.

An increased emphasis on strategic planning drives all of these enhancements. Such a thrust is predicated on the long-range view, helping to recognize new opportunities and avoid future obstacles.

In addition to being at the forefront of education, recognition, and rewards, Jostens proudly maintains its community leadership. The Jostens Foundation administers one of the largest external scholarship programs in the nation, contributing to college-bound students on the basis of demonstrated leadership and academic achievement.

The company also is the primary founder

ABOVE: Jostens produces many of the customized awards treasured by champion athletes throughout the world. These include Olympic medals and Super Bowl, World Series, Stanley Cup, NBA, Canadian Grey Cup, and NCAA championship rings.

TOP: A mother and father experience the impact of Jostens Learning's integrated systems on their child's development. © Doug Baartman Photography, Minneapolis

ously of their skills, dollars, and time.

Jostens has long observed strong social and corporate values. Now but a short step away from its second century, Jostens and its employees are already planning the creation of meaningful new traditions.

Hypro Corporation

Not unlike a military ally, Hypro Corporation's "Long Blue Line" of agricultural pumps has always been at the front with American farmers in their winning battle for increased crop production and a cleaner, more fertile environment.

Founded in 1947, the company enjoyed early growth based on a new nylon "roller" pump, invented by its founder, that combined moderate cost with enduring, high-volume performance in agricultural spraying applications. Hypro (the name is an acronym for high production) can look back on the lifetime manufacture of some 25 million pumps, now sold in more than 60 countries around the world.

Hypro's administrative headquarters and flagship operations are located in New Brighton, Minnesota. Its Sherwood Division, founded in 1903, is located in Detroit, Michigan. Formerly a division of Lear Siegler, Hypro is now privately owned.

As the company's chairman and president, W. Ted Dudley, points out, Hypro's internationally recognized products are segment leaders in the fields of agricultural spraying, marine engine cooling, pressure washing (for autos, farm implements, buildings, and industrial cleaning systems), and foam proportioning for the most effective fighting of fires in aviation, forestry, and large municipalities. In addition, the firm's high-pressure, low-volume plunger and piston pumps are being increasingly used in the improved preflight deicing of commercial jets, mandated by stringent new FAA regulations.

Top quality, backed up by responsive customer service, is a high priority at Hypro, where small quality-assurance "focus" teams rigorously test each new pump as it comes off the assembly line. "We take deep pride in our products," says John Goode, vice president of operations. "We build the highest possible level of quality into each item we produce. Our customers know they can count on us for the highest-quality pumps in each of our markets."

The head of the company's Agricultural Products Division, Don Jorgensen, points out that Hypro pumps have played a significant role in reshaping agriculture by enabling the use of low-rate, low-residual chemicals, helping to save both soil and water. "Today's crop chemicals are measured in ounces instead of gallons," he says. "Our ability to accurately apply those sub-

ABOVE: The firm's Detroit-based Sherwood Division is a leading manufacturer of industrial and marine pumps.

TOP: Hypro's administrative headquarters and flagship operations are located in New Brighton.

stances is now vastly improved. It's a 'win-win' proposition for both farm economics and the general environment."

The use of Hypro pumps is increasing in Eastern Europe—the former USSR, Poland, and Hungary—where wheat farms sometimes come close to U.S. and Canadian spreads in size. "But we also sell lots of products in Western Europe," says international marketing manager Deb North. "Smaller acreages there, and the wider use of high-pressure insecticide sprays, demand different kinds of pumps."

Hypro is engaged in large volumes of international trade—both as exporter and importer. "We make constant use of the air freight carriers at MSP," North says. "Fast, dependable service is vital in our competitive markets."

The company's Pressure Cleaning Products Division includes internationally manufactured items in its product offering. Bob Edlund, who heads the division, says that "Hypro, as a market-driven company, is positioning itself to take full advantage of the growing market in pressure cleaning applications.

These applications range from consumer and light industrial units to heavy-duty hot and cold water pressure cleaners, for a wide variety of cleaning and surface preparation requirements."

Recently the company demonstrated its responsiveness to end users and their market by structuring an award-winning approach to packaging. "We brought consumerism into the pump market," explains Dudley, "by spelling out everything the ultimate consumer needs to know—performance parameters, installation, and the like—right on the package, much like the data on a cereal box. This reassures the purchaser of the excellence of the product and furthers our emphasis on quality."

Hypro's Detroit-based Sherwood Division is a leading manufacturer of circulating, lubricating, and cooling pumps that fill a variety of needs in industrial and marine applications. The 90-year-old unit's rubber impeller products are used for engine cooling on marine power plants of from 20 to 750 horsepower. Sherwood's industrial pumps are of the gear, centrifugal, and turbine varieties.

Dri-Steem Humidifier Company

If ever an engineer-inventor fit the definition of entrepreneur, that person is Bernie Morton, founder and president of Dri-Steem Humidifier Company of Eden Prairie. His firm's edge is innovation. Its products are uniquely positioned to fill an essential humidity-control niche within the vast heating, ventilation, and air-conditioning (HVAC) industry.

"Our existence is due to two markets for precisely metered humidification," he explains. "One is the area of health care. The other includes a spectrum of manufacturing processes in which moisture, or the lack of it, can be counterproductive, or even downright hazardous to success."

Each sector provides about half of Dri-Steem's revenues: Hospitals seek reliable, mid-range humidity to speed the healing process and curb the growth of harmful bacteria. In the clean rooms of electronic plants, one spark of static electricity can destroy any number of costly computer components. Dri-Steem has grown as it developed solutions to these problems, becoming a rich source of new technology in the process.

A farm boy from northern Minnesota with a tour of duty in the Korean Conflict, Morton came to the Twin Cities to study engineering. He stayed to work in air con-

enhanced the absorption of steam into an air stream. This advance prevented the wetting of dust within air-conditioning systems, which created an ideal breeding ground for germs that carry Legionnaires' and other virulent diseases.

The recent proprietary Ultra-Sorb™ discovery, a design that allows steam to absorb instantaneously, led to a whole family of patents, with the result that Dri-Steem devices are increasingly being written into job specifications by HVAC contractors and architects. (Even now, the American Institute of Architects is working on a new hospital construction code heavily skewed toward higher quality of the indoor air.)

Dri-Steem prides itself on creating products to fit systems, rather than expecting engineers to design systems that fit its products. "We differ from the competition by delivering energy-saving, water-conserving, environmentally sound equipment at competitive prices," Morton says. "All of

RIGHT: Bernie Morton, founder and president of the firm.

BELOW: Dri-Steem's manufacturing facilities and corporate offices are located at 14949 Technology Drive in Eden Prairie.

requires unwavering humidity control. Even the major auto companies aren't exempt; humidity glitches can ruin whole ranks of new-car paint jobs.

The firm's 50,000-square-foot attractively modern building houses its manufacturing facilities and corporate offices. In addition, it contains a very well-equipped research and development center that includes air-handling systems, steam boilers, and various computer-monitored test-

ing and measuring devices. Morton believes that continual research that results in unending innovation is essential to ongoing success in the ever-changing HVAC industry.

Dri-Steem, which holds a "significant share" of its small but essential segment of the HVAC industry, markets its products through independent manufacturers' representatives domestically and internationally. It finds its proximity to the many air freight services at Minneapolis-St. Paul International Airport crucial in meeting

ditioning, and wound up founding the business in the family garage, at Hopkins, in the mid-1960s.

Dri-Steem was already in the vanguard of the industry when, in the 1980s, it met the challenge of Legionnaires' disease by designing a multiple-tube humidifier that

our products are customized; none comes straight off the shelf."

Dri-Steem's customer list includes many *Fortune* 500 companies. The most demanding include such pharmaceutical manufacturers as Merck & Co., Upjohn, and Glaxo. The stability of drug products

urgent customer demands. In regard to location, the strong regional work force, and the all-around quality of life, Morton hails Minnesota as an ideal place to site a business. "We probably wouldn't be as successful as we are today if we'd located anywhere other than the Twin Cities," he says.

Advantek Incorporated

Q: What do Ki-Heung, Korea; Kaohsiung, Taiwan; Penang, Malaysia; Osaka, Japan; Bangkok, Thailand; Singapore, Singapore; East Kilbride, Scotland; Nijmegen, Netherlands; Vimercate, Italy; and Frieburg, Germany, all have in common?

A: Bullish implications for the U.S. economy and its balance of payments, via their trade with a Minnetonka firm that's become an essential supplier to the worldwide electronic assembly industry.

Until 1985 the assembly of circuit boards for computers and other high-tech hardware seemingly owed more to the buggy whip days than the exploding electronic era and all of its marvels. Called "through-hole" assembly for obvious reasons, the existing technology involved the insertion of the leads of components through the holes of perforated circuit boards, which were then soldered on the back side—hardly an elegant process 150 years after Edison.

But then came a system that brought precision mass production to the assembly of ever-smaller electronic devices. The advance can be credited in no small part to the key participation of Advantek Incorporated, a 15-year-old Minnesota-bred corporation that has gained a dominant share of the surface-mount component packaging materials market. It's a total systems approach, including proprietary materials, pioneered by a devoted group of employees.

"What our product does," says chief

Advantek's new 93,000-square-foot building in Minnetonka.

executive officer Jim May, "is deliver surface-mountable semiconductors and other components to the circuit board assembly line in a unique packaging medium." The surface-mounting technology provides unerring high-speed robotic pickup and mounting on now-solid circuit boards imprinted with solder pathways. The approach permits simultaneous delivery of multiple components to a single PCB (printed circuit board), a tremendous cost and labor saver that provides more reliable electronics at significantly lower prices for consumers.

For Advantek sales manager Tim Cowen, what May's company did was to implement the classic example of the razor and its blades: "The high-utilization blade is our surface-mount tape, die-formed to the specifications of each component carried. The razor is our line of machines used to package customers' components and deliver them in tape to the point of circuit board assembly."

Advantek customers include the who's who of worldwide high-tech electronic manufacturing—IBM, Motorola, Intel, National Semiconductor, Philips, Siemens, Texas Instruments—plus many offshore buyers. Competitors include 3M Company and the Japanese giant, Sumimoto. "But we're the only company that manufactures *all* of our products in the United States, right here in Minnetonka, in our brand-

new 93,000-square-foot headquarters," says Cowen.

How Advantek came to this prominent position is an instructive story in itself. Jim May is a native Twin Citian who was employed by a local firm for some 15 years, working with representative organizations all over the world. May decided to strike out for himself, in 1978, handling a line of test equipment from Japan.

"I started with some good products," he recalls, "and some even better relationships, many going back 15 years. My old friends were very supportive."

Next, May was off and selling, contacting every potential customer in the United States. "It was an amazing response," he says. "I'm sure that I received orders because my contacts wanted me to succeed. Particularly in the Pacific Rim countries, most things are done on trust, which is more important than contractual relationships."

Advantek's global leadership in the specialty of embossed carrier tape and equipment is reflected in the company's rapid growth. Today's employee roll, worldwide, is pushing 200, compared to fewer than 25 in 1985. As indicated by the lead-in to this story, it has a strong presence in Europe as well as Asia. The most visible sign of Advantek's success is its handsome new headquarters building near the intersection of highways 62 and I-694.

Privately held, the firm chooses not to disclose performance figures. Sources who know say that perhaps 70 percent of Advantek sales are overseas, the majority in the Far East. All of its activities contribute to the nation's gross domestic product and the economic well-being of the Upper Midwest. Advantek has offices in Japan, Germany, Singapore, and Taiwan.

If its proprietary forming machines and tapes are the building blocks of Advantek, the mortar that makes it a seamless whole is, according to May, quality people and outstanding service. Advantek history is replete with examples:

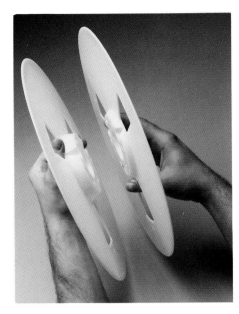

■ Intel, one of the largest factors in computers, recently called regarding a supplier it desired to have establish a distribution center in Southeast Asia. However, Intel was leery about the firm's paucity of experience there. Can we have them contact you at Advantek, so you can teach them how to operate there? "Of course we did," says May. "We always strive to help our loyal customers."

■ IBM Japan called Mr. Fujita, Advantek's managing director there, saying that it needed a special tape, available only from Advantek in the Twin Cities, the very next day. The company immediately had Northwest Airlines fly the product

counter-to-counter to Honolulu, where Fujita-san, who'd flown down from Osaka, picked up the consignment and hand-delivered it to IBM squarely on time.

To May and company, Minneapolis-St. Paul International Airport and NWA are absolutely essential to Advantek's leading global position. But it's not always easy doing business here, according to May, due to Minnesota's tax and corporate governance policies. "It's tough, expensive, and sometimes troublesome," he says, adding that the firm is frequently courted to move to the four states adjacent, even locations in the Deep South. Why then does it stay here? "Primarily because of the people, our saving grace. It's simply the very best work force we know."

In the area of international relations, a business friendship recently led to a peak experience for May. In 1991 Advantek provided financial help for five Britons—led by D.K. (Kim) Hempleman-Adams, the son of

ABOVE: Advantek's patented two-piece packaging reel is produced in Minnesota and shipped worldwide.

TOP LEFT: Lokreels® are easily snapped together with a simple twist. They are packed stacked and offer enormous savings in shipping costs and storage space.

BELOW: Advantek's embossed carrier tape and cover tape for surface-mount component packaging has become a standard product used by the world's major electronic component manufacturing companies.

a longtime business associate—who became the first adventurers to reach the Geomagnetic North Pole on foot. (May flew to the pole to photograph the ceremony.) One of the party, a Royal Air Force pilot who flew helicopters in Operation Desert Shield, later presented May with the swagger stick of an Iraqi general. May's representative, his daughter, also attended a small picnic Queen Elizabeth II held for the team, and talked with British Prime Minister John Major.

At home in Buckingham Palace or the ultracompetitive international circuit board marketplace, the Advantek team makes continuing contributions to Minnesota's industrial and political economy and renders a vital service in keeping the United States in the vanguard of the global electronic assembly enterprise. Advantek salutes the Metropolitan Airports Commission on its 50th anniversary and achievement in maintaining a world-class airport at MSP.

Horton Holding, Inc.

The many interests of Hugh K. Schilling—public and private, civilian and military—all seem to coalesce around aviation: first as a young aerial gunner in the U.S. Army Air Corps during World War II, then as a leading industrialist early to recognize the advantages of corporate aircraft, today as chairman of the Metropolitan Airports Commission, the administrative agency that oversees Minneapolis-St. Paul International Airport and its extensive system of six reliever airports.

In the public arena, Schilling is a past chairman of the Aviation Committee of the Greater Minneapolis Chamber of Commerce. He also represented the chamber on the pathfinding Metropolitan Aircraft Sound Abatement Council (MASAC) and served as a member of the Minnesota Advisory Council on Metropolitan Airport Planning.

In his private persona, Schilling is president of Horton Holding, Inc., of Minneapolis, a diversified, eight-division company based on a small enterprise he co-founded more than 40 years ago, not long after finishing college after his discharge from the Air Corps.

"We're in the stopping and starting business," he says, explaining that Horton Manufacturing, one of two major entities, is a maker of industrial drive components, clutches, and related devices for the control of in-plant heavy machinery. Use of the product line is international, with sales and licensing agencies in the United States, along the Pacific Rim, and all of Western Europe.

A second, outgrowth company is Horton Industries. Its major product is a bet-

ter-known proprietary item. Called the "Fan Clutch," it was designed as a fuel- and noise-saving accessory for big, "Class-8" over-the-road trucks. Temperature-sensed, it declutches the radiator fan, required only part of the time by the big rigs. Thus it makes possible fuel savings of up to 10 percent (a major overhead item in trucking), and reduces wear and tear on human ears. "After combustion and tires, engine fans are the biggest noise-makers on large trucks," explains Schilling. "So we do our part for the aural environment." Fan

clutches are sold directly to engine and truck manufacturers, or for separate retrofitting.

Horton employs some 400 workers at its several worldwide locations. Clutch plants are located in the Twin Cities, western Wisconsin, near Detroit, and in Britton, South Dakota. Closely held, it does not release financial figures. However, Schilling concedes that the firm is a "dominant manufacturer" in its primary field.

With its far-flung locations in the

region, Horton has long found it cost effective to maintain and fly its own corporate aircraft. "We've kept our two planes at St. Paul Downtown Airport for years and years," says Schilling, "long before anyone else. We were the first to put up facilities on the new, west side of the field. I just don't know why more corporate customers don't opt for Holman. It's a terrific facility, and ease of access is its secret."

Schilling acknowledges that Horton's salutary experiences with a corporate fleet led to his becoming a leading advocate of aviation in the region, and a practical activist in charting a smooth future course for that mode of transportation, insofar as

ABOVE LEFT: Horton Manufacturing makes industrial drive components, clutches, and related devices for the control of in-plant heavy machinery.

BELOW: Horton Industries' major product is the "Fan Clutch," a fuel- and noise-saving accessory for big rigs.

economic conditions allow.

"A good airport is a tremendous economic driver of the community to which it is attached, regardless, almost, of its size. We at Horton will not locate a plant close to a city without an airport," he says, citing the small community of Britton, South Dakota (population 1,590), as an example.

Similarly, Schilling is committed to the public quest for better air transportation to guarantee the growth of the region and its economy.

The Bergquist Company

Meet Carl R. Bergquist II, the very person who made it possible for automobile manufacturers to squeeze more and more of those complex little components under the hood of your new car.

What's that you say? You'd appreciate a little less crowding and a lot more space inside there? Then let Bergquist, a respected inventor and founder of companies, explain himself:

"Smaller cars are ordained in the interest of fuel economy," he says, "meaning the utilization of every scrap of space. Our contribution has been to downsize such things as electric ignitions and alternators, via our heat-defeating insulators that permit the use of much smaller, high-power components than were even dreamed of before."

His Bergquist Company is now known the world over as a manufacturer and distributor of heat-beating electronic devices, notably two proprietary ones: Thermal Clad™ thermal management substrates, and Sil-Pad™ thermally conductive insulators. They have earned the firm sole-source supplier status with some of the world's foremost electronic companies.

"We're fortunate enough to have a very high market share in this niche we created," says the modest president and chief executive officer. A business major turned manufacturer's representative who started his own firm 25 years ago, Bergquist says: "I was smart enough to hire some very fine chemists who managed to 'beat the heat' generated by high-performance semiconductors confined in very tight places. Without our advancements in chemistry, many of those components would literally self-destruct."

The feat did not go unrewarded. Annual sales at the closely held Bergquist Company are $37 million. The firm employs 255 people at its 26,000-square-foot headquarters and production plant in Edina, plus other domestic facilities in Bloomington and Cannon Falls, Minnesota, and Fort Jones, California, and a new European headquarters in Hamburg, Germany.

Carl R. Bergquist II, president and chief executive officer of The Bergquist Company.

Bergquist has also built a new facility in Big Fork, Minnesota. The company has sales representatives in the Far East, Australia, Israel, and Canada.

In addition to thermal materials, Bergquist also makes membrane switches. One of these high-tech devices played a life-saving role when an employee's family was rocked by a near-fatal motorcycle accident in 1992. For 14 days human resources manager Bonnie Lyles sat at an intensive-care bedside watching her son while a Bergquist "Smart Switch" was working to keep him alive. It was programmed to respond to changing data in predetermined ways: a meticulous control of everything from IV infusions, including four different antibiotics, to a special bed cooler adapted to fight a raging fever in her injured son, Jeff, 20.

Later, a thankful Bonnie Lyles wrote the medical equipment firm that employed her company's switch: "You sit for hours watching it all, hoping beyond hope that no one makes a mistake or a piece of equipment fails. You reflect at length on your colleagues and are thankful they are dedicated to producing the finest-quality

switches money can buy."

Carl Bergquist tells of a corporate policy that financially supports an anonymous employee contributions program to benefit the less fortunate, a nondenominational program based upon Judeo-Christian ethics. "It's the loaves and fishes sort of thing," he says, "devoted to community betterment by uplifting neighbors who have less than we."

The company also met a burgeoning illegal drug problem at one of its plants by moving in with its own private investigators to expose the pushers, then offering victimized employees their jobs back after they had successfully completed courses aimed at eliminating drug abuse.

"It is our commitment that we will never again allow any employee to be exposed to the hazards of illegal drugs, insofar as we are able," says Bergquist, pointing to a stylized "No Drugs Here" sign that is the first thing to greet drivers entering the headquarters parking lot.

Dotronix, Inc.

"We make lots of dots," says Dotronix's Bill Sadler. "Dots vital to displays on medical imaging systems, to high-tech industrial processes, and absolutely essential to the airlines and their passengers—who must get to the correct gates before their planes leave."

Dotronix also bears the American flag in feverish international electronics competition. The firm is the only significant U.S. manufacturer of those ubiquitous flight information displays (FIDs) found in airports around the world.

"We're always head to head with giants like Sony and NEC," he explains. "I'm proud that the airport at Seoul, Tokyo's branch of the Bank of America, and the railroad station in Taipei all use our imaging equipment. Each is in a so-called 'homeland' of low-cost TV monitors. We must be doing something right."

At home, Dotronix has been a major

TOP: Dotronix's 10-inch 9V high-resolution C2400 color display used for industrial applications.

RIGHT: The firm's DSV flight information display is used in airports worldwide to provide airline gate information.

BELOW: An actual application using the C2400 display in a flight-control system. The C2400 is mounted in the lower console.

player in flight information and derivative large-screen color displays. Its FIDs are a fixture at most major U.S. terminals, including Minneapolis-St. Paul International Airport (MSP), one of its initial customers. A parallel relationship still exists

with Northwest Airlines.

Sadler tells of complaining to former NWA chief Donald Nyrop that the main trouble with his Dotronix displays was that "they last too darn long. I'd like to sell you more!" (Nyrop, an executive of the old school, smiled thinly.) Some of those monitors still glow with flight information after a quarter-century, the only maintenance an occasional worn picture tube.

Lately, Dotronix was pleased when American Airlines called from Miami International Airport to say that rain from Hurricane Andrew had collapsed a concourse ceiling, sending tons of debris down onto the vendor's FID system. "But not to worry," said the Floridians. "We just dried it out, turned it on, and everything worked perfectly."

Sadler is a born inventor-entrepreneur: After studying college engineering throughout high school, he graduated into World War II, serving as a young Coast Guard communications officer in 32 convoys on the perilous North Atlantic, including deadly runs to the USSR port of Murmansk. With the peace, he put San Francisco's first TV station on the air, in 1947, as an amateur hobbyist whose total outlay for war surplus equipment was $400.

That feat led to jobs at the Bay City's KPIX and KRON commercial TV stations, and, later, as chief engineer for Stanley E. Hubbard's video empire, particularly KSTP-

TV in the Twin Cities. (Sadler's engineering permitted the station to carry the December 10, 1953, edition of *Dragnet* in glowing color, a full decade ahead of competing stations.) While there he founded as a sideline Miratel Corporation, a maker of industrial cathode ray tube displays (CRT) and closed-circuit television systems (CCTV).

Miratel was the first company to supply solid-state displays to "Complex 39," the Moon-Launch project, and NASA's Manned Space Flight Center. Even Gary Francis Power's ill-fated U2 carried a Miratel viewfinder for its high-resolution camera when it

was shot down in 1960 over the USSR.

Today successor Dotronix is a publicly held, $22-million firm (its NASDAQ symbol is "DOTX") with more than 260 full- and part-time employees in manufacturing plants at New Brighton, Minnesota, and Eau Claire, Wisconsin.

President and treasurer Sadler emphasizes his company's commitment to transportation and the "home" airport, MSP. "As business people we use it all the time," he says. "As suppliers we are proud of our long association with the Metropolitan Airports Commission and its airline tenants here. We trace our progress with theirs in the growth of commercial aviation in the United States."

Looking ahead, he sees strong demand for information display: In medicine, with super-sensitive diagnostic equipment; in "video-walls" (Dotronix has supplied several at the local Mall of America) and similar spectaculars, made by the firm's multimedia product line; and widening niches for high-resolution displays.

"Give us an electrical signal and we'll turn it into a recognizable image," says Sadler. "That's our commitment and capability. We can be sure the next 25 years will be much more dramatic than the last."

Paramax, A Unisys Company

The 50th anniversary of the Metropolitan Airports Commission (MAC) is of special significance in the annals of aviation electronics.

Because 1993 also marks current quantum improvements to Minneapolis-St. Paul International Airport's basic flight safety system, the occasion recalls a legendary Minnesota computer company synonymous with aircraft safety: first as inventor of automated air traffic control (ATC) for the Federal Aviation Administration (FAA) in the era following World War II; then as developer of MSP's first computerized terminal control system, installed in 1973; and now as architect of the 1993 updated version.

The contemporary firm is Paramax of suburban Eagan, Minnesota, a Unisys Company that traces its roots back to the

computer, light years ahead of all others in reliability, the Model 1011 gave Paramax a lead it has never relinquished in the design and installation of automated terminal air traffic control systems around the world.

Paramax has been the pathfinder, ever since the FAA took its first inevitable steps to computerize the skies in 1956. That year, a Univac File Computer went on line in five U.S. airport locations, processing and expediting flight information to keep safe the intervals among aircraft.

The firm took part in the first Automated Radar Terminal System (ARTS) in

The firm also produced 128 ARTS IIA systems for the nation's low- to medium-density airports, making Paramax the major supplier of terminal automation systems. Paramax provides more than 500 Digital Bright Radar Indicator Tower Equipment (DBRITE) displays for all FAA towers and many DOD control centers, as well as the Mode Select (Mode S) monopulse secondary surveillance radar system, which is being installed at MSP in 1993.

Dr. William Marberg, vice president of air traffic control for Paramax, says that Mode S offers great safety implications for the future: "Mode S provides more accurate data on the location of aircraft in and around major airports. It also provides an air-ground data link that can be used to reduce controller work load. Mode S is compatible with the current secondary radar system to provide an extra safety margin."

He also sees the extension of Mode S to the automation of airport ground control: for collision avoidance on visibility-reduced runways and for accelerating surface traffic back and forth from gates to active runways. The result will be advanced flight safety and reduced costly consumption of jet fuel by aircraft delayed in becoming airborne.

Paramax headquarters in Eagan, Minnesota.

Twin Cities of 1946. Its various names over the years have been Engineering Research Associates (ERA), then Remington Rand Univac, Univac, Sperry, Unisys Defense Systems, and today Paramax.

Founded in a drafty World War II plywood glider plant in St. Paul's Midway district, ERA was the center of Minnesota's electronics industry (an original hotbed of the technology), where Sperry's famous Model 1011 was conceived.

As the world's first commercially produced, general-purpose electronic digital

Atlanta in 1965. The FAA awarded Univac a contract for the design and manufacture of the 1963 prototype, which upon its completion two years later charted new directions in the modernization of terminal air traffic control.

From that system, designated ARTS I, the company developed and installed ARTS III systems at 64 U.S. airports, one of them MSP. Designed to reduce aircraft holding time, optimize the use of available airspace, and increase the capacity of terminal airspace, ARTS III epitomizes the FAA's mission of maintaining the world's safest skies.

Still another step into the future may be "heads up" displays in FAA control towers, similar to the see-through viewers that permit "Top Gun" pilots to watch the skies while simultaneously receiving a steady input of graphic information.

There is little that seems beyond the ever-quickening progress of flight safety—an area in which Paramax, the most venerable pioneer, remains the leading innovator.

Foley-Belsaw Company

Founded 65 years ago by an entrepreneurial "Johnny Appleseed" who traveled the Upper Midwest planting the ideal of personal enterprise, the Foley-Belsaw Company has never forgotten its core competence, nor family ideals, in forging a strong national position as a medium-size group of fascinating niche businesses.

The name, Foley-Belsaw, offers a clue. Remember the marvelously versatile Foley Food Mill? More than 50 years ahead of the juicing-mincing-dicing devices now occupying endless infomercial-minutes on TV, it represents one taproot of the firm. The other lead is more oblique, but has to do with wood—the cutting, shaping, and saw-sharpening requirements thereof.

Put it all together and it spells out a closely held family enterprise employing some 400 "associates" in places as diverse as northeast Minneapolis, western Wisconsin, mid-Missouri, Upstate New York, and Michigan's forest-covered Upper Peninsula.

In downtown Minneapolis, chairman Walter Ringer, Jr., assisted by sons and vice chairmen John Ringer and Walter (Joe) Ringer III, oversees the business begun in 1926 by the late patriarch, Walter Marden Ringer, as Foley Saw and Tool Co. The elder Ringer, always looking for a better

way, made the move after wide experience in marketing, then inventing Wheaties and establishing the package cereal division for Washburn Crosby Co., precursor of today's General Mills.

"Dad had this vision of making new sales for Foley, over and in addition to its housewares, by creating a whole new business," says Walter Ringer, Jr. "We might safely say that he pioneered the 'income opportunity' segment." Implementation was swift, ads being placed in *Popular Mechanics* magazine (an arrangement still in effect), small but powerful "Saw Filing Pays" displays offering the prospect of a profitable small business via the purchase of a Foley saw filter and setter.

The home study-implementing hardware concept later was expanded to include locksmithing, small engine repair, VCR repair, computer repair, even upholstering. Surprisingly, the idea has not withered in our modern "disposable" culture, wherein it's often easier to throw something than to seek out marginal repairs. That and the economy have produced an army of recruits from among retirees (and the early retired) plus generations of the craft-oriented who seek out the tools and techniques to produce things of beauty and enduring value.

"At one time we reckon we had up to

ABOVE: Foley-Belsaw tool maintenance equipment.

LEFT: Company founder Walter M. Ringer, Sr., at 100 years, wearing a Foley-Belsaw hat and holding a Twins baseball.

TOP RIGHT: A Foley-PLP product display.

BOTTOM RIGHT: A Foley-Martens product display.

60,000 alumni and follow-up customers. That number probably hasn't dwindled much because those sole proprietorships are often passed down within the family," says John Ringer. Also notable is that such an enterprise is not only recession-proof, but might actually be driven by crunch times like the present, when people seek new or extra sources of income.

The same is true for the Foley line of housewares. Founder Ringer best described it in his remarkable as-told-to autobiography, *Keeping Everlastingly At It Brings Success*, as an assortment of "juicers, drainers, strainers, shredders, graters, slicers, choppers, sharpeners, and other kitchen aids." They and the famous Foley food mill were the recipient of a coveted government "E for Excellence" for their contribution to the World War II effort—and were income savers during the Great Depression, when almost all were forced to cook from scratch. History has repeated itself, to a small degree, and again there is little stint in the demand for similar products.

Today's Foley-Belsaw breaks out into the following enterprises:

■ The home-study dimension, marketed by Foley-Belsaw Institute of Kansas City since 1967, founded in 1926, the same year as Foley Manufacturing.

■ Foley-United of River Falls, Wisconsin, manufacturer of grinding equipment and other tool maintenance equipment originally developed by Foley Manufacturing.

■ Foley-Martens of Kingsford, Michigan, a housewares concern making cutting boards and chopping blocks from the finely grained hardwoods of the Upper Peninsula.

■ Foley-PLP of Rochester, New York, whose lawn-mower blades, replacement parts, and small-engine repair kits serve a burgeoning national do-it-yourself business.

General Mills, long before starting Foley. He was among the first frequent flyers with Northwest Airways, as the carrier was known when it began scheduled passenger service at MSP in mid-1927. It's almost certain he was flown by NWA chief pilot and aviation legend Charles "Speed" Holman on the original Chicago route, in a three-place Stinson Detroiter at a one-way fare of $40.

"All of us travel nearly as much now," says John Ringer, "and to this day my father sends holiday gifts to some of the veteran skycaps at Lindbergh Terminal."

Keeping abreast of sensitive markets and remaining customer-driven in the widest sense are other aspects of the firm's operating philosophy. "But we are also very sensitive to the numbers," adds Joe Ringer. "We've sought out top professional managers to make sure we perform up to expectations and maintain the growth of the businesses."

Looking ahead, the company admits to looking for new niche markets in accordance with the proven Foley-Belsaw approach of breeding success all around. As the Ringers explain: New customers gain confidence via hands-on practice with Foley materials according to the thorough learn-at-home material provided. Soon they are gaining new income, purchasing more materials, and profiting further from the marketing support provided by the source company.

Company founder Walter M. Ringer died in 1987, at the age of 100-plus, shortly after the last out, as his beloved Minnesota Twins won their first World Series Championship. In addition to his leadership of industry and community, he will be long remembered for his service to the cause of education in the Upper Midwest and as a volunteer member of several governmental commissions appointed by the President of the United States.

"When you call Foley-Belsaw at its family headquarters, it's likely that a Ringer will pick up the phone," says vice chairman John, explaining how the company has grown both by expanding its historic businesses and successfully entering new but related fields.

"All three generations have been inveterate travelers," he adds. "We are 'touchy feely' in regard not only to our business

customers but the end-users who have gotten to know and trust us down through the years." Reams of correspondence received by Foley-Belsaw proudly relate tales of long-successful family businesses begun by fathers or grandfathers who learned from Foley.

Patriarch Walter M. began traveling tradition in the best "Yankee drummer" tradition as a young sales rep for Swift and

Minntech Corporation

Minntech Corporation is one of those quintessential Minnesota medical companies that sprang from the vision of one person, pulling itself up by the bootstraps (starting in a warehouse in this case) to emerge as a vital force in the health care industry.

It has prospered by realizing its founder's extraordinary flair for invention within a high-value-added market. Driven by the goal of becoming the low-cost producer of top-quality products through integrated manufacturing, it has also acquired an expertise in selling in domestic and overseas markets.

Take care of those things, it seems, and performance takes care of itself.

"Analysts expect us to have sales of $43 or $44 million in 1993," says executive vice president and treasurer Bob Rosner. "Net earnings should exceed $4.5 million. That would be an increase of 20 percent over 1992."

Minntech products are world leaders among the precision devices essential in open-heart surgery and the dialysis treatment of individuals with kidney failure, both growing segments of health care. All have come from an unmatched technological mix of electronics, chemicals, plastics, and exotic fibers. So many of its products are proprietary that Minntech recently added a full-time patent attorney to the staff.

Minntech was founded in 1974, when Dr. Louis Cosentino—chairman, chief executive officer, and president of the firm—left his job as head of advanced R&D at Medtronic, Inc., the world's leading manufacturer of cardiac pacemakers, to build better artificial kidney products. He called his enterprise Renal Systems, Inc., and set up business in an old Minneapolis warehouse.

Cosentino was a perfect neo-Renaissance person for the job. A Ph.D. in bioengineering with heavy job experience at Hoffman-La Roche, he's a Brooklyn, New York, native who learned how to fix almost anything at an early age. "I learned common sense from my father," he recalls. "We always looked for ways to make things simpler."

Renal Systems outlasted the 1974 recession while inventing whole new technologies, precursors to the company's innovative line of dialysis products. One was a blood access device: Implanted under a kidney patient's skin, it permitted dialysis sans the large needles that damaged tissues.

Minntech has grown almost from the start, as its innovative products broke new

ABOVE: Minntech is one of the world's largest manufacturers of oxygenators used during open-heart surgery.

RIGHT: Minntech's sophisticated manufacturing facility produces hemodialysis concentrate for treating patients with kidney failure.

ground and mature ones gained market share. Rosner also credits Cosentino's confident mindset—"Never be afraid of technology or manufacturing"—for the company's profitable growth via vertical integration.

"We have our own injection molding and extrusion departments," Rosner says. "Both work three shifts, five days a week. We can go from raw resin material to finished products under one roof, speeding new products to the market. An outstanding example is our revolutionary new membrane blood oxygenator. We believe we are *the* low-cost producer in the field, thanks to integrated manufacturing."

Minntech's growth is reflected in its heightened presence in Europe. A new headquarters and technical service center near Frankfurt, Germany, will serve as home base for the company's own sales people, replacing former sales representatives.

The culture at Minntech, which employs some 300 people in headquarters and manu-

facturing facilities in the Minneapolis suburb of Plymouth, embraces several incentive plans not always available at times of economic slowdown. A stock option plan encourages the purchase of company stock at 15 percent off the market price, while a new profit-sharing plan has made disbursements equal to 4 percent of each person's compensation during each of the past two years.

Minntech has a strong vested interest in Minneapolis-St. Paul International Airport. Explains Rosner, "With visitors coming from all over the world, we couldn't be located in a better community." Other geographical pluses are proximity to the Medical School and Hospital and the Institute of Technology of the University of Minnesota, a major "market infrastructure" of many medical devices companies, plus a ready work force of educated, highly trained people.

DataCard Corporation

Plastic cards have reshaped the way we live. Today Americans carry more than one billion credit cards—issued by an assortment of financial institutions, retailers, and petroleum companies—and use them to buy gas and groceries, make hotel reservations, secure cash advances, and conduct countless other financial transactions.

These six-gram pieces of plastic are a cornerstone of business in every part of the world. Yet, for all the fame and popularity of plastic cards, the company behind them is relatively unknown to the people who use them.

That company is called DataCard Corporation. And while cardholders may not be familiar with this privately held, Twin Cities-based company, major card issuers around the world are well aware of DataCard's leadership and success in the credit card business.

DataCard helped pioneer the financial card market in 1969, when it developed the world's first fully automated card personalization systems for American Express, Sears, Bank of America, and other fledgling card issuers. Today DataCard employs nearly 3,000 people and is responsible, in one way or another, for a majority of the world's credit cards—including the ones in your purse or wallet.

Some companies purchase card person-

alization equipment from DataCard and issue cards on their own. Others rely on the firm's service bureaus to handle card issuance for them. But no matter how it's done or where it's done, if a credit card is issued, DataCard is usually involved.

In fact, for nearly 25 years, card issuers in the financial, retail, and petroleum industries have recognized DataCard as the world leader in plastic card equipment, products, and services.

This reputation—along with a commitment to total quality and complete customer satisfaction—has earned DataCard

its leadership position in the credit card industry.

But financial transaction cards only account for part of DataCard's $300 million in annual revenues. Today's plastic cards— with new features such as full-color photos, built-in computer chips, bar codes, and magnetic stripes—have become a powerful platform for a variety of business applications.

Airlines, car rental companies, and other businesses use plastic cards to track participation in frequency marketing programs. Amusement parks, casinos, and other entertainment organizations count on cards to attract and retain customers. Direct marketers rely on the plastic card to add value and increase response to their solicitations.

Hospitals use them to identify patients and track charges. Colleges and universities have taken advantage of photo capabilities for student ID applications. Health insurance companies rely on plastic cards to promote and administer their programs. Fitness clubs and associations use them to identify members.

The list goes on and on. And in each case, you're likely to find a DataCard system hard at work. It's been that way since 1969.

DataCard also manufactures products used to capture card-based transactions. When a merchant swipes your credit card through a terminal or inserts it in an imprinter, there's a good chance that piece of equipment will have a DataCard logo on it. Plus, the company manufactures nearly 500 million plastic cards each year in its worldwide production facilities.

This quarter-century of success has made DataCard an international power and one of the top high-tech companies in the Twin Cities area. With plastic cards becoming more central to our way of life and more prominent in our daily activities, it appears the next 25 years will bring even more opportunity—and perhaps less anonymity—to the quietly successful company called DataCard.

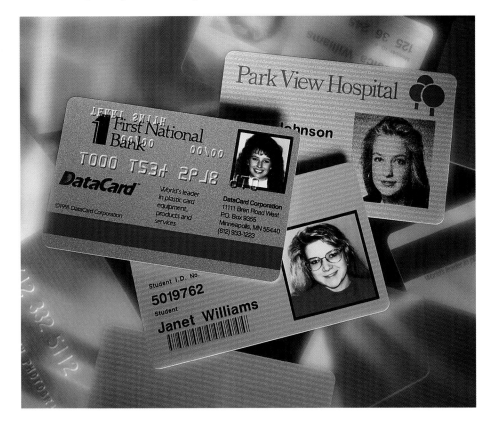

TOP: The firm manufactures nearly 500 million plastic cards each year in its worldwide production facilities.

LEFT: DataCard provides a wide range of photo ID card solutions for business and government.

Metal-Matic, Inc.

Snuggled down beside the Mississippi River in old St. Anthony, where Minneapolis was born, Metal-Matic, Inc., while contemplating a major expansion, continues to build a better mousetrap in the manufacture of top-quality steel tubing.

Without its unglamorous but essential product, cars would not run as well, homes would be far less homey, and Minneapolis-St. Paul International Airport (MSP) would undoubtedly be a facility without all of its present bustle.

"We are bullish about our position because we produce the best-quality electric welded and cold-drawn tubing that can be purchased anywhere in the world," says family-owned Metal-Matic president and chief executive officer, Gerald J. Bliss.

The company has fared well in the global economy, meeting or beating competition from far-away places such as Japan, Germany, Italy, and other countries. However, Bliss is less sanguine about adding significant manufacturing capacity in Minnesota.

Metal-Matic's main plant is located under Minneapolis' 10th Avenue Bridge. Another is nearby and a third plant is in North Minneapolis. All have long operated for three shifts a day. But having exhausted its own land and finding acceptable vacant property hard to find elsewhere in Min-

neapolis, the firm is currently seeking plant sites in other states. An Illinois plant site, for example, would put Metal-Matic closer to steel sources, which could result in a major savings.

It is a complex decision, tugging at Metal-Matic from opposite directions. "Make no mistake," says Bliss, "our Minnesota work force is simply the best there is. Many of our 425 people have worked for no other employer. Some have been here for the full 43 years of our existence."

Countervailing forces, however, are strong: a desire to be nearer to major customers, many in the Great Lakes and parts of the country to the east and south. There is an obvious economic advantage in moving closer to the greater Chicago area.

Bliss also hesitantly acknowledges tempting offers from several nearby states. All have displayed aggressive industrial development attitudes and, seemingly, less animus against an expansion-minded existing industry than manifested by certain departments of Minnesota government.

Metal-Matic was begun in Minneapolis in 1951 as an offshoot of Acro Metal Products, which had been sold a year earlier by Jerome Bliss, the founder of both firms. Bliss, who brought many key employees

from Acro to the new company, was a Minnesota inventor with a flair for products requiring tight, exacting tolerances. Early activity included model shop work for Honeywell and the making of tools, dies, and jigs.

Founded as a research and development company, Metal-Matic in 1954 became involved in the design and development of

RIGHT: An aerial view of the Metal-Matic Minneapolis headquarters.

ABOVE RIGHT: Metal-Matic has a fleet of trucks serving the nation.

TOP: A welding wheel automatically provides a continuous weld on a piece of tube.

primers and burster tubes for U.S. Army 150-millimeter field pieces, later used in the Vietnam War.

But there was one major difficulty: None of the tubing then available measured up to the rigorous Pentagon ordnance standards, especially exacting because a firing mishap could result in the loss of American lives. Tube suppliers also proved to be unreliable, forcing frequent shutdowns due to strikes and failures to deliver.

Metal-Matic's solution was to begin manufacturing its own tubing in 1957, launching the tradition of excellence that still distinguishes the firm. "Our sensitivity to the quality imperative began with that project," says Gerald Bliss, explaining that military work calls for extremely close tolerances, voluminous documentation, and thorough testing at every manufacturing step—all ensuring goods to time-after-time consistency.

As government contracts burgeoned, Metal-Matic became convinced that it could manufacture even better tubing stock than the kind it was then making. It began by crafting much of its own equipment to produce a better grade of steel tubing. Today the company has a multitude of tubing mills and peripheral equipment, all serving to assure that its quality remains the finest in the industry.

To this day, Metal-Matic dramatizes its commitment to unmatched service by keeping a corporate fleet of 16 sleeper tractors and 36 trailers to assure "just in time" shipping between Minneapolis and its distant customers. Company trucks are operated in round robin style, delivering finished products, then returning with steel coils, thus maximizing transportation efficiency and helping to keep the company competitive. Further savings are effective by using low-cost barge service on the Mississippi.

Gerald J. Bliss, president and chief executive officer of Metal-Matic.

Aviation too, has a significant place in the company's transportation mix. First vice president Jerry Bliss, Jr., tells of the gratitude of a key customer in South Korea who was air expressed the prototypes and rush parts to keep production lines going. Customers and business guests from all over the United States as well as China, Japan, Germany, Switzerland, and India, among other countries, have flown to the Twin Cities to visit Metal-Matic.

Tragedy struck in August 1964, when Jerome Bliss narrowly escaped death by accidental electrocution while working in the plant. Severely burned over the upper 20 percent of his body, he lingered until his death the following summer. Gerald Bliss, who had served in various positions, then assumed control of Metal-Matic and has been chief executive officer and president ever since.

Gerald Bliss takes special pride in the fact that 1964 was the last year in which Metal-Matic lost money. "After that," he jokes, "we had everyone throw away their red pencils!"

By then, Metal-Matic customers had come to include some of the nation's top manufacturers: all of the major auto companies, John Deere and Caterpillar of the tractor segment, Whirlpool and Sony in home appliances, also Singer—to name but a few.

In Detroit, Metal-Matic steel tubing is held in such high regard that routine receiving inspection has been waived, permitting the product to go straight to the auto assembly line. "The secret," says Bliss with a measured smile, "is to take a prospect's tolerances, cut them in half, then give the client superior goods and services that no

alternative supplier can match."

It's his opinion that the old adage—that someplace there is somebody who can make the tubing cheaper— doesn't apply very well when user production lines are shut down because of shoddy substitutes.

In addition to wide use in the automotive industry—for both tubular members and all kinds of high-pressure conduits and connections (including the passenger-side air bag containers)—Metal-Matic steel tubing is employed as columns in a wide variety of household appliances—vacuum cleaners, washing machines and dryers— and as industrial components that are truly too numerous to mention.

In the late 1980s Metal-Matic purchased all of the tube mill equipment used by Ford Motor Company in its Ypsilanti, Michigan, plant. It was of the same type and superior quality that Metal-Matic had developed over the years—the two companies having forged a strong relationship because of Ford's demand for absolute quality assurance. Now that equipment, used for less than four years, cries out for employment, while Metal-Matic runs three shifts, six days a week—and its customers anxiously inquire about new capacity.

"It simply doesn't make sense to have such equipment lie fallow," says Bliss. Although the company would keep its main plant and most present operations in Minnesota, the de-mothballed hardware seems destined to anchor a new, "green field" (built from the ground up) factory, built in another state and the potential employer of more than 300 Metal-Matic tube makers.

"The year 1992 was our best ever," says Jerry Bliss. "I'm convinced that we'd never have attained that mark without our Minnesota dimension. But I'm equally sure we can't progress much further without the expansion that appears impossible here.

"It's an ironic footnote to a great success story. Perhaps we can work something out. We'll try as long as we can, but the outcome is anything but clear at this time."

Dresser-Rand Electric Machinery

"Every day we slug it out with the largest electrical manufacturing firms around the world." Though a part of the community for more than 100 years, many of its neighbors may not know this manufacturer of heavy machinery, a veteran of global competition for decades. That community is the Twin Cities, and the organization is the Electric Machinery (EM) operation of Dresser-Rand Company.

As a world leader in highly engineered equipment (used both to generate electrical energy and also to harness it with an array of amazingly powerful motors), EM enjoys an outstanding reputation with its customers. Although it isn't widely known by consumers, industrial customers have known Dresser-Rand and have relied on EM for decades. The firm is proud that it has been able to improve its competitiveness enough to grow and keep heavy manufacturing here, to the benefit of both the Twin Cities community and the nation.

EM dates from the day James Boustead opened a small repair shop in 1891, when electric power itself was still a scientific wonder. His original Central Avenue location was ideally adjacent to the Minneapolis milling district and the Falls of St. Anthony. One of his first customers was Minneapolis Mill Co., which later became the Hydro Division of Northern States Power Company.

That relationship has grown even closer in the ensuing century, during which EM products—custom engineered for sophisticated, demanding applications—have earned their unparalleled reputation in the face of scores of competitors, including such household names as General Electric and Siemens. It hasn't been easy. As EM points out, "There is no U.S. government support for making highly engineered motors and generators, in contrast to support for agriculture and many firms serving the defense industry."

EM serves myriad customers, in everything from aerospace rocket fuels to zinc mining, leading the industry in the sale of meticulously made slow-speed synchronous motors. Its major niche is "medium-size" motors and generators in the 10,000- to 40,000-horsepower range. EM counts among its valued customers some of the most respected names in the electric utility, chemical and petrochemical, forest prod-

ABOVE: Dresser-Rand's 900-horsepower, 400-rpm variable-speed synchronous motor in use at a water-treatment plant.

TOP: The firm's 7,000-horsepower, 327-rpm synchronous motor on the job at a paper mill.

ucts, and mining industries—regionally, nationally, and internationally.

Long an innovator, EM recently installed the world's only running motor/generator in a compressed air energy storage (CAES) facility, a 110-kilowatt installation atop the salt domes of Alabama. EM's equipment drives massive compressors to squeeze air into huge caverns in the salt domes. When that air flows back through expanders made by a sister operation, the generator produces enough electricity to power more than 100,000 homes. Company officials were pleased to hear competitors admit their firm was the "only game in

town" that could meet such demanding applications.

EM helps meet challenges of the U.S. Clean Air Act by devising the motors, controls, and ancillary equipment that play a major role in regulatory compliance. Its products drive forced-draft induction fans for flue gas desulfurization, helping to cut plant emissions, while electrostatic precipitators and scrubbers powered by its motors release a purer air by extracting the particulate matter. EM also powers some of the new water-treatment facilities going in to clean up effluent.

As a supplier to a market of demanding clients who are highly conversant with the business, EM prides itself on a special amalgam of expertise and informed responsiveness. "Our engineering and marketing team is in direct contact with customers from day one. It's always a collaborative, iterative process. We're constantly improving how well we serve our customers' needs, up to and including delivery and installation."

The company also sees itself as a conscientious, cost-effective bridge between its customers and suppliers. This often results in important innovations such as the fabrication of new and highly specialized fuses and the development of motor diagnostics that don't interrupt customers' operations.

Essential to such responsiveness is EM's dedication to "The Total Quality Process." EM likens it to the golf pro who improves **how** a student swings, rather than merely pointing out dubbed shots. "We focus on every stage of the task. Our aim is to create enthusiastic customers by involving everyone in doing the job right the first time, and in continuously improving upon our capabilities. That policy applies to every member and function of our organization."

With this dedication and track record, look for EM to be living proof that global competitiveness can be a reality in this area, even in heavy manufacturing.

McLaughlin Gormley King Company

MGK is the only North American refiner of pyrethrum, a natural insecticide extracted from a daisylike flower grown in Africa and Austral-Asia.

If there were a hall of fame for unsung hero firms making natural products, a charter member would certainly be McLaughlin Gormley King (MGK®), a major supplier of pesticide concentrates sold in the $500-million consumer product market. It is also the only North American refiner of natural pyrethrum, a substance extracted from a daisylike flower that yields a series of chemicals that are low in mammalian toxicity.

The fourth-generation company, based in the Minneapolis suburb of Golden Val-

ABOVE: Three generations of MGK leadership: chairman William D. Gullickson, Sr. (seated); George McLaughlin (portrait); and president and chief executive officer Bill Gullickson, Jr.

BELOW: MGK's new state-of-the-art production facility in Chaska, Minnesota.

ley, has a state-of-the-art production facility in Chaska, Minnesota, and employs 65 persons. It exports its products to more than 45 countries on six continents and is a worldwide market leader in its segment of the chemical industry.

Founded in 1902 by spice merchant and pharmaceutical maker Alexander McLaughlin (when the Wright Brothers were still a couple of flightless bicycle makers), MGK has flourished to see one of its products remain the insecticide of choice for two huge federal agencies.

Both the Pentagon and the Federal Aviation Administration use the material to destroy insects entering the United States on planes, ships, and on bases, lest the bugs impair the nation's health and food supply. Northwest Airlines and its customers are beneficiaries of this MGK contribution to public health.

In the 1920s MGK's Charles Gnadinger devised the first standard for the analysis of pyrethrum, a natural bug killer extracted from a flower found widely in Africa and Austral-Asia. "Until he came up with this method, the standard mixture was one pound of blossoms in a gallon of kerosene," says MGK president and chief executive officer Bill Gullickson, Jr., a great-grandson of McLaughlin. William D. Gullickson, Sr., is chairman of the firm.

MGK kept improving its formulations, reducing where possible the level of the active ingredient while maintaining strong entomological activity. After World War II the company began marketing synthetic pyrethroids, as safe and effective as their natural predecessor, but at lower concentrations. The firm developed MGK® 264 Insecticide Synergist, a biological agent that facilitates activity of pyrethroids at safer, lower concentrations.

Intensive research has kept MGK ahead of the industry, yielding stable synthetics that permitted the use of water-based delivery systems in spray cans and pump applicators. Such aqueous systems are less intrusive environmentally than solvent carriers.

The company's newest product is NYLAR®, an insect growth regulator (IGR) that disrupts natural insect life cycles, rendering them incapable of reproduction. NYLAR® shows great promise in controlling a wide range of pests—including mosquitoes, flies, cockroaches, and fleas.

Total customer service distinguishes MGK, essential in a business where each new product is rigorously tested at each stage of development before being formally registered by the EPA. MGK provides hands-on assistance in its own labs, as well as helping with packaging, shipping, and merchandising.

"If customers prefer, we can work with them through the product development process, from the initial concept to the retail shelf," says Gullickson.

MGK's pride is its new $18.5-million manufacturing plant in Chaska, a 100,000-square-foot facility set into a hill for energy conservation and employing the latest environmental and safety devices. The interior is pressure balanced so air never migrates from more-hazardous areas, all process piping is welded to reduce the chance of leaks, and chemical storage tanks are nitrogen blanketed for content stability and reduced flammability.

The plant has a "zero discharge" drain system and storm runoff receives primary treatment. All drains are channeled into the facility's two-tank containment system for reduction and recycling.

"Every measure exceeds current federal and state environmental standards but the time and expense were all worth it," says Gullickson. "The plant has worked perfectly from its first batch."

Precision Associates, Inc.

ABOVE: View of one of four different molding departments on separate floors in the 155,000-square-foot PAI facility. Courtesy, Greg Ryan/Sally Beyer

RIGHT: A mold, rubber O-rings, and calipers for measuring dimension. Courtesy, Greg Ryan/Sally Beyer

In one year as many as one billion separate synthetic rubber oil- and gas-resistant parts come out of the molding machines at Precision Associates. Industry-standard products such as O-rings, U-Cup rings, and Back-Up rings plus plating masks and plugs account for some 64 percent of the company's production. The other 36 percent involves custom products manufactured to a client's often exacting specifications. More than half are sold through independent distributors, the balance direct to the end users.

In 1954 an alumnus of Minnesota Rubber Co. was seeking investors for the forming of a new rubber company. He learned about Arnold Kadue through an executive search agency. He then persuaded Kadue and his wife to risk almost their entire lifetime savings in this new molding enterprise. As the former production manager of a valve and faucet factory in Ohio, Kadue had been impressed by the spectacular savings being accomplished by the use of O-rings as replacements for braided packing seals. He was attracted by the vision of being on the cutting edge of the vastly improved technologies in gaseous and liquid sealing.

In 1955 and early 1956 Kadue took part in the new business only by writing sales solicitations and visiting some prospective Twin Cities customers. His most vivid memory from that time was a visit with a purchasing executive at Honeywell's Fourth Avenue headquarters in Minneapolis, when Kadue was bluntly told that it was "silly" to even think about starting another rubber company in Minnesota since there were already many such firms active in the state. The only possible niche would be for a company that could specialize in super-high-quality vulcanizates.

What a splendid quality clue this was— and coming from a world-famous company! The mission objective of this infant new rubber company must be excellent quality forever, in every tiny detail. That truly has happened, to the delight of a constantly growing legion of satisfied customers.

The corporate name of "Precision Associates" already had been selected from a Connecticut undertaking organized by Kadue in 1944. Only two other firms named "Precision" were listed in the Minneapolis telephone book. (Today there are 63.) Cofounder Kadue wanted the business philosophy to be different from the old "boss and employee" and "management and labor" makeup. The new company should be a group of achievement-minded people, enthusiastically "associated" together to create strictly top-quality products with dependable deliveries at competitive prices. Annual employee profit sharing has been in effect for decades.

In the happy "Nordeast" part of town, more than 160 associates work in spirited cooperation with each other in an economical six-story concrete structure at 740 North Washington. Another dozen operate in another location, manufacturing the high-precision steel molds needed to turn out quality moldings. That department also produces molds for other

administration, is active as the executive vice president of Precision Associates, Inc.

Back in 1982 Paul had won the hand of a brilliant lady engineer, Chris Sanford. Together in Wisconsin they worked in separate manufacturing establishments for several years in their respective engineering specialties. As part of sound business continuity planning, Paul is scheduled eventually to become chief executive officer of Precision Associates. By fortunate coincidence, Chris has an extensive marketing background, working for Honeywell, and has tremendous knowledge in that field to share with Paul. Thus, the very same world-class company that helped Precision in 1955-1956 to grasp the vision and determination for strictly top-quality products continues to inspire the unrelenting dedication of the energetic workers of Pre-

cision Associates today.

Precision's company letterhead displays an engraving of the American Liberty Bell in Philadelphia, famous for the ringing it pealed in 1776. The word "ring" is symbolic at Precision Associates because of all the rings the firm makes:

C-Rings	Diamond Rings
D-Rings	Pyramid Rings
L-Rings	Breadloaf Rings
O-Rings	Grommet Rings
U-Rings	Bushing Rings
V-Rings	4-Corner Rings
X-Rings	Multiseal Rings
Oval Rings	Rod-Wiper Rings
Seal Rings	Wiper-Cup Rings
Flare Rings	Valve Seat Rings
Pruva Rings	Gasket Rings
R-T-M Rings (Rubber-to-Metal)	

firms in the rubber business when such companies are in need of extremely high-quality tooling.

The father of three sons, Kadue has had all of them busily laboring in his factory throughout their high school and college weekends and summers. Two left the rubber business for the professions of medicine and law, but Paul, with a master's degree in engineering and another in business

RIGHT: Mark Anderson operates a new 700 series O-ring molding press, designed and constructed in-house by Precision Associates. Courtesy, Greg Ryan/Sally Beyer

TOP RIGHT: Arnold Kadue (center), president of Precision Associates, Inc., flanked by marketing director Chris Kadue (left) and executive vice president Paul Kadue (right). Courtesy, Greg Ryan/Sally Beyer

PATRONS

The following individuals, companies, and organizations have made a valuable commitment to the quality of this publication. Jostens Publishing Group and the Metropolitan Airports Commission gratefully acknowledge their participation in *America's North Coast Gateway: Minneapolis-St. Paul International Airport.*

Adolfson & Peterson, Inc.*
Advantek Incorporated*
Air Cargo Center
Alexander & Alexander, Inc.
American Amusement Arcades*
Anchor Paper Company
Anderson Trucking Services, Inc.
Apcoa, Inc.
The API Group*
AT&T*
Bell Mortgage Company*
The Bergquist Company*
David Braslau Associates, Inc.
Browning-Ferris Industries of Minnesota
Budget Rent A Car of Minnesota
Calhoun Maintenance Company/St. Paul
    Flight Center*
Carlson Companies
    Carlson Travel Network ■ Carlson
    Hospitality/ Radisson Hotels International*
Cedarberg Industries, Inc.
Cedars Edina Apartment Community*
Central Engineering Company*
Ceridian Corporation*
Control Data Systems*
Controlcom Systems, Inc.
Courage Center*
Dain Bosworth*
DataCard Corporation*
Diversified Dynamics Corporation*
Dotronix, Inc.*
Dresser-Rand Electric Machinery*
Dri-Steem Humidifier Company*
Electronic Components Group
Filtration Engineering Company
Foley-Belsaw Company*
HealthEast
HealthSpan Health Systems Corporation*
Hidden Creek Industries
HNTB Corporation
    Architects Engineers Planners*
Holiday Inn Airport #2*
Horton Holding, Inc.*

Host Marriott*
Hotel Capital Group*
Hubbard Broadcasting*
Hypro Corporation*
IncStar Corporation
Industrial Fabrics Corporation
InterNatural Designs, Inc.*
Inter-Regional Financial Group
Jostens, Inc.*
KLM Royal Dutch Airlines*
Kraus-Anderson Companies*
Kurt Manufacturing Company
Bruce A. Liesch Associates, Inc.*
McLaughlin Gormley King Company*
MacQueen Equipment, Inc.*
Marsh & McClennan Incorporated
Mayo Foundation*
Mesaba Aviation, Inc.
    A Wholly Owned Subsidiary of AirTran
    Corporation*
Metal-Matic, Inc.*
Miller & Schroeder Financial, Inc.*
Minneapolis and Suburban Yellow Cab
Minneapolis-St. Paul Airport Hilton Hotel*
Minnesota Community College System*
Minnesota Office of Tourism
Minnesota World Trade Center
Minntech Corporation*
Naegele Outdoor Advertising Company*
National Interrent*

National Trade Trust*
Nippon Express, USA, Inc.
Northern States Power Company*
Northwest Airlines*
Norwest Bank Minnesota N.A.
Oppenheimer Wolff & Donnelly*
Palm Beach Beauty Products
Paramax, A Unisys Company*
Precision Associates, Inc.*
Residence Inn By Marriott
    Minneapolis/Eden Prairie*
RFA/Minnesota Engineering*
Robins, Kaplan, Miller & Ciresi*
Ron-Vik, Incorporated
SBM Company*
Schenkers International Forwarders
Smarte Carte, Inc.*
S.T.S. Consultants, Ltd.
Toltz, King, Duvall, Anderson and
    Associates
Twin City Testing Corporation
United Parcel Service
Wenck Associates, Inc.*
Woodward-Clyde Consultants*

*Participants in Part Two of *America's North Coast Gateway: Minneapolis-St. Paul International Airport.* The stories of these companies and organizations appear in Chapters 7 through 13, beginning on page 105.

Members of the MAC are (left to right): Nick Mancini, Mark G. Brataas, John Himle, Patrick O'Neill, Laurel Erickson, Virginia Lanegran, Jan Del Calzo, Kenneth Glaser, Hugh Schilling, Faye Petron, Jack Mogelson, Tommy Merickel, Alton J. Gasper, and Paul Rehmkamp. Not shown: Tim Lovassen. Photo by Alvis Upitis

BIBLIOGRAPHY

BOOKS & BOOKLETS

Aviation Planning Associates Inc. *Regional System Reliever Airports Study.* Cincinnati: Metropolitan Council (St. Paul), June 1990.

Berman, Lael, and Frieda Rich. *Landmarks Old and New: Minneapolis and St. Paul and Surrounding Areas.* Minneapolis: Nodin Press, 1988.

Brooklyn Historical Society. *History of the Earle Brown Farm.* North Central Publishing Co., 1983.

CityBusiness. *CityBusiness Book of Lists.* Minneapolis: 1993.

Hartsough, Mildred Lucile. *The Twin Cities as a Metropolitan Market.* Minneapolis: University of Minnesota, 1925.

Herberg, Amy, and Lisa Leet. *Minneapolis-St. Paul International Airport Factbook 1991.* Minneapolis: Metropolitan Airports Commission, 1992.

Mainstreet Antique Mall. *A Million Miles Without an Accident.* Hopkins, MN: 1991. (Originally published by Northwest Airways, 1929.)

Metropolitan Airports Commission. *Minneapolis-St. Paul International Airport Factbook 1991.* St. Paul: 1992.

Metropolitan Airports Commission. *The Local and Regional Economic Impacts of the Minneapolis-St. Paul International Airport.* Lancaster, PA: Martin O'Connell Associates, 1991.

Metropolitan Council. *Metropolitan Aviation Development Guide Chapter.* St. Paul: January 1990.

Metropolitan Council. *The Twin Cities Economy in Profile.* St. Paul: 1991.

Mills, Stephen E. *More Than Meets the Sky.* Seattle: Superior Publishing Co., 1972.

Minneapolis Community Development Agency. *Profile Minneapolis.* Minneapolis: 1990.

Minneapolis-St. Paul Metropolitan Airports Commission. *Early Aviation, Metropolitan Area, 1911-1943* (Vol. 1). Minneapolis: MSP and MAC staff.

Minnesota Department of Trade and Economic Development. *Compare Minnesota.* St. Paul: 1992.

Minnesota Department of Trade and Economic Development. *Minnesota Living.* St. Paul: 1991.

Minnesota Department of Trade and Economic Development. *Profile Minnesota.* St. Paul: 1991.

Minnesota Department of Trade and Economic Development. *Resource Minnesota.* St. Paul: 1991.

Minnesota Trade Office. *Minnesota Trade Statistics: A Factbook of Exports and Foreign Direct Investment.* St. Paul: 1992.

MSP International Airport, Airport Director Technical Support Office. *Minneapolis-St. Paul International Airport Annual Highlights, 1950-1991.*

Peirce, Neil R., and Jerry Hagstrom. *The Book of America.* New York: W.W. Norton and Co., 1983.

Ruble, Kenneth D. *Flight to the Top.* Viking Press, 1986.

Serling, Robert. *Ceiling Unlimited: The Story of North Central Airlines.* Marceline, MO: Walsworth Publishing Co., 1973.

Wirth, Theodore. *Minneapolis Park System, 1883-1944.* Minneapolis: City of Minneapolis.

INTERVIEWS

Mark Abels (vice president for corporate communications, Northwest Airlines)

Randy Adamsick (executive director, Minnesota Film Board, St. Paul)

Jon K. Andersen (International Resource Group Inc., Minnetonka, MN)

Milton Andersen (retired Northwest Airlines station manager, Minneapolis-St. Paul)

Don Anderson (sales director, Dresser-Rand Electric Machinery, Minneapolis)

Jon Bream (music critic, *Star Tribune*, Minneapolis)

Vincent Doyle (retired Northwest Airlines pilot and historian)

Jack Eberlein (Crystal Airport manager)

Arlene Englert (travel management services manager, 3M Company, Maplewood, MN)

Greg Fries (St. Paul Downtown Airport manager)

Tom Getzke (vice president, St. Paul Convention and Visitors Bureau)

Jeff Hamiel (executive director, Metropolitan Airports Commission)

Abigail McKenzie (director of information and analysis, Minnesota Department of Trade and Economic Development, St. Paul)

Greg D. Ortale (president and CEO, Greater Minneapolis Convention and Visitors Association)

Kenneth B. Peterson (director, St. Paul Department of Planning and Economic Development)

Dick Reid (Medtronic, Inc., Minneapolis)

Robert M. Rosner (vice president, Minntech Corporation, Plymouth)

Dorothy Schaeffer (retired assistant to the director, Minneapolis-St. Paul International Airport)

Gary Schmidt (Metropolitan Airports Commission Reliever Airports manager)

Harold Stassen (former governor of Minnesota)

Robert Swan (northern region general manager, KLM Royal Dutch Airlines)

Interviews with various fixed-base operators and other aviation businesspersons on the six MAC reliever airports.

NEWSPAPERS

Minneapolis Journal, 1923-1941.

Minneapolis Morning Tribune/Minneapolis Tribune, 1919-1941

Minneapolis-St. Paul CityBusiness

Minneapolis Star Tribune, 1941-1992

St. Paul Pioneer Press, 1919-1941, Feb. 3, 1992

St. Paul Pioneer Press-Dispatch, 1941-1992

PERIODICALS

Business Week (May 21, 1990)

Career Pilot (Feb. 1992)

Contact (Wold-Chamberlain-Twin City Airport Memorial Issue). Vol. II, No. 3 (Aug.-Sept., 1923)

Corporate Report (Dec. 1990)

Electronic Business (April 20, 1990)

Forbes (Nov. 12, 1990)

Fortune (Oct. 22, 1990)

Minnesota History, Vol. 50, No. 3 (Fall 1986)

Minnesota Motorist (Aug. 1961)

Money (Sept. 1990)

National Geographic (Nov. 1980)

Newsweek (Feb. 6, 1989)

Sales and Marketing Management (1990)

World Trade (July 1990)

OTHER SOURCES

Greater Minneapolis Convention and Visitors Association (various publications)

Metropolitan Airports Commission, St. Paul (various publications)

Minneapolis City Hall Archives

Minneapolis Park Board annual reports, 1929-1944

Minneapolis Park Board records

Minneapolis-St. Paul Metropolitan Airports Commission Archives, Minnesota History Center, St. Paul

Minnesota Department of Trade and Economic Development, St. Paul (various publications)

Minnesota Division of Aeronautics Archives, Minnesota History Center, St. Paul

Minnesota Film Board, St. Paul (various publications)

Northwest Airlines, Eagan, MN

Northwest Airlines annual reports, 1950-1970

St. Paul Convention and Visitors Bureau (various publications)

Sun Country Airlines, Eagan, MN

Wold-Chamberlain Field dedication program (July 10, 1923)

INDEX

TWIN CITIES ENTERPRISES INDEX

Adolfson & Peterson, Inc., 154-155
Advantek Incorporated, 188-189
American Amusement Arcades, 129
API Group, The, 156-157
AT&T, 122
Bell Mortgage Company, 167
Bergquist Company, The, 191
Calhoun Maintenance Company/St. Paul
    Flight Center, 128
Carlson Companies: Carlson Travel Net-
    work * Carlson Hospitality/Radisson
    Hotels International, 172
Cedars Edina Apartment Community, 175
Central Engineering Company, 148
Ceridian Corporation, 180-181
Control Data Systems, 182-183
Courage Center, 143
Dain Bosworth, 162-163
DataCard Corporation, 197
Diversified Dynamics Corporation, 178-
    179
Dotronix, Inc., 192
Dresser-Rand Electric Machinery, 200
Dri-Steem Humidifier Company, 187
Foley-Belsaw Company, 194-195
HealthSpan Health Systems Corporation,
    136-137
HNTB Corporation: Architects Engineers
    Planners, 146
Holiday Inn Airport #2, 173
Horton Holding, Inc., 190
Host Marriott, 126-127
Hotel Capital Group, 165
Hubbard Broadcasting, 120-121
Hypro Corporation, 186
InterNatural Designs, Inc., 112-116
Jostens, Inc., 184-185
KLM Royal Dutch Airlines, 108
Kraus-Anderson Companies, 134-135
Liesch Associates, Inc., Bruce A., 151
McLaughlin Gormley King Company, 201
MacQueen Equipment, Inc., 160-161
Mayo Foundation, 140-141
Mesaba Aviation, Inc., A Wholly Owned
    Subsidiary of AirTran Corporation, 109
Metal-Matic, Inc., 198-199
Miller & Schroeder Financial, Inc., 166
Minneapolis-St. Paul Airport Hilton Hotel,
    174
Minnesota Community College System,
    147
Minntech Corporation, 196
Naegele Outdoor Advertising Company,
    123
National Interrent, 117
National Trade Trust, 158-159
Northern States Power Company, 118-119
Northwest Airlines, 106-107
Oppenheimer Wolff & Donnelly, 138-139
Paramax, A Unisys Company, 193
Precision Associates, Inc., 202-203
Residence Inn by Marriott:
    Minneapolis/Eden Prairie, 170-171
RFA/Minnesota Engineering, 142
Robins, Kaplan, Miller & Ciresi, 144-145
SBM Company, 164
Smarte Carte, Inc., 130
Wenck Associates, Inc., 149

Woodward-Clyde Consultants, 150

GENERAL INDEX
Italicized numbers indicate illustrations.

Abels, Mark, 88, 91
Aero Club of Minneapolis, 14, 15, 18
Airbourne Express, 90
Aircraft Electronics, 53
Aircraft Sales Inc., 56
Air Express, 33
AirLake Airport, 56, *58-59*
Airline industry deregulation, 45
Air mail service, 13, 14-15, 16, 18, 21, 29,
    81
Airport (motion picture), 42, *43*
Air traffic control, 23, *24*
Air Wisconsin, 43
Allegheny Airlines, 43
American Air Center, 53
American Airlines, 21, 39, 90
American Airlines Cargo, 33
American Airways, 21
American Aviation Company, 56
American Express, 19
American Swedish Institute, *68,* 70
America West, 90
Amtrak, 63
Andersen, Elmer L., 39
Andersen, Jon K., 91
Andersen, M.E. (Milton), 19, 23
Anderson, Don, 91
Anoka County, 33, 35, 41, 42, 49, 53
Anoka County/Blaine Airport, 52, 53, *53,* 54
Anoka Flight Training, 53
Apple Valley, 75
Aquatennial, 75
ASI/Modern Aero, 54, 55
Augsberg College, 97
Aviation Maintenance Inc., 52

Bald Eagle Lake, 75
Bandana Square, 74, 78
Baseball Museum, 74
Bastis, A.G., 30
Bellonte, Maurice, 20
Bennett, A.C., 13
Benson Airport, 59
Blackmon, Harry, 97
Blaine, 53, 74
Bloomington, 46, 49, 75
Bloomington Airport, 32, 49
Blues Saloon, 70
Bolduc Aviation Specialized Services, 53,
    54
Braggen, Van, 69
Braniff International, 39 45, 47
Bream, Jon, 69
Brittin, L.H., 16, 21
Brooklyn Center, 56
Brooklyn Park, 56
Brooklyn Township, 30
Brooks, W.F., 15, 16
Brown, Earle, 14
Brown, Walter F., 21
Buffalo Municipal Airport, 59
Burger, Warren, 97
Burgum, Harry P., *31*
Burlington Express, 90
Butanes Soul Revue, 69

Cambridge, 59
Cambridge Municipal Airport, 59
Capital Airlines, 36

Cargill, 95, 97
Carlson, Curt, 99
Carlson College, 97
Carlson Companies, 99
Carlson Travel Network, 99
Carlton Municipal Airport, 59
Carr, Hal N., *35,* 36
Castle, Lewis, *31*
Cedar Airport, 32
Centennial Showboat Theatre, 74
Central Iowa Airlines, 43
Ceridian Corporation, 97
Cessna Pilot and Service Center, 58
Chamberlain, Cyrus Foss, 15, *16*
Chamberlain, F.A., 15
Chanhassen, 100
Children's Museum (St. Paul), 68, 74
Children's Theatre Company, 68
Christianson, Theodore, 17
Cirrus Flight Operations, 53
Civil Aeronautics Act of 1938, 23
Civil Aeronautics Administration (CAA),
    27, 28, 50
Civil Aeronautics Board (CAB), 35, 36, 38,
    40, 84
Civilian Pilot Training program, 27
College of St. Catherine's, 97
Committee of 100, 18
Como Lake, 76
Como Park, 75
Confederate Air Force, 52
Continental Airlines, 45, *46-47,* 90
Control Data Corporation, 97
Coste, Dieudonne, 20
Cray Research, 97
Crystal, 56
Crystal Airport, 49, 56
Crystal Shamrock, 56
Crystal Skyways, 56
Curtiss, Glenn H., 8, 13
Curtiss Northwest Airplane Company, 16

Dakota Bar and Grill, 70
Dakota County, 42, 46, 56, 59, 102
Dasburg, John, 81
Dayton-Hudson, 78, 97, 100
Defense Plant Corp., 28
Delta Airlines, 45, 90
DePonti, Angelo "Shorty," 21, *22*
DePonti Aviation Co., 23, 28, 33, 39
Depression, Great, 22
de Waart, Edo, 69
DHL Airways, 90
Dickenson, Charles, *17*
Dickinson, Charles "Pop," 16
Doolittle, James, 8
Doyle, Vince, 23, *24*
Dresser-Rand, 91
Dudley Riggs' Theatre, 66
Duffy, Jim, 55
Duluth, 31, 36, 98
Dunwoody Institute, 14
Durst, W.A., 17
Dylan, Bob, 68, 69

Eagan, 84, 90
Earhart, Amelia, 8
Eastern Airlines, 21, 39
Eastern Air Transport, 21
Eden Prairie, 49, 54
Elliott Flying Service, 55
Elmo Aero, 58
Emery Worldwide, 90
Englert, Arlene, 91

FAA, 40, 45
Faribault, 59
Faribault Municipal Airport, 59
Farmington, 56, 59
Federal Aid to Airports Act, 35
Federal Express, 45, 90, 100
Festival of Nations, 78
Fine Line Music Cafe, 70
Firefighters Memorial Museum, 74
First Avenue (blues club), 70
First National Bank, Minneapolis, 15
Fitzgerald, F. Scott, 67; residence of, 63
Fitzgerald, Zelda, 67
Fleming Field, 32, 49, 52, 58
Flying Cloud Airport, 49, 54-56
Flying Cloud Executive Aviation/Aviation
    Charter, 55
Flying Scotchman, 56
Flying Tigers Line, 33, 42
Flyteline, 58
Ford, Henry, 16
Forest Lake Airport, 59
Fort Snelling, 9, 23, 27, 28, 38
Foshay Tower, 66
440th Fighter Bomber Wing Reserve, 53
Fries, Greg, 51
Frontier Airlines, 45

Galtier Plaza, 78
General Aviation Services, 56
General Mills, 95; products of, *97*
Getzke, Tom, 100, 101
Gilbert, Cass, 63
Glam Slam, 70
Glencoe, 59
Glencoe Municipal Airport, 59
Goodhue County, 59
Governor's Mansion, 63
Grain Belt Brewery, 66
Grand Casino, 78
Grand Rapids, 90
Great American History Theatre, 67
Great Circle route, 10, 35, 37, 86, 89
Greater Minneapolis Convention and Visi-
    tors Association, 101
Great Northern Railway, *9,* 10
Green, William, 30
Griggs, Milton W., *31*
Gross, Francis A., *31*
Guthrie, Tyrone, 66
Guthrie Theater, Tyrone, 66, *67,* 69, 70

Hamiel, Jeffrey W., *8,* 88, 90
Ham Lake, 41
Hamline University, 97
Hammond, Lawrence D., 19, 22
Hanford Airlines, 22, 23
Hanford Tri-State Airlines, 21
Harris, Jimmy Jam, 69
Hartsough, Mildred Lucile, 66
Heart of the Beast Puppet and Mask The-
    atre, *66,* 67
Hedberg-Freidheim, 22
Heine, Alexander T., 8
Helicopter Flight, 56, *57*
Hennepin Center for the Arts, 67
Hennepin County, 31, 42, 49
Hibbing/Chisholm, 36
Hill, James J., mansion of, 63
Hinck Flying Service, 33
Hinckley, 78
Holman, Charles "Speed," 8, *12-13,* 18, 19,
    50; death of, 20
Holman Field, *10,* 12, 20, 29, 30, 31, 32,

49, 50, 53. *See also* St. Paul Downtown Airport
Honeywell, 97, *98,* 99
Hoover, Herbert, 21
Hughes, Howard, 23
Humphrey, Hubert, *33, 35, 36,* 44
Hunter, Croll, 35
Hunter, Howard, 23
Husker Du, 69

Illusion Theater, 67
Inland Aviation, 35, 36
International Multifoods, 95
International Resource Group Inc., 91
Inver Hills Community College, 52
Irvine Park, 66
Isanti County, 59

Jefferson Airways, 19
Jemne Building Galleries, 70
Johnson, John O., 13
Johnson, L.A., 23
Johnson, Prudence, 70
Johnson, Roy, 22, *24*

KCAQ, 20
Keillor, Garrison, 70, 93
Kelly Act, 16
Kidder, William, 16
Kidder's Field, 16
Kline, Marvin L., *31*
KLM Royal Dutch Airlines, 80-89, 90
Koerner, Ray and Glover, 70
Korean Airlift, 37
Kottke, Leo, 70
KPBC, 27

Lake Calhoun, 13, *14*
Lake Central Airlines, 36
Lake Elmo, 58
Lake Elmo Airport, 48, 49, 58
Lake Harriet, 75
Lakeland Skyways, 33
Lake Minnetonka, 8, 13, 75
Lake Phalen, 75
Lake Superior, 9, 98
Lakeville, 56, 59
Landmark Center, 63, 64, 74, 75, 76, *77*
Landmark Center Galleries, 70
Land O' Lakes, 95
Lao Family New Year, 78
LeSueur, 59
LeSueur County, 59
LeSueur Municipal Airport, 59
Levine, Carole, *36*
Levine, Len, *36*
Lewis, Terry, 69
LifeLink III, *52*
Lindbergh, Anne Morrow, 10
Lindbergh, Charles, 8, 10, 17, 18
Little Canada, 99

Macalester College, 95, 97
McDonough, John J., *31, 33*
McLeod County, 59
Mall of America, 78, *79*
Maplewood, 91
Marriott, 45
MATS Airlines, 43
Maxwell Aircraft Service, *56*
Mayer Aviation, *48-49,* 58, *59*
Mayo Clinic, 100
Mayslack's Polka Lounge, 78
Medtronic, Inc., 97, 100

Mesaba Airlines, 43, 45
Mesaba Aviation, 90, 131; planes of, *90, 131*
Metrodome, Hubert H. Humphrey, 74
Metropolitan Airports Commission, 8, 30, 32, 33, 36, 41, 43, 46, 47, 50, 53, 54, 56, 58, 88; airport system of, 33; and Federal Aid to Airports Act, 35; dual-track planning process of, 102; first meeting of, *31*; first members of, *31*; first proposed airport system of, 49; importance of Northwest Airlines to, 102; legislation creating, 31; 1988 capital improvements budget of, 45; noise abatement efforts of, 45-46; noise reduction plan of, 45; reliever airports, 35, 42, 48-59, 98; responsibilities of, 31
Metropolitan Council, 41, 46, 49
Metropolitan Transit Commission bus system, 98
Michaud, W.B., 18
Mickey's Diner, 78
Mid-Continent Airlines Inc., 23, 27, 28, 35, 37, 39. *See also* Hanford Airlines
Midstate Air Commuter, 43
Midway Airlines, 45
Military flight training, 14, 27
Mille Lacs Lake, 75
Minneapolis, 13, 14, 15, 16, 17, 18, 20, 22, 24, 29, 30, 31, 32, 33, 41, 56, 59, 67, 68, 70, 74, 75, 78, *92-93,* 94, 97, 100; appreciation of performing arts in, 68; architecture of, 63, 66; art galleries/-museums of, 70; as financial/retailing center, 92; blues music in, 69-70; downtown, 50, 51, 53, 59, 66, 67, 70, 74, 78; downtown business district of, 58; first flight over business district of, *8*; popular music scene in, 69-70; rock music in, 69; suburban, 67; Uptown area of, 78; West Bank area of, 78; West Bank Theatre District of, 66. *See also* Minneapolis-St. Paul *and* Twin Cities
Minneapolis City Council, 24
Minneapolis City Hall, 8, 63
Minneapolis Civic and Commerce Association, 14, 17
Minneapolis Community Development Agency, 68
Minneapolis Convention Center, 61, 98
Minneapolis Honeywell Regulator Co., 28, 32
Minneapolis Institute of the Arts, *69,* 70
Minneapolis Morning Tribune, 13, 18
Minneapolis Municipal Airport, 18, 19, 20, 22, 23, 24
Minneapolis Park Board, 16, 17, 18, 19, 20, 23, 24, 27, 29, 30, 32
Minneapolis-St. Paul, 8, 9, 10, 13, 35, 36, 38, 39, 40, 45, 47, 49, 63, 74, 75, 84, 88; advertising industry in, 98; architecture of, 63, 66; art scene of, 66; as early transportation hub, 9-10; as international multimodal transportation hub, 98; audio production industry in, 98; boating in, 75; camping in, 75; canoeing in, 75; casinos in, 78; children's theater in, 67, 68; dining in, 78; diverse economy of, 97; economy of, 102; festivals in, 75, 78; film/video production industry in, 98; fishing in, 75; gambling in, 78; high-tech industries in, 97; highways in,

63; hotels in, 61; hunting in, 75; Indians in, 9; live theater in, 66-68; manufacturing in, 97; museums (nonart) in, 70, 74; office space growth in, 98; parks in, 75; performing arts in, 66-70; picnicking in, 75; population of, 93; railroad development in, 9-10; railroads in, 63, 98; restaurants in, 78; restored theaters in, 68; retail sales in, 78; road development in, 9; service industry in, 97; shopping and shopping centers in, 78; sports in, 74; trucking firms in, 98; voyageurs in, 9
Minneapolis-St. Paul International Airport (MSP), *2-3, 5,* 10, 12, 13, 36, 37, 39, 41, 42, 43, 45, 46, 49, 50, 51, 53, 54, 61, 63, 80, 81, 88, 90, 98, 101, 102; air cargo activity at, 43; air cargo growth at, 90; air traffic controllers at, *7*; and Gatwick Airport (London), *84, 85*; Blue Concourse construction at, *37*; Blue Concourse of, 39, *44*; cargo airlines at, 90; charter airlines at, 90; expansion programs at, *36-37,* 38, 42, 47; Gold Concourse of, 42, *44,* 45, 46; Green Concourse of, 39, 42, 43, *44,* 45, 46; Hubert H. Humphrey International Charter Terminal, 43, *44,* 45; importance of to business, 91; international air service at, 100; Les Voyageurs restaurant at, 42; Lindbergh Terminal at, *38-39, 42-43,* 45; McDonald's restaurant at, 45; major passenger carriers at, 90; modernization of, 40; 1949 open house at, 37; 1963 control tower at, *40*; 1962 new terminal dedication at, 38; 1962 terminal interior at, *38*; noise problems from, 42; nursery in terminal at, 37; observation decks at, 38, 39; operating conditions at, 89-90; profitability of, 89; quality air service at, 90-91; Red Concourse of, 39, *44,* 45; role of in economic development, 101; Servicemen's Center at, 42; small carriers at, 43; snow-removal crews at, 90. *See also* Wold-Chamberlain Field
Minneapolis-St. Paul International Airport/Wold Chamberlain Field, 35. *See also* Minneapolis-St. Paul International Airport (MSP)
Minneapolis-St. Paul Metropolitan Airport/Wold Chamberlain Field, 32. *See also* Minneapolis-St. Paul International Airport (MSP)
Minneapolis Sculpture Garden, *68-69,* 70
"Minneapolis sound," 69
Minneapolis Star Tribune, 69
Minneapolis Tribune, 14, 15
Minnehaha Falls, 75, *76-77*
Minnesota: agricultural exports from, 97-98; airports, 61, 63; education in, 94; exports from, 97-98; image of, 61; importance of air service to Pacific Rim and, 88; international investments in, 98; Japanese investments in, 98; nickname of, 61; population figures, 9; tourist industry of, 61. *See also* names of individual cities in Minnesota *and* Twin Cities
Minnesota Air National Guard, 16, 19
Minnesota Airport Commission, 36
Minnesota Amateur Sports Commission, 74
Minnesota Aviation Sales and Service Co., 21, 23. *See also* DePonti Aviation Co.

Minnesota Clean Indoor Air Act, 43
Minnesota Department of Trade and Economic Development, 98
Minnesota Jet, 52
Minnesota Landscape Arboretum, 75
Minnesota Museum of Art, 66, 70
Minnesota Mutual Life, 97
Minnesota National Guard, 14, 18, 20; 109th Observation Squadron of, 15, 50, 53
Minnesota Office of Tourism, 61
Minnesota Opera, 68
Minnesota Orchestra, 69
Minnesota Public Radio, 70
Minnesota Renaissance Festival, 78
Minnesota River, 9, 10
Minnesota River Valley, 75
Minnesota State Capitol, *60-61, 63*
Minnesota State Fair, *75,* 78
Minnesota State Fairgrounds, 13, 16
Minnesota Supreme Court, 32
Minnesota Timberwolves, *70,* 74
Minnesota Twins, 70, 74
Minnesota Valley Wildlife Refuge, 75
Minnesota Vikings, 74
Minnesota Zoo, 75
Minnetonka, 91, 99
Minntech Corporation, 97, 100
Mississippi River, 9, 10, 50, 51, 63, 72, *74,* 75, 94, 98
Mixed Blood Theater, 66
Modern Avionics, 55
Mohawk Airlines, 43
Multiflight, 58
Murphy, Willie, 69
Mystic Lake Casino, 78

Naftalin, Arthur, 39
Nancy Hauser Dance Company, 68
National Aeronautics Association, Greater Twin Cities chapter of, 49
National Scenic Riverways System, 75
National Sports Center, 74
Naval Air Station, 28
Naval Reserve Aviation Base, 25, 28, 29
Naval Reserve Aviation Squadron, 18, 19, 20, 22, 23
New Brighton, 49
New Dance Ensemble, 68
New Richmond, 59
New Richmond Municipal Airport, 59
New Riverside Cafe, 78
New York Air, 45
Nicollet Airport, 32
Nicollet Mall, 78
9th Naval District, 18
Nokomis Lake, 75
Nokomis Park: father-child run at, *95*
North Central Airlines, 35, 36, 39, 43, 45, 47; construction of main base of, *41*
Northern Aviation, 53
Northern States Power substation, 39
Northfield, 97
Northland Aircraft Services, 56
Northland Aviation Company, 21, 22
Northport Airport, 59
Northport Field, 28
Northwest Aerospace Training Corporation, 84
Northwest Airlines, 10, 12, 17
Northwest Airlines, Inc., 21, 23, 24, 25, 27, 28, 30, 33, 35, 39, 40, 44, 45, 47, 63, 88, 90, 91, 97; and KLM Royal Dutch Airlines, 80-89; and Sydney, Australia,

as destination of, *86-87;* Boeing 747 of, *40;* Boeing Stratocruiser of, *34,* 35; DC-3 of, *25;* Frankfort-Main International Airport and, *86;* hangars of, 23, 45; Holman Field overhaul facilities of, 37; Kingsford Smith Airport and, *86-87;* training facilities of, 52
Northwest Airways, Inc., 16, 17-18, 19, 20, 21, 29, 50; air mail hangar of, 19
Northwestern Aeronautical Corp., 28, 33
Northwestern National Bank, 15
Norwest, 97
Norwest Center, 66
Nyrop, Donald, *40*

Oakdale, 49
Oldenburg, Claus, 69
Oldfield, Barney, 14
Old Log Theater, 67
Orchestra Hall, 68, 69
Ordway, J. G., 15
Ordway Music Theatre, 64, 67, 68, 75
Original Coney Island, The, 78
Orpheum Theater, 68
Ortale, Greg D., 101
Osceola Airport, 59
Ozark Airlines, 39, 45

Paisley Park Studios, *100*
Pan Am, 40
Paramax, 97
Parker Aviation, 33
Parranto, William A., *31*
Partridge, Elmer, 16
Paulson, Gerald F., 39
Pelli, Cesar, 66
Penumbra Theatre Company, 67
PeoplExpress, 45
Peterson, Kenneth B., 101
Phalen Park, 75
Phillips 66 Performance Center, 58
Pillsbury, 95
Planes of Fame Air Museum, 54, *55*
Plymouth, 100
Pond, Bob, 55
Powderhorn Park, *66,* 65
Prairie Home Companion, A, 68, 70
Prince, 69, 100
Puckett, Kirby, 70, *71*
Purdy, E.A., 14

Questionable Medical Devices Museum, 74
Quitu, Henry, 40

R.C. Avionics, 52
Radisson Hotels, 99
Ramsey, Alexander: house of, 63
Ramsey County, 31, 32, 59
Ramsey County Courthouse, 63
Red River, 9
Red Wing, 78
Regent Aviation, *50-51*
Reid, Dick, 100
Replacements, the, 69
Republic Airlines, 44, 45, 47
Rice Park, *64-65,* 75, 76, *77*
Richfield, 46
Richfield Airport, 33
Rickenbacker, Eddie, 8, 14, 15, *21*
Robbinsdale, 49
Robbinsdale Airport, 32, 49
Robinson, Hugh, 13-14
Rochester, 100
Roosevelt, Franklin D., 21, 27

Rosner, Robert M., 100
Ryan, John, 16

St. Anthony, 9
St. Cloud, 36
St. Croix Meadows, 78
St. Croix River, 58, 78
St. Croix River, upper, 75
St. Jude Medical, 97, 99
St. Olaf College, 97
St. Paul, 9-10, 14, 15, 16, 17, 18, 20, 29, 30, 32, 33, 41, 48, 49, 50, 56, 59, 62, 63, 67, 74, 75, 78, 93, 97; appreciation of performing arts in, 68; architecture of, 63, 66; art galleries/museums of, 70; as host to 1992 World Congress on Bovine Medicine, 101; downtown, 16, 51, 53, 59, 64, 75, 78; downtown business district of, 58; first nighttime airmail flight from, *17;* "Frogtown" neighborhood of, 70; Lowertown District of, 78; Midway District of, 78; Mississippi River waterfront of, *94-95;* popular music scene in, 69-70; private colleges in, 95; state capitol in, *60-61.* *See also* Minneapolis-St. Paul *and* Twin Cities
St. Paul Airport, 50
St. Paul Association, 14, 16
St. Paul Cathedral, *62,* 63
St. Paul Center, 78
St. Paul Chamber Orchestra, 67, 68
St. Paul City Hall and Courthouse, *63*
St. Paul Civic Center, 61
St. Paul Convention and Visitors Bureau, 100-101
St. Paul Downtown Airport, 12, 16, *18,* 20, 21, 22, 23, 43, 50, *51,* 52, 58. *See also* Holman Field
St. Paul Flight Center, 51-52
St. Paul Hotel, 64, 75
St. Paul Pioneer Press, 18
St. Paul Public Library, 64, 75
St. Paul Winter Carnival, 75, 76, *77,* 78
St. Thomas University, 97
Schaeffer, Dorothy, 22, *36,* 38
Schmidt, Gary, 51, 53, 54, 56, 58
Schubert Club, 68; Musical Instrument Museum of, 74
Science Museum of Minnesota, 70
Settende Mal festivities, *78*
Shakopee, 78
Skelly Oil Co., 19
Sky Freight Line, 33
Slick Airways, 33
Smith, Big Walter, 69
Smith, Mary Jo, *25*
Snelling Field Corp., 15, 18
Snelling Speedway, *14-15. See also* Twin City Motor Speedway
Soo Line Railroad, 98
Southdale Mall, 78
Southern Airways, 45, 47
South St. Paul, 32, 49, 58
South St. Paul Airport, 58
Special Olympics, 1991, 51
Speedway Field, 15
Spirit of St. Louis, 18
Stassen, Harold, 29, *30,* 31
State Theater, 68
Stillwater, 58, 75, 78
Sun Country Airlines, 45, 90
Super Bowl, 1992, 51, 74
Super Valu, 97

Surplus Property Act, 33
Swan, Robert, 88
Symphonies for the Cities, 69

Target Center, 70, 74
Target discount stores, *100*
Texas International Airlines, 45
Theatre de la Jeune Lune, 67
Theatre Exchange, 67
Thompson, Benjamin, 68
Thorshov & Cerny Inc., 39
3M Company, *91*
Thunderbird Aviation, 55
Thunderbolt Aviation, 53-54
Times Bar, 70
Torrance, Ell, *31*
Trans-Continent Air Express, 33
Transcontinental Airlines, 21
Treasure Island Casino, 78
Truax, Fred M., *31*
Turner, O.H., 16
TWA, 45, 90
Twentieth Century Airlines, 33
Twin Cities, 21, 59, 49, 67, 81, 86, 102; agribusiness industry in, 95, 97; convention industry in, 61, 100; dance companies in, 68; ethnic holiday celebrations in, 78; first airmail flight in, *14;* first public airplane flight in, 13; folk music in, 70; food-processing industry in, 95, 97; gospel music in, 70; higher education in, 94-97; jazz in, 70; medical products industry in, 99-100; street and highway system in, 98; technology-intensive firms in, 99; tourism in, 100-101; tourist attractions in, 60-79. *See also* Minneapolis-St. Paul *and* Minneapolis *and* St. Paul
Twin Cities Marathon, *72-73,* 74
Twin City Aero Corporation, 15, 16, 18
Twin City Motor Speedway, 14, 15; remnants of, *20*

U.S. Army, 21, 28, 32, 33
U.S. Army National Guard, 50
U.S. Army Reserve, 50
U.S. Customs and Immigration, 39
U.S. Department of Agriculture, 23
U.S. Department of Commerce, 19, 20, 21, 22
U.S. Department of Interior, 41
U.S. Marine Reserve Squadron, 20
U.S. National Figureskating Championships, 1991, 74
U.S. Navy, 18, 28, 31, 37
U.S. Post Office Department, 17, 23
U.S. Senate, 21
U.S. War Department, 23, 28, 38, 50
United Airlines, 39, 90; hangar of, 43, 44
United Express, *90*
Universal Air Lines Inc., 19, 20, 21. *See also* American Airways
Universal Studios, 42, 43
University Airport, 32, 49, 53
University of Minnesota, 53, 54, 66, 74, 75, 94, 95, *96,* 97
University of Minnesota-Twin cities, 94-95
Upholstery Shop, 56
UPS, 90
USAir, 90

Van Dusen Aircraft Co., 28
Veterans Administration, 38
Viennese Sommerfest, 69

Walker Art Center, 69, 70
Washington County, 42, 58, 59
Webster, Byron G., 18
Western Airlines, 21, 36, 39, 40, 45
White Bear Lake, 13, 28, 59, 75
Wilcox, Ralph D., 13
Wiley Enterprise, 56
William Mitchell College of Law, 97
Wilson, August, 67
Wings Inc., 52
Winona, 14
Winsted, 59
Winsted Municipal Airport, 59
Wirth, Theodore, 18, 19, 20
Wisconsin Central Airlines, 35, 36, 39
Wold, Ernest Groves, 15, *16*
Wold, Theodore, 15
Wold-Chamberlain Field, 15, 16, 17, 18, 19, 20, 21, 22, 23, 24, 25, 26, 27, 29, 30, 31, 35, 36, 41, 43, 49, 50; air cargo activity at, 33; A1A rating of, 20; B29 Super Fortress at, *26-27;* controlled field designation of, 23; conversion of back to civilian operations, 32; dedication ceremonies for, 15; expansion plan of 1940 for, 25; first scheduled jet flight through, 39; improvements to, 19-20, 22-23, 24, 27, 28, 29, 39; municipal ownership movement of, 16-18; municipal takeover of, 32; national defense role of, 26; 1949 open house at, *26-27;* passenger service at, 20, 21, 24, 27, 33; postwar military flights and, 33; runway construction at, 22-23; sightseeing flights from, 20, 21, 23, 24; snow removal at, 22; terminals at, 39; visitors to, 20, 24; weather broadcasting operations from, 20; weather bureau service at, 21; widebody air service at, 39; World War II military operations at, 24, 26-28
Wolf, Stephen, 47
Wolff, Hugh, 68
Works Project Administration (WPA), 23, 25, 50
World Theater, 68
World War I, 14, 16
World War II, 8, 24, 25, 26, 32, 33, 36, 84
Wright Brothers, 8, 13, 14
Wright County, 59

Youth Performance Company, 68
Ysker, John, 54

Zantop, 90
Zenon Dance Company, *67,* 68